TA T'UNG SHU

HISTORY, PHILOSOPHY, ECONOMICS

CHINA: HISTORY, PHILOSOPHY, ECONOMICS

TA T'UNG SHU

The One-World
Philosophy of K'ang Yu-wei

K'ANG YU-WEI
AND
LAURENCE G THOMPSON

Routledge
Taylor & Francis Group

LONDON AND NEW YORK

First published in 1958

Reprinted in 2005 by
Routledge
2 Park Square, Milton Park, Abingdon, Oxfordshire, OX14 4RN

711 Third Avenue, New York, NY 10017

Routledge is an imprint of the Taylor & Francis Group

First issued in paperback 2011

© 1958 George Allen & Unwin Ltd

The publishers have made every effort to contact authors/copyright holders
of the works reprinted in *China: History, Philosophy, Economics*. This has not
been possible in every case, however, and we would welcome
correspondence from those individuals/companies we have been unable to
trace.

These reprints are taken from original copies of each book. In many cases
the condition of these originals is not perfect. The publisher has gone to
great lengths to ensure the quality of these reprints, but wishes to point
out that certain characteristics of the original copies will, of necessity, be
apparent in reprints thereof.

British Library Cataloguing in Publication Data
A CIP catalogue record for this book
is available from the British Library

Ta T'ung Shu

ISBN 13: 978-0-415-36156-9 (hbk)
ISBN 13: 978-0-415-61240-1 (pbk)

China: History, Philosophy, Economics

TA T'UNG SHU

The One-World
Philosophy
of
K'ang Yu-wei

TRANSLATED FROM THE CHINESE
WITH INTRODUCTION AND NOTES

BY

LAURENCE G. THOMPSON

LONDON
GEORGE ALLEN & UNWIN LTD
RUSKIN HOUSE MUSEUM STREET

CONTENTS

PREFACE

IN the first issue of the quarterly journal, *Philosophy East and West*, one author remarks that, 'as a result of the devoted study of so many philologists, the most important texts are available in translations and can be used as a starting-point for later phases in the evaluation'.[1] The desire of that author is to see studies in Oriental thought progress beyond the basic stages, and reach the level of comparative philosophy. This desire is understandable, and is shared by an increasing number of students. However, his statement as to the availability in translation of 'the most important texts', applicable though it perhaps may be to the Indian philosophers, is certainly far from correct, so far as Chinese philosophy is concerned. The only period well represented in translation is the most ancient one, although even there such important texts as the *Ku Liang Commentary on the Tso Chuan* and the *Huai Nan Tzu* remain untranslated. For the period since the Latter Han dynasty (about A.D. 200), there is a great emptiness, broken only by a solitary sampling here and there. Unfortunately for our wish to rise above the basic work of translation, the fact is that a tremendous work of translation must yet be done before we can make bold to essay a serious comparative study of philosophy.

The present writer is convinced from his experience thus far in the study of Chinese thought, that the most important contribution the student can make, at the present stage of scholarship, is to add what he can to the presently meagre store of translations. Upon the quality and range of translations depends the possibility of developing our understanding of Chinese thought. I hold no confidence in the view that we can acquire such understanding merely by reading the texts in the Chinese, even provided we have that ability. The labour of providing an accurate translation, familiar to all who have attempted the task, is proof enough that only such thorough study and detailed work as is necessary to produce a translation faithful to the original, will guarantee an adequate comprehension of the text. Nor, to be realistic, can we hope that such a competence in reading classical Chinese will be developed among foreign students, as will assure that more than a handful of the most able can in a short life-time actually read many of these texts in the original. No, we shall depend upon the translations in all possible cases. Much therefore depends upon the quality of the translation. And there is perhaps no language offering such possibilities of mistranslation as classical Chinese. A poor translation from classical Chinese is really worse than none.

It is the present translator's purpose therefore to bring to the Western student of Chinese thought an accurate and reasonably literate rendering of one of the major works of modern Chinese philosophy. He is far from supposing his rendering to be free from faults of misinterpretation or clumsiness. He does trust that it is clear and precise enough to assure that the reader is actually receiving the ideas which the author sent forth.

The original suggestion that *Ta T'ung Shu* should be made available to Western readers was made to me by Katherine Hughes. I am very grateful to her for having put me on the track of such a reward-ing subject. It is an obligation and a pleasure to own a pupil's debt of gratitude to professors Ch'en Shou-yi and E. R. Hughes. While in Taipei from 1951 to 1953, I was fortunate enough to make the acquaintance of the eldest son of K'ang Yu-wei and of his third wife; they kindly supplied me with some materials which would not otherwise have been available. I am further indebted to Professor Shen Kang-po (沈剛伯), then of National Taiwan University, for his generosity in giving me his personal copy of the Chung Hwa edition of the text, which, despite its recent date of publication (1935), has become a 'rare book'. Professor T. S. Wei (衛挺生) has also placed me in his debt by pointing out several corrections which needed to be made in the manuscript.

[1] J. Kwee Swan Liat, 'Methods of Comparative Philosophy', *Philosophy East and West* (quarterly), vol. I, no. I, April 1951, p. 12.

BOOK ONE

INTRODUCTION

CHAPTER I

Biographical Sketch of K'ang Yu-wei

Note: The following material might in part almost be called an autobiographical sketch. It is taken, unless otherwise identified, from Chao Feng-t'ien's *Draft Chronology of Mr. K'ang Ch'ang-su,* 康長素先生年譜稿, which is in turn based (for the first forty years of the story) on the subject's own *Self-Compiled Chronology of the Gentleman from Nan Hai* 南海先生自編年譜(cited hereafter as *Chronology*). Mr. Chao's work is by far the most detailed biography of K'ang Yu-wei yet to appear.

(Page citations below refer to Chao's article.)

K'ANG YU-WEI was born in the eighth year of the Ch'ing Hsien Feng Emperor, on the fifth day of the second month (corresponding to March 19, 1858). His natal place was Kwangtung province, Nan Hai *hsien*, Yin T'ang *hsiang*, Tun Jen *li* (廣東 南海縣銀塘鄉敦仁里). According to his own *Chronology*, he was carried by his mother for eleven months before birth—an infallible sign of a prodigy.

He early demonstrated his intellectual capacities: by the age of five he was able to recite several hundred T'ang poems. The following year he began his studies of the regular curriculum, comprising such works as *Ta Hsüeh, Chung Yung, Lun Yü,* and *Hsiao Ching.* When he was eleven his father died, and he was sent to Lien Chou (連州) to study with his grandfather. At fourteen he was again living in Yin T'ang *hsiang*, his studies facilitated by the large family library collected by his great-grandfather. His independent spirit manifested itself as early as the age of fifteen, when he rebelled at the task of composing the 'eight-legged essays'[1] set for him by his teacher.

At seventeen, he states (*Chronology*), he first read the *Brief Description of the World* 瀛環志畧(compiled by Hsü Chi-yü 徐繼畬 in 1848),[2] and learned something of the history and geography of foreign nations. Two years later (1876) he began studying under a teacher of real stature, Chu Chiu-chiang 朱九江. In this same year he was married.[3] The following year, upon the death of his grandfather who had cared for him since he was a child, K'ang Yu-wei observed the mourning period for him as for his father.

In 1878, when he was twenty-one, he underwent a sudden revulsion against the arduous studies he had been pursuing for so long. He records in his *Chronology* the following significant experience:

'While sitting in meditation, I suddenly saw that the ten thousand creatures of Heaven and Earth and I were all of the same body; a great light dawned (literally, I [received] great enlightenment), and I believed I was a sage: then I laughed with joy. Suddenly I thought of the sufferings of life: then I cried with melancholy. Suddenly I thought of the parent I was not serving —how could I be studying?—then forthwith I packed up and went back to dwell by his grave.'[4] (p. 181.)

He thus gave up his instruction under Chu Chiu-chiang, and we find him in his twenty-second year living alone on a mountain to the south of Yin T'ang *hsiang*, named Hsi Ch'iao Shan (西樵山), in the Cave of the White Clouds (白雲洞). Here, according to his *Chronology*, he spent his time in studying Buddhist and Taoist books, and in meditation and spiritual clarification. During this time he became intimate with a scholar named Chang Yen-ch'iu (張延秋), and the two men spent long hours together, discussing the affairs of the day, the new books, and the old learning. Such was the importance of his friendship with Mr. Chang that K'ang Yu-wei said: 'From my teacher, Mr. Chiu-chiang, I was introduced to the Great Way of the sages and worthies;[5] from my friend, Mr. Yen-ch'iu, my interpretation of our original written records was enlarged.' (p. 181.)

It was in the winter of this year (1879) that he first went to Hong Kong. Prior to this trip he had read several works on foreign lands in addition to the *Brief Description of the World*; his *Chronology* mentions a *Concordance of Modern Western History* 西國近事彙編, a *New Account of a Tour of the World* 環遊地球新錄, 'and others'. Now, when he visited the British Crown Colony, he

'saw the elegance of the Westerners' houses and the good order of the streets, and for the first time realized that the governments of the Westerners had laws. He read again the *Illustrated Gazeteer of the Countries Across the Seas* 海國圖志 and the *Brief Description of the World*, bought a map of the world, and gradually acquired [more] books on Western learning so as to investigate the basis of Western learning.' (p. 181.)

In 1882, when K'ang Yu-wei was twenty-five, his old teacher, Chu Chiu-chiang, died, and K'ang took part with his other pupils in collecting his writings. It was also in this year that K'ang first travelled to Peking, to take part in the triennial examinations for the second degree. He was not successful. On the return journey he passed through Shanghai, where, according to his *Chronology*, he observed the prosperity of this city, and realized all the more that the Western methods of government had [sound] basic principles. So he purchased many books on Western learning, and became a serious student of that learning.[6] (p. 182.)

In 1883, at the age of twenty-six, he undertook his first venture in practical reform by organizing an Anti-Footbinding Society in his native place. This was the first such society in China, and it was later followed by his South China Anti-Footbinding Society, and his memorial to the Throne of 1898, in which he urged the prohibition of this inhuman practice.[7] This year saw further steps in his intellectual development: he bought the *World News*[8] 萬國公報, studied Western sciences, read on foreign history, geography, and travels. He now became interested solely in practical studies, and no longer devoted himself to preparing for the examinations.

It was during the years 1884 and 1885 that K'ang Yu-wei wrote the '*Li Yün*' *Annotated* 禮運注 and the first draft of the *Ta T'ung Shu*. Thus it was at the age of twenty-seven that his ideas crystallized into a conception of a world in the future, in which the sufferings of mankind would be ended, and the Universal Society established. The first draft of the work was entitled *Universal Principles of Mankind* 人類公理. It had only just been completed in the second month of 1885, when the author (who was then again in Peking) was attacked by head pains so severe that they seem very nearly to have cost him his life. He remained in his room for several months without emerging, and seemed resigned to die: '*The Universal*

Principles of Mankind was already finished, the polity of the *Ta T'ung* was already formulated, and the Teacher contemplated death without regret.' (p. 184.)

In 1887 he revised the manuscript of the *Universal Principles*, considering such matters as the establishment of the world language institute, the world parliament, a world army, etc.

The following year he went for the third time to the capital, where he arrived in time to find his old friend Chang Yen-ch'iu dying. It was in November of this year that he addressed his first memorial to the Throne, urging reforms—a memorial which was not brought to the Emperor's attention. He remained in Peking until the fall of 1889, taking the triennial examination for the second degree, and this time winning first place.

In 1890 K'ang Yu-wei was thirty-three, and living in Yang Ch'eng (i.e. Canton). It was during this year that Ch'en Ch'ien-ch'iu (T'ung-fu) 陳千秋 (通甫) and Liang Ch'i-ch'ao (Jen-kung) 梁啓超 (任公) came to study with him; and the following year he began lecturing at Chang Hsing *li* 長興里 in the provincial capital of Kwangtung. According to Liang Ch'i-ch'ao's *Biography* (Chapter III),

'in teaching his students, [Mr. K'ang] took as the matter Confucian, Buddhist, Sung, and Ming (i.e. neo-Confucian) scholarship; he took as the method history and Western studies. He taught solely by fostering a spirit of determination, by expanding upon essentials, by aiming at knowledge in a broad way.'

While the school at Chang Hsing *li* was not organized like schools of the present day, in spirit, Liang states, it was like Western schools.

During these past few years K'ang Yu-wei had been writing various things, and in 1891 was printed the first book that was to bring fame—not to say notoriety—to him: *Forged Classics of the Hsin Period* 新學偽經考 . In the following year he set his ablest students to helping him revise the manuscript of a work which he had first begun in 1886: *Confucius as a Reformer* 孔子改制考 . In these books he tried to establish the position of the so-called 'new text school' as against the 'old text school',[9] and to picture Confucius as a reformer rather than a conservative. While these two works created a turmoil in scholarly circles that has not yet completely died down, their real objective seems to have been to furnish a sanction from the sacred texts for the author's intended programme of reforms.

In the practical difficulties of reform he had his first lesson during 1893. In attempting to correct evils in the local administration of his native place, he and his pupils incurred the enmity of officials protecting their vested interests; the upshot was that the reforms failed, his favourite pupil, Ch'en T'ung-fu, fell ill, and K'ang himself was forced to flee to Kweilin (Kwangsi). Thus he came to realize that it is not easy to abolish evils and bring about good conditions.

The next year, when he was thirty-seven, he made his third trip to Peking, but stayed there this time for only three months. His *Forged Classics of the Hsin Period* was attacked as sacrilegious and unscholarly by high officials, and at their request the blocks were burned. K'ang Yu-wei also suffered the loss of a favourite pupil, Ts'ao Chu-wei (曹著偉). After returning from the capital, K'ang busied himself with attempting to improve standards of education in Kweilin. Then, on August 1, the Sino-Japanese War broke out. K'ang had pointed out in his memorial of six years before the dangers of the existing situation of unpreparedness on the part of China, and now his fears were realized.

The death of Ch'en T'ung-fu in February of the next year was a severe blow to K'ang, whose most brilliant and trusted pupil he had been. But he had little time to brood over this tragedy, as he had now returned to Peking once more, and was embroiled in the turbulent affairs of state then taking place. Learning that the government was negotiating a treaty to end the war with Japan, which treaty would involve a heavy indemnity including cession of Taiwan and Liaotung, the officials in Peking were overcome by dismay and anger. Perceiving the temper of these officials, K'ang Yu-wei and Liang Ch'i-ch'ao organized the graduates from the eighteen provinces into a mass meeting lasting for a day and two nights, which produced a petition asking for rejection of the peace and strengthening of the military forces, removal of the capital, and a general reform of the laws. This petition was handed to the Court of Censors on April 8; but the treaty had already been signed. The officials in power, fearing the repercussions of the agitation among the graduates, saw to it that the Emperor and Empress Dowager were persuaded to honour the treaty, and that the joint petition was not brought to their attention.

In the fourth month of the same year K'ang himself succeeded in taking fifth place in the examination for the third degree (chin-shih), forty-eighth place in the Palace Examination (an examination of chin-shih conducted personally by the Emperor), and second place in the Court Examination (examination of chin-shih for admittance to the Academy, called Han-lin). According to what K'ang heard from Weng T'ung-ho (翁同龢), the Imperial Tutor and Associate Grand Secretary, he had actually been first in both the chin-shih and Court examinations, but his standing had been changed because of the opposition of two high officials. He was appointed to office in the Board of Works, but did not accept the appointment.

At this time, on his third attempt to memorialize the Throne, he succeeded. This memorial was a redraft of previous recommendations, urging broad reforms in the government. While this memorial was published, a fourth one was suppressed by his enemies. He wanted to return to the south, but upon the urging of his friends remained a short time longer, publishing articles in a paper put out with his pupils Liang Ch'i-ch'ao and Mai Meng-hua (麥孟華). He also organized a group called the Society for Studying Strengthening [of the Nation] (強學會), and this began to attract a number of the scholars in the capital. It was also at this time that Timothy Richard[10] first joined the reform movement in Peking. Although there were many powerful officials who supported this reform group and supplied financial backing, there were likewise highly placed enemies of its objectives. K'ang soon departed for Shanghai, where he opened another study society and started up a paper. But a decree from Peking forced both of the societies to close down, and the Shanghai paper as well. In the twelfth month K'ang returned to Kwangtung.

The following year he taught at the provincial capital, continued his always prolific writing, travelled throughout Kwangtung and Kwangsi, and founded another paper at Macao with Ho Sui-t'ien (何穗田), called Know the New (知新報). This paper continued publication for over two years. His Confucius as a Reformer was put into final form, and he began a Bibliography of Japanese Books

(日本書目志). This was based on the numerous Japanese works he had by that time collected, which he had had his eldest daughter translate.[11] K'ang realized that the strength of the Western countries lay in their specialization in studies, and he believed that China must import this specialized learning in order to become strong. But since it was difficult to learn Western languages, the solution lay in acquiring the Western learning through the Japanese translations by then available in large numbers. (p. 193.)

In 1897 K'ang went to Kweilin, where he started up another study group, and busied himself with teaching and writing. His *Bibliography of Japanese Books* was completed, and along with *Confucius as a Reformer* and a study of Tung Chung-shu's interpretations of the *Ch'un Ch'iu*, was printed by the newly founded Ta T'ung Translation Bookstore in Shanghai. At this time, he had become concerned with the problem of over-population in China, and was sponsoring a plan to develop emigration to Brazil. He therefore travelled north to Peking once again; but the sudden occurrence of the Kiaochow affair[12] changed his objective into a new effort to bring about governmental reforms so as to save China from disaster. He presented another memorial pleading for reform, started up another society like the previously established one, and joined his voice to those who were advocating an alliance with England and Japan to oppose Russian aggression. He urged the opening of all of China's ports to international trade as being the best method of utilizing the power of the foreign nations to preserve Chinese territorial integrity. It was also in this year that K'ang took a second wife.[13]

In 1898, when K'ang Yu-wei was forty-one, there occurred his sudden rise to great power, and his equally swift fall to defeat and exile. The story of this affair has been told in English in such writings as Bland and Backhouse's *China under the Empress Dowager*, Meribeth Cameron's *The Reform Movement in China*, and the great biographical dictionary edited by Arthur Hummel, *Eminent Chinese of the Ch'ing Period*, to name three of the more important studies.[14] It does not seem necessary, therefore, to discuss the events of 1898 here, all-important though they were in the life of K'ang Yu-wei. As is well known, the young Kuang Hsü Emperor had become convinced that the reforms advocated by K'ang and his party were essential, if

China were to survive; taking the bit in his teeth, he began to issue one reform edict after another, based on the programme spelled out by K'ang Yu-wei. The latter was, for a few months, to all intents and purposes the legislator of the Chinese Government.

The brief hour of power was brought to an end by the Empress Dowager, who had been watching this revolution with increasing alarm. Acceding to the pleas of the reactionary and conservative elements at Court, she deposed the Emperor and entered upon her third Regency. K'ang Yu-wei, along with his most prominent colleagues, was of course condemned to be executed. Six of the reformers actually suffered execution (including K'ang Kuang-jen, Yu-wei's younger brother, and T'an Ssu-t'ung, still respected both for his voluntary acceptance of martyrdom in this affair, and for his book, *Jen Hsüeh*; but K'ang himself made his escape from Peking, and eventually to Japan, as did Liang Ch'i-ch'ao.

K'ang was in Japan from the ninth month of 1898 to the second month of 1899. Liang Ch'i-ch'ao, with others of the reform party, founded a paper in Yokohama to carry on the fight. At this time Sun Yat-sen was also working in Japan with his revolutionary group. He wished to join forces with K'ang and Liang, but K'ang refused to meet with the revolutionary leader. This was only the first manifestation of the fundamental cleavage between the two men: Sun believed a revolution must be brought about, to replace the decadent Ch'ing dynasty and the entire imperial system with a republican government; K'ang believed that the best hope for China was to bring about reforms within the framework of the traditional system, with the modification of the absolute monarchy into a constitutional monarchy. He knew that the young Emperor was willing to carry out these reforms if given the chance, and so he bent his energies to the task of restoring the Emperor to power. In 1899 K'ang went to Canada, where he founded the Society to Preserve the Emperor (保皇會). The one attempt at forceful action made by K'ang's group occurred in the next year, when, hoping to take advantage of the chaotic conditions of the moment (largely due to the Boxer troubles), an army was formed under T'ang Ts'ai-ch'ang (唐才常), which was to take over the southern provinces. The plan miscarried, and the resulting arrests and executions caused K'ang to abandon any further thoughts of using violence in the pursuit of his aims.

During these several years following the Hundred Days of Reform, K'ang's life was very unsettled. He was constantly on the move, living in Hong Kong, Japan, America, England, Japan again, Penang, Singapore, India. He was very much a wanted and hunted man, with the fear of assassination ever present. He was preoccupied with the raising of funds and other activities connected with the movement to restore the Emperor; at the same time, he continued to write, completing such works as *Mencius Analysed* (孟子微), *Lun Yü Annotated* (論語注), and *Ta Hsüeh Annotated* (大學注).

It was in Darjeeling, India, in 1902, when K'ang Yu-wei was forty-five years old, that he finally completed the work now entitled *Ta T'ung Shu*.[15] At the time this may not have seemed as important to him as a letter which he received from the overseas Chinese members of the Society to Preserve the Emperor. These people had become discouraged at the lack of success in accomplishing restoration of the Emperor, and were now in favour of stronger measures. Even K'ang's own disciples were becoming impatient, and were beginning to think along revolutionary lines. K'ang wrote open letters to these two groups, stating his firm conviction that a constitutional monarchy was the only answer to China's problems, and rejecting the revolutionary thesis.[16]

With the death of his arch-enemy at Court, the Empress Dowager's kinsman Jung Lu (榮祿), K'ang felt it safe to return to Hong Kong in 1903. On the way there he visited Burma and Java. He did not remain for long in Hong Kong, but departed early in 1904 for an extended tour of the West, which lasted for some five years and took him to eleven different countries. During 1907 he took a third wife.[17]

The sudden death of the Kuang Hsü Emperor in 1908—which was immediately followed by that of the Empress Dowager—profoundly shocked K'ang Yu-wei. Although to this day the circumstances of the Emperor's death are not clear, K'ang was convinced that he had been poisoned by Yüan Shih-k'ai. He poured out his hatred of Yüan[18] in several writings, accusing him of the dastardly crime and crying for revenge upon the traitor.

During the next three years K'ang lived in Singapore, Penang, Hong Kong, Germany, and Japan. He once narrowly escaped assassination. He watched events at home moving with increasing momentum towards a revolution, and did not cease to counsel constitutional monarchy-plus-reform as the better alternative. However, in the tenth month of 1911 the Republic of China was declared, with Dr. Sun Yat-sen as provisional president.

It was 1912, and K'ang Yu-wei was fifty-five. While he had deplored the revolution, and considered it the wrong solution for China's problems, he did not fight against the new Republican Government. His attention was directed instead upon the dangers which threatened from within and without. He implored the northern and southern factions to unite, lest China be partitioned among the foreign powers. He pointed out that it was no longer a question of Chinese revolutionaries versus Manchu court, but of the Republican Government versus Yüan Shih-k'ai. Unity of the nation was the essential thing. The territories of Mongolia and Tibet had declared their independence and they were in imminent danger of being taken over by foreign powers. K'ang also wrote on the necessity of basing the financial policy of the new government soundly on metal. Again, he came out against the proposed banking loan to be obtained from the Powers. This year Liang Ch'i-ch'ao returned to China from his long exile; while Hsü Ch'in, a faithful disciple of K'ang, was elected by overseas Chinese as a member of the new parliament.

The following year K'ang started publication of a monthly magazine entitled *Compassion* (不忍雜誌). This title was meant to indicate his feelings as he considered the sufferings of his nation in the present day. The contents, written by K'ang himself, comprised writings on government, [Confucian] teachings, his travels throughout the world, and literary pieces including poetry. Many of these were earlier writings, such as 'Confucius as a Reformer'. The magazine was issued from February to November of 1913. K'ang later added two issues, and had the whole published in two bound volumes, in 1917.

In 1913, also, his mother died in Hong Kong, at the age of eighty-three. K'ang had just undergone an operation for ulcers in Tokyo, and was unable to return immediately; so that it was not until the eleventh month of the year that he arrived in Hong Kong, and thence journeyed to Yang Ch'eng, where the interment took place accompanied by manifestations of respect from the governor of the province and local authorities. This was the first time that K'ang Yu-wei had set foot on the soil of his native land since fleeing for his life in 1898. He was now fifty-six.

His old enemy, Yüan Shih-k'ai, whom he had so bitterly denounced as the murderer of the Kuang Hsü Emperor, had now replaced Dr. Sun as president of the new Republic. Yüan sent three successive telegrams to K'ang, asking him to join the government. The latter refused on the ground that he was in mourning for his mother.

The next year he suffered two additional losses in the deaths of his sister I Hung (逸 紅) and his young third wife, Ho Chan-li. Along with these personal tragedies there continued a series of national misfortunes which caused him deep anguish and compassion. The great European war broke out, and while China declared its neutrality, Japan entered against Germany, and used this as a pretext to seize German-held Tsingtao and the province of Shantung. Then in 1915 Japan served China with the notorious 'Twenty-one Demands'. In addition, Yüan Shih-k'ai had scarcely been elected president that he attempted to make himself emperor. Civil war broke out as Sun Yat-sen and his followers hastened back from Japan to take up arms against Yüan; while K'ang, for once in sympathy with Sun, came out against this would-be emperor. His disciple Hsü Ch'in, with the financial backing of K'ang's wife, Madam Chang, raised a flotilla of warships and attacked Kwangtung.

Yüan soon disavowed his imperial designs; but K'ang was sure that he intended to monopolize control of the government in fact. Therefore he wrote a letter to the governors of the seven southern provinces, urging them to hold fast and to maintain neutrality in the interests of the entire nation. In the second month of 1916 he also wrote a lengthy essay suggesting the adoption of three policies: the institution of an hereditary presidency without real powers; the establishment of a council of elder statesmen elected from all the provinces and dependencies, which would have in its hands the real powers of government; a figure-head monarch, performing the same function as the British monarch. K'ang considered the American and French forms of republicanism as impossible to carry out in China;

he pointed out that the essence of republicanism lay not in the existence or non-existence of a monarch, but in the extent of the rights of the people.

Upon the death of Yüan Shih-k'ai in June of this year, K'ang had become hopeful of actually bringing an end to the chaos within the country—due, as he thought, to the unsuitability of the new form of government—by a restoration of the Ch'ing dynasty. He wrote an open letter on this matter to his followers; he also corresponded with General Chang Hsün, urging him to take advantage of the circumstances, and to rally to the support of the legitimate emperor. As before, however, K'ang was doomed to failure in the realization of his plans. The restoration was a fizzle. He was forced to take sanctuary in the American Legation, where he remained for half a year, occupying the time by writing a book expounding his criticisms of republican government. A glance at the mandate he issued during the few days of his incumbency as an official of the 'restoration government' shows that his ideas on reforms had not changed in any essentials from those of 1898. (p. 232.)

At the year's end he was convoyed out of the capital by American officials, and returned to his home in Kwangtung. It was the end of his active participation in public affairs. He maintained his interest in the political situation, sending telegrams to one and another of the powerful men in the arena of civil conflict, ever urging unity of the nation. He never abandoned his loyalty to the cause of a constitutional monarchy or to the memory of the Kuang Hsü Emperor who once, so long before, had tried to carry out the policies which K'ang believed would save China.

In 1922 his wife, Madam Chang, for many years his faithful helpmeet in all the difficult situations of his unsettled life, died at the age of sixty-seven. In the second month of 1927 his former pupils and followers gathered from near and far in Shanghai to celebrate the teacher's seventieth birthday. Liang Ch'i-ch'ao wrote a special essay for the occasion, recalling the inspiring days when he was a student of K'ang Yu-wei in the 'Thatched Hall in Ten Thousand Trees' and eulogizing his teacher as the man who opened up the new era in China's history. The Hsüan T'ung Pretender sent him a scroll with the words 'Peak of peaks, deep and clear' (嶽峙淵清), in recognition of his lifetime of loyalty and fidelity.

Twenty-five days after the celebration, on the twenty-eighth day of the second month (March 31), 1927, death ended the career of K'ang Yu-wei: a man of singular genius, unswerving high principles, and noble compassion; a man whose vision places him among the greatest of those who have dreamed of a world in which there shall be happiness without suffering.

REFERENCES

[1] A kind of literary exercise of a very artificial type, but formerly required in the examinations.

[2] Teng, Fairbank, and Sun say of this work: 'It was not so long and less broadly discursive, compared with Wei Yuan's *Hai-kuo t'u-chih* [海國圖志 , 1844]; as a straight summary of world geography based on Western sources it was more handy and succinct—one might say "scientific".' [It was printed in 1850, and reprinted by the Tsungli Yamen in 1866.] (See *China's Response to the West*, p. 62.)

[3] The first wife, *née* Chang (張), was two years his senior. She had been betrothed to him when he was eight.

[4] The duty of a filial son included this dwelling by the grave. From Mencius we learn, for example, that the disciples of Confucius remained by his grave for three years; and that one of them, Tzu-kung, could not bear to leave for an additional three years. (*Mencius*, III, A, 4.13.)

[5] 賢 A word for which there is no adequate English equivalent. The term indicates a man of moral eminence, who is yet not quite to be ranked as a sage. Thus, Confucius, of course, is a sage, while his seventy-two disciples are called 'hsien'. (On these terms, and the general subject of official Confucian titles, see John K. Shryock, *The Origin and Development of the State Cult of Confucius*, New York, 1932, especially Chapter IX, and Appendices.)

[6] Liang Ch'i-ch'ao tells us (*Biography of K'ang Yu-wei*, Chapter III) that the books which K'ang purchased at that time were those published by the Kiangnan Arsenal and the missionary societies. He remarks that these translations were all on 'elementary, common studies, and technology, military methods, and medicine; if not, then they were only the Christian scriptures and commentaries. On political science, there was nothing whatsoever'.

[7] The first foreign-sponsored organization for this purpose was the Anti-Footbinding Society founded by Mrs. Archibald Little in Shanghai, in 1895. (See Richard, *Forty-Five Years in China*, pp. 226–8.)

[8] Often rendered as *A Review of the Times*. An influential journal founded by the Rev. Young J. Allen in 1875, and edited by him until his death in 1907. During the latter half of this period, it was the organ for the Christian Literature Society. It was an important agent in spreading information about the 'outside world' among the intellectuals of China.

[9] These names derive from a controversy which arose first during the Han period (206 B.C.–A.D. 220), concerning the authenticity of certain texts basic in the Chinese curriculum. The 'old text school' became dominant, and for many centuries there were but few proponents of the 'new texts'. One of the principle subjects of study by scholars in the Ch'ing period (1644–1911) was the matter of the authenticity of texts; K'ang Yu-wei is generally considered the last and most influential of the latter-day champions of the 'new text school'. (For a good discussion of the Han controversy, see Tjan [Tseng], *Po Hu T'ung*, vol. I, Section 36: 'The New Text and Old Text Controversy', pp. 137–45. For the philosophical developments based on the two schools, see Fung-Bodde, *History of Chinese Philosophy*, vol. II, Chapters II, IV, and XVI.)

[10] Timothy Richard reached China in 1870 under the auspices of the English Baptist Missionary Society. He became widely known and respected by the intellectual class throughout China as a man of scholarly attainment, deep sympathies for China, and personal integrity. His influence on the reform movement was undoubtedly important, although as yet it has not been analysed in any study of which I am aware. As an indication of this importance we can cite the fact that in a publication of the Peking reform society of February 1898, entitled a *New Collection of Tracts for the Times*, thirty-eight of the essays were by K'ang Yu-wei, forty-four by Liang Ch'i-ch'ao, and thirty-one by Richard. In 1898, during his brief period of power, K'ang invited Richard to become a foreign advisor to the Emperor. (On Richard, see Soothill's *Timothy Richard of China*, and Richard's own *Forty-Five Years in China*.)

[11] (p. 193.) Mr. K'ang's eldest son informs me, however, that this daughter is not able to read Japanese. But if we suppose that these Japanese translations were written in the 'Sinico-Japanese' style, it would then not be impossible for a Chinese student to grasp the meaning sufficiently well to make an adequate translation.

[12] An incident involving the murder of two German priests in Kiachwang, Shantung, which served as the pretext for Germany's forcing upon China a series of demands; these demands led to Germany's assuming a position of economic and military dominance in the rich province of Shantung.

[13] The second wife, *née* Liang (梁), is at the date of this writing living near Taipei, Formosa, aged seventy-five.

[14] See also Bibliography, Section 3.

[15] (p. 217.) This is stated by Liang Ch'i-ch'ao in a note in *Anthology of Poems of the Gentleman from Nan Hai* (南海先生詩集), published Hsüan T'ung, third year (1911), *chüan* 1, p. 1.

[16] A discussion of this matter is found in Sung Yün-pin's *K'ang Yu-wei*, Chapter V, Section 2. (This author is strongly biased against K'ang and his views.)

[17] The third wife, *née* Ho (何), was an intelligent girl who had gone to America to pursue her studies. She had admired K'ang for a long time, keeping his picture on her wall. She became his concubine at the age of seventeen, with her parents' permission. (p. 228.)

[18] Yüan, one of the prominent figures in the history of this period, had been directly responsible for the downfall of the reformers and the *coup d'état* of the Empress Dowager in 1898: entrusted by the Emperor with the crucial task of removing the Empress Dowager from the scene, and of executing Jung Lu, Yüan instead passed on a warning of these plans to the latter, who was his chief. Thus K'ang Yu-wei's hatred of him was from the most understandable of reasons.

'Ta T'ung Shu': The Book

As we have noted in the first chapter (p. 13), the work which is now entitled *Ta T'ung Shu* was originally called *Universal Principles of Mankind* (人類公理), when K'ang Yu-wei wrote the first draft in 1884–5. This draft is not now extant, so far as is known,[1] nor is the whereabouts of any other, later draft known to me. That the author made changes at later times is known. According to his own *Chronology*[2] he revised the *Universal Principles of Mankind* in 1887. The text itself contains mention (on p. 267) of the death of President William McKinley, which occurred in September 1901. Liang Ch'i-ch'ao, in a note in the *Anthology of Poems of the Gentleman from Nan-Hai* (南海先生詩集) which was published in 1911, states that (what had now been titled) *Ta T'ung Shu* was completed in 1902, while K'ang Yu-wei was residing in Darjeeling, India.[3] Aside from the fact that Liang Ch'i-ch'ao was in a better position to know the facts than almost anyone else, due to his long and intimate relationship with Mr. K'ang, this date is reasonable from the evidence of the text as we now have it.[4]

In his *General Discussion of Ch'ing Dynasty Scholarship*, Liang Ch'i-ch'ao tells us that it was only he and Ch'en Ch'ien-ch'iu who, as young students of K'ang Yu-wei, were given the opportunity to see this work; but that the teacher refused to permit its publication, on the ground that its ideas were too advanced for the times.[5] In his school at the 'Thatched Hall in Ten Thousand Trees', Mr. K'ang did not lecture on *ta t'ung*. The world being as yet in the 'Age of Disorder', he was only concerned to discuss with his students the problems of the present era.[6]

It was not until 1913 that Liang Ch'i-ch'ao prevailed upon his teacher to publish the first two parts of *Ta T'ung Shu* (comprising about one-third of the whole work) in the pages of Mr. K'ang's magazine, *Compassion*.[7] The published portions contained plenty of ideas which were radical at the time, but these were not yet so extreme as what were contained in the remainder which Mr. K'ang still refused to publish. According to the Preface of the San Francisco edition of the book (published in 1929 and also including only the first two parts), Mr. K'ang was asked by a Columbia University professor[8] to have the entire work translated into English, but this he would not consent to do. President Wilson was also said to have made the same suggestion in vain.[9] It was not until 1935, eight years after K'ang Yu-wei's death, that the complete book was published, under the care of Mr. Ch'ien Ting-an (錢定安), a former pupil of Mr. K'ang, by the Chung Hwa Book Company.

Thus far the name of the work under consideration has been given only in a transliterated form. It is time that an explanation of this name and an indication of the contents be given. As is the case with so many concepts originating in a culture which has developed apart from the West, a mere translation will not serve our understanding, and we require an elucidation.

So, then, we will recall that in 1884-5, when K'ang Yu-wei was writing his first draft of the *Universal Principles of Mankind*, he also completed another essay, entitled *'Li Yün' Annotated*.[10] That these two studies were undertaken at the same time is not an accident. For it is in the 'Li Yün', one of the sections of the canonical *Li Chi*,[11] that the conception of *ta t'ung* is set forth.[12] It may be interesting, if only to show how differing translations of classical Chinese can be, to quote this passage in the versions of four different translators. Confucius is made to say the following words.

(According to James Legge):

'When the Grand course was pursued, a public and common opinion ruled all under the sky; they chose men of talents, virtue, and ability; their words were sincere, and what they cultivated was harmony. Thus men did not love their parents only, nor treat as children only their own sons. A competent provision was secured for the aged till their death, employment for the able-bodied, and the means of growing up to the young. They showed kindness and compassion to widows, orphans, childless men, and those who were disabled by disease, so that they were all sufficiently maintained. Males had their proper work, and females had their homes. (They accumulated) articles (of value), disliking that they should be thrown away upon the ground, but not willing to keep them for their own gratification. (They laboured) with their strength, disliking that it should not be exerted, but not exerting it (only) with a view to their own advantage. In this way (selfish) schemings were repressed and found no development. Robbers, filchers, and rebellious traitors did not show themselves, and hence the outer doors remained open, and were not shut. This was (the period of) what we call the Grand Union.' (*Li Ki*, 'Li Yün', pp. 364–6.)

(According to Tsuchida Kyoson):

'When the Great Way is realized, the following will surely take place: all the world will be a common possession; the wise and the able are elected; all people will be bound by equal ties of intimacy so that no man sees only his father as father nor only his son as son; the old keep their case, the ripened youth has his responsibilities; the boy and the girl are trained up, widows, orphans, the disabled and the like are respectively cared for; men take their respective parts while women respectively marry; as for property, while one would hate to let it go to waste, he will not wish to have it in private possession; as for man's talents, while he would hate not to have exercised them, he will not necessarily expend them on himself; and thus plots will come to an end, thieves and brawlers will not be seen, so that people will come to leave every door open: such an age should be called *Ta T'ung*.' (*Contemporary Thought of Japan and China*, pp. 194–5.)

(According to Wu Kuo-cheng):

'When the great principle prevails, the whole world is bent upon the common good. The virtuous and able are honoured, sincerity is praised, and harmony is cultivated. Hence, the people not only treat their own parents and children as they should be treated, but others' as well. They provide that all the old are given comfort, all the adults are given work, all the young are given development, all the widowed, orphaned, helpless, disabled and defective people are given nourishment. For every male there is a division of land; for every female there is a home. The people dislike to have wealth wasted; but they do not like to hoard it up for themselves. They dislike to have their strength unemployed; but they do not like to work solely for themselves. Hence, all cunning designs become useless, and theft and banditry do not exist . . . This is called "the age of Great Universality".' (*Ancient Chinese Political Theories*, pp. 299–300.)

(According to Fung Yu-lan, as edited by Derk Bodde):

'When the great *Tao* was in practice, the world was common to all; men of talents, virtue and ability were selected; sincerity was emphasized and friendship was cultivated. Therefore, men did not love only their own parents, nor did they treat as children only their own sons. A competent provision was secured for the aged till their death, employment was given to the able bodied, and a means was provided for the upbringing of the young. Kindness and compassion were shown to widows, orphans, childless men, and those who were disabled by disease, so that they all had the wherewithal for support. Men had their proper work and women their homes. They hated to see the wealth of natural resources undeveloped, [so they developed it, but this development] was not for their own use. They hated not to exert themselves, [so they worked, but their work] was not for their own profit . . . This was called the great unity.' (*Short History of Chinese Philosophy*, pp. 202–3.)

We shall not in this place consider the philosophy of history underlying the above description.[13] But it will be apparent from the passage that, whether the translator has rendered it in the future or in the past tense, 'Confucius' is picturing an ideal state of society and of human nature. This ideal state is called *ta t'ung*. The question for the translator is, how to express that idea concisely in English. From the various authors who have essayed to do this, we may secure the following suggestions:

1. 'The Great Unity'.[14]
2. 'Grand Union', or 'Grand Course'.[15]
3. 'Cosmopolitan society'.[16]
4. 'The same social ideal as in Western communism or anarchism'.[17]
5. 'The Great Commonwealth'.[18]

6. 'The Great Similarity'.[19]
7. 'The age of Great Universality'.[20]
8. 'Era of "world brotherhood"'.[21]
9. 'The Great Communion'.[22]
10. 'Grand Harmony'.[23]
11. 'Great Similitude'.[24]
12. 'Great Similarity'.[25]
13. 'Cosmopolitanism'.[26]

Even if it were granted that all of the above were really true to the Chinese original, it is sure that most of them do not indicate to the reader in the slightest the connotation of the term of which they profess to be a translation. Of them all, number one is the most literal, and possibly the most accurate.

Another translation which would occur to the Westerner reading K'ang Yu-wei's book about *ta t'ung* is Utopia. The present author was rather tempted to adopt this translation. However, *Ta T'ung Shu* does not quite fit into the pattern of the Western utopias, whether of the type exemplified by Plato's *Republic*, by More's *Utopia* or by Butler's *Erewhon*. Perhaps the essential difference is in the spirit of completely realistic planning which motivates the Chinese work. Granting the visionary quality of the whole scheme, it is nevertheless logically developed from the world as it is, and offers solutions to human problems which may in truth be otherwise insoluble. It is a 'utopia', therefore, only in the sense in which a serious treatise, dealing with universal human problems and social problems in particular, and conceived on a grand scale, may be called utopian.

Under the ever-increasing specialization of modern scholarship, we will no doubt be inclined to disapprove of any such sweeping treatment of problems which we have become aware are so hugely complex. And yet, such organizations as the League of Nations and the United Nations are evidence that sweeping measures must be taken to cope with these problems. One feels that a Woodrow Wilson and a Wendell Willkie would have hailed K'ang Yu-wei as a guide and prophet, could they have read his book. Willkie's 'One World' is a phrase which contains in its implications for us in the present day pretty much what *ta t'ung* meant to K'ang. These terms both connote a world of political, social, and economic unity and equality; a world in which the age-old barriers between man and man, and group and group, have been done away with.

Ta T'ung Shu, or *One World Book*, in its printed form, as published by the Chung Hwa Book Company in 1935, is a long work, occupying four hundred and fifty-four pages, with certainly well over one hundred and fifty thousand Chinese characters. The style is the concise literary style which conveys ideas in much more abbreviated form than would be required for expression in English; so that a full English translation would require many more words than there are Chinese characters. In only a few places has the author affected a recondite manner; the great bulk of the text is written in a clear, expository way. While K'ang Yu-wei is not the brilliant writer that his pupil Liang Ch'i-ch'ao is, he does have a knack of hammering away at his point with force and persistence. The book is organized into ten parts, with chapters and sections subsumed. So that the reader may get some idea of the subject-matter as a whole, together with the relative amount of space devoted to each topic, the Table of Contents is reproduced below in translation, with pagination indicated.

Such, in outline, are the major topics discussed by the author in this work. In the second part of the present work, the reader will find the material itself, in the form of translations and summaries. In the chapter immediately following this one we shall undertake a summary and analysis of that material.

REFERENCES

[1] Mr. K'ang Shou-man (康壽曼), eldest son of K'ang Yu-wei, so stated to me.

[2] As cited by Chao Feng-t'ien in his *Nien-p'u* (see above, Chapter I, n. 1). The original *Chronology* exists in two manuscript copies now in

private hands, according to Mr. Chao (*Nien-p'u*, p. 239). It covers the first forty years of K'ang Yu-wei's life.

[3] See above, Chapter I, p. 19.

[4] Ch'ien Mu, in an elaborate critique of K'ang's writings, concurs in the reasonableness of the dates 1884 and 1902 (see his *History of Chinese Scholarship during the Last Three Hundred Years*, pp. 699–700, and chart, pp. 111 and 116). The following places in the text indicate additions possibly later than 1902: the mention (on p. 399) of the 'opening' of the Panama Canal (begun in 1880 by the French; first work begun by the United States in 1904; actual construction started in 1907; first ship went through in 1914; officially opened in 1915), the description (on p. 442) of the appearance of the earth from a balloon (see below, Book Two, Part X, n. 4); the author's notes mentioning enactment of the Russian constitution (1905) (p. 130) and the loss of Korea (which came increasingly under Japan's control from 1895 to 1909) (p. 133); and the remark about 'flying ships' becoming more common (p. 136).

[5] Liang Ch'i-ch'ao, *General Discussion of Ch'ing Dynasty Scholarship*, p. 136.

[6] See reference cited in n. 5.

[7] Tseng Yu-hao, in a note on p. 48 of his *Modern Chinese Legal and Political Philosophy*, gives the first publication of *Ta T'ung Shu* as 1885 (Canton, Shanghai, Chang Hsing Book Store 長興書局), but this is certainly mistaken.

[8] The name of this professor is given as 'Hsia-te' (夏德), i.e. [Friedrich] Hirth, a well-known sinologist and first professor of Chinese at Columbia. This story is repeated by Lung Chieng-fu, in his dissertation on *The Evolution of Chinese Social Thought*, p. 316. Lung may have drawn it from the San Francisco edition's Preface.

[9] This is found in the same sources.

[10] That '*Li Yün*' *Annotated* actually was composed at this date has been seriously questioned by Ch'ien Mu (see his *History of Chinese Scholarship during the Last Three Hundred Years*, pp. 697–701). However, it is not within our province here to examine this question. Whether or not '*Li Yün*' *Annotated* was written only as a later bulwark to K'ang's views, the conception of *ta t'ung* does come from the famous passage in the '*Li Yün*'. (One might perhaps observe that, although Ch'ien does make a strong case for his opinion that '*Li Yün*' and its *ta t'ung* ideal were not important in K'ang's thinking as early as 1884–5—for example, the title

of his book was then *Universal Principles*, and not *Ta T'ung Shu*; yet, how is one then to account for the frequent use of the term *ta t'ung* within the text? It seems hardly likely that the author would have interpolated this term in so very many places, at a later date.)

[11] Authorship of 'Li Yün' is unknown; modern scholarship places collection of the *Li Chi* writings in the Former Han dynasty, and authorship at various unknown dates prior to that time.

[12] This term is first found in *Shang Shu*, 'Hung Fan 洪範', in a passage referring to divination: 'Now you consent . . . the tortoise consents, the milfoil consents, the dignitaries and noblemen consent, the common people consent; that is called the *great concord*' (Karlgren's rendering, in *The Book of Documents*, reprinted from *Museum of Far Eastern Antiquities Bulletin* 22, Stockholm, 1950, p. 33, italics mine). It has been a common expression, used for names of places and emperors' reigns, and is still current today, in the Nationalist anthem, for example.

[13] See below, Chapter III.

[14] Fung, *Short History of Chinese Philosophy*, p. 324.

[15] Thomas, *Chinese Political Thought*, p. 44, uses the second; Legge, *Li Ki*, p. 366, uses the first.

[16] Teng, Fairbank, and Sun, *China's Response to the West*, p. 392.

[17] Tsuchida, *Contemporary Thought of Japan and China*, p. 196.

[18] Lung, *Evolution of Chinese Social Thought*, p. 315; Lin, *Men and Ideas*, p. 32.

[19] Chen, *Economic Principles of Confucius and His School*, p. 16; F. W. Hummel, *The Role of Historical Criticism in the Chinese Renaissance of Today*, p. 48.

[20] Wu, *Ancient Chinese Political Theories*, p. 300.

[21] A. W. Hummel, *Autobiography of a Chinese Historian*, p. xiii.

[22] Wilhelm, *The Soul of China*, p. 78.

[23] Tseng, *Modern Chinese Legal and Political Philosophy*, p. 46.

[24] H. B. Morse, *International Relations of the Chinese Empire*, vol. III, p. 132, London, 1918. (Cited in Tseng, loc. cit.)

[25] Hsü, *Political Philosophy of Confucianism*, p. 237.

[26] Ibid., Bibliography, p. 250.

[27] This chapter title was inadvertently omitted from the printed text.

[28] 天民 From *Mencius*. Legge renders: 'Heaven's plan in the production of mankind is this:—that they who are first informed should instruct those who are later in being informed, and they who first apprehend

principles should instruct those who are slower to do so. I am one of Heaven's people who have first apprehended . . .' Again: 'Heaven's plan in the production of mankind is this:—that they who are first informed should instruct those who are later in being informed, and they who first apprehend principles should instruct those who are slower in doing so. I am the one of Heaven's people who has first apprehended . . .' (James Legge, *The Four Books: The Works of Mencius*, II, A, 7.5, p. 804 and pp. 813–14. I have used the photolith edition, n.p., n.d.)

29 工黨業主.

30 太平 This term, as used by K'ang Yu-wei, in many cases connotes either, or both, of the meanings here given. The hyphenated compound is a translator's dodge.

31 仁 Despite all efforts, this word defies the translators. The latest suggestions, offered by Peter Boodberg (see his 'The Semasiology of Some Primary Confucian Concepts', in *Philosophy East and West* [Quarterly], vol. II, no. 4, January 1953, pp. 317–32), are 'hominimity', or 'co-humanity', which do not seem likely to me to replace previous renderings, inadequate though those may be. There is really no reason why the Chinese term should not become common philosophical tender in the same way that many Buddhist terms, for example, have done; since *jen* is a concept of great importance in the history of Chinese thought, and offers new points of view to philosophers of other backgrounds.

CHAPTER III

A General Discussion of the One-World Philosophy of K'ang Yu-wei

THE purpose of offering a translation is to afford the inquirer an opportunity for seeing, as clearly as possible through the imperfect medium of the translation, just what an author actually said, and how he said it. In this way the reader is enabled to make his own analysis, to form his own judgments, and to feel confident that he has a real grasp of the author's thought. The present discussion is not intended, therefore, as a 'clarification' of what our author has said, since the translator feels that the author was quite capable of making his own presentation in a form suitable to the best communication of his ideas. The reader will, by having the text available for examination, no doubt feel on his part as competent to draw his own conclusions as the translator.

It may be convenient, however, for us to have a bird's-eye view of One World, preparatory to examining the text in detail. And there are a number of points with regard to our author's One-World philosophy which it is within the translator's province to bring to the reader's attention. In a work as long, varied, and unusual as *Ta T'ung Shu*, there is indeed material for a great deal of discussion. The present chapter will thus touch only upon certain matters which have struck the translator as especially interesting and noteworthy.

One World: A bird's-eye view

One World *is* one world because all the boundaries which created divisions (and hence oppositions) have been abolished. It is called the Age of Complete Peace-and-Equality. It is a polity in which, as far as is possible on this earth, the causes of suffering have been done away with, and all creatures are happy. The keyword of this polity is 'public', as opposed to 'private' (which is the same word in the Chinese as 'selfish'). The sole criterion for the rightness or wrongness of things in this world is whether or not they contribute to happiness. In every way the organization of this world is intended

37

to provide every individual with the maximum possible independence and freedom.

The child is born into this world within a public institution, and receives his nurture and education within various public institutions for the first twenty years. Thereby two things are provided for: first, that he does not have the responsibility for requiting his parents for their care, and second, that all persons will receive an equal physical, mental, and moral start in life. On the other hand, the father and mother are relieved of the burdens of providing for children, and are free to pursue their own careers as individuals. Of course, the principle of requital cannot be avoided, and the citizen of the world will be expected to repay the public for his twenty years of care and training by performing twenty years of service in some capacity of benefit to the public weal. However, this is not at all the same thing as the private burden of the old family system, since everyone requites this public debt by the mere fact of working at his job, whatever that may be.

The individual will have been prepared for a vocation by practical studies during his later school years. Upon graduation from college (which will be attended by all), he will face no problem of employment, since all occupations and all the work of the world is under (what we nowadays would call) a planned economy. Agriculture, industry, and commerce are all publicly owned and operated, as indeed are all other activities. And this world is not an 'economic world', nor is its citizen the 'economic man'. Money actually plays a small part in the lives of the people of One World, since almost everything which money now buys is then provided for by the system of the public institutions.

When our people fall in love they will find that the matter of sexual relations and marriage is regarded by One World in a completely practical way. Practicality, in the sense of that time, means the criterion of happiness or suffering. When people fall in love they may form alliances, which are for no longer than one year. For it is recognized that human nature is seldom satisfied for a long period of time with the same object. Therefore it is provided that the sufferings caused by compelling people who do not wish to remain together to stay married is abolished. Of course, those who do wish to stay married may renew their contracts for as long as they are happy together. One World will not apply any moral ban to the practice of homosexuality, either, since, judged by its criterion of happiness or suffering, no harm is done to others by the practice, and there will always be those who are happier in it than in the normal relationship.

The men and women of One World are entirely equal. Through the abolishment of the family, women are no longer burdened with the age-old duties of caring for children, nor are they merely playthings for men. There being no essential differences between men and women as human beings, women are not regarded any differently than men when it comes to work or to holding office.

By the very name of it, we know that in One World there will no longer exist such private divisions as the old states. Over all the globe, the public government holds authority, while most of the actual administration of government is in the hands of degree governments and local self-governments. In the public government there is the public parliament, to which members are elected by each of the degrees. The public parliament consists of an upper and a lower house,[1] but there is no higher officer such as a president. Besides the public parliament, there are the various ministries. The degree governments are semi-autonomous in operation, and their organs are similar to those of the public government. The degrees are units based on arbitrary division of the globe's surface into areas of measurement and have no other significance. They are a practical way to solve the problems of administration and elections, and are not, therefore, sovereign political entities. The local self-governments comprise the individual farms, factories, and stores. They are pure democracies, through their local councils in which every person has the right to express his views. On all levels, questions will be decided by public discussion and voting. Thus, there will be no political leaders, no political parties, and no individuals holding arbitrary legislative or decision-making powers. High office, in One World, is more a matter of honour than of actual authority. The governments of the various levels exist for only one purpose: to assure equality and efficient planning on a world-wide scale.

If one has noticed the absence of the judicial branch in our One World government, this is not an unintentional omission. For such will be the favourable social environment in this time that crimes and punishments will have been abolished. It is as a result of the conditions of the environment that men are forced into crimes, so that when the environment is favourable, criminal behaviour will automatically cease. Anti-social behaviour is treated in this age by what is called dishonouring the name. A more severe punishment is to hold the offender ineligible for office. Only in the case of such heinous crimes as abortion (heinous because its wholesale practice would endanger the survival of the species), or plotting to revive old institutions like the State or military force, would there be punishment by imprisonment.

Life as lived in One World is pleasant for all. Machines have done away with long hours of toil, and everyone has ample leisure time. The people of this time love to travel, and can do so with comfort in vehicles travelling on land, sea, and in the air, propelled by electricity, or perhaps by some new fuel. The climatically unsuitable regions of the earth have been evacuated as areas of habitation, and the public institutions are situated in the most healthful and pleasant locations. In these institutions, as well as in the various farms, factories, and stores, the people live on a communal basis, and everything is provided for them in the way of recreational and educational facilities, as well as gardens, zoos, and the like.

With life so secure in every way, and the public institutions providing every social benefit, will our citizens not become lazy, and may not this system degenerate? With no outlet for the competitive drive in business, politics, or military activity, how can this world continue to progress? The answer is that the competitive drive has been channelled into constructive action. The honours and rewards of this society are given to those who help to advance the arts and sciences of civilization, and to those who are outstanding for their *jen* (which, if we must have a translation, let us here render as goodness). The striving of men of this age is for constant betterment of civilization, and to encourage it there are awarded both honours and cash. (The latter is to free them entirely from other considerations so that they can devote all of their energy to additional work in the service of civilization.)

Supreme in this time is the science of medicine. The medical authorities are the ones to whom the lives and health of all are entrusted, and they have the final say in every phase of life, from

supervision of the public institutions to approval of building construction. Medical science has eliminated infectious diseases, and
indeed there are few persons in the public hospitals except for those
injured in accidents and for the aged who are dying. The latter may
be mercifully put out of their sufferings if it is agreed by the
physicians that there is no hope of recovery. To such an extent is
the health of all persons guarded that a daily physical check-up is
provided.

The power of the medical people being so great, it is necessary that
we be watchful for the rise of some medical Napoleon, who might
gather together a great following, and become a world ruler. And
the possibility of any person being idolized and thus heading a great
following is one of the few real dangers to One World. We do not
permit the formation of political parties, of medical parties, or even
of religious parties. The idolization of an individual and the formation of a group which follows him faithfully would be a sure way
to bring an end to One World, as it would inevitably give rise to
inequalities and other evils of the Age of Disorder.

For all human beings are entirely equal in this time. The races
have become blended into one great race. Women and men are not
distinguished even by the clothing they wear. Government officials
are merely citizens who, having demonstrated their superior knowledge and *jen*, have been chosen by their fellow-citizens to occupy
positions of honour. And in One World, so far as it is possible, *jen*
is extended even to the birds and beasts. However, there is a practical
limit to this extension: the limit is reached when it becomes a choice
between perfection of *jen* or the survival of the human species. Since
man must live, he cannot help but kill both those creatures dangerous
to him and those creatures which are inadvertently trampled on, or
breathed in. But all other creatures are kindly treated. The eating of
meat is no longer a human practice. The most intelligent animals
(monkeys) are even trained as servants.

Upon the attainment of this One World of Complete Peace-and-
Equality, the ideals of Confucius have been realized. The religions
of Christianity and Islam have been left behind, in the progress of
civilization. The utmost 'Law of this world' is One World. There
remain ahead only the studies of the art of immortality (that is,
Taoism), and of becoming a buddha. Persons who have returned to

the public their twenty years of service may thereupon follow their own inclinations in undertaking such studies. The study of buddha-hood is higher than that of becoming immortal, and still higher than the study of buddhahood is the study of 'roaming through the Heavens'. But with such studies we have left the Law of this world, and we enter another sphere.

The world of suffering: K'ang's ideas, and Buddhism

The title of the first part of *Ta T'ung Shu* tells us in itself what impelled K'ang Yu-wei to write the book. It has also given rise to such statements as that he merely borrowed this idea from Buddhism and is not, therefore, original.[2]

The realization that beneath the surface manifestations of happiness man's life is basically suffering is not, of course, at all novel. And as a student of Buddhism, K'ang of course knew that the Buddhist philosophy of life is founded on this fact of suffering. (And of course any social philosopher starts from the sufferings or unhappiness of mankind as his reason for philosophizing.) But it is quite obvious that K'ang is not really indebted to Buddhism for anything more than the *emphasis* on the fact of suffering—and that it is most probable he would have been struck by this fact, even without having studied Buddhism. Let us demonstrate this briefly:

The Buddhist premise is that life is suffering; the Buddhist analysis is that the cause of suffering is desire; the Buddhist solution is the extinction of desire.

K'ang's premise is that life is suffering; his analysis is that the cause of suffering is the nine boundaries;[3] his solution is the abolishing of these nine boundaries. He specifically rejects the Buddhist solution. Not only does he point out that the extinction of desire would lead to the vanishing from the earth of the human species, but he positively holds the *gratification* of the desires to be the Good:

'Therefore, [the nature of] human life depends upon what men consider to be the Way; [what] depends upon man's Way is simply pain and pleasure. What is schemed for by men is simply to abolish pain so as to find pleasure. There is no other Way[4] . . . The establishment of laws, and the creation of teachings [of the Way] which cause men to have happiness (i.e. pleasure) and to be [entirely] without suffering: [this] is the best [form] of the Good.'[5]

K'ang cannot, as the Buddhist does, abandon his family, his country, and the world. He cannot, because he feels an obligation for what he has received from them,[6] and because he feels love and compassion for other beings. In a word, K'ang is completely Confucian, rather than Buddhistic, in his attitude towards the problem of suffering. And he transcends the Confucian attitude in that he looks beyond Chinese society to embrace the whole world—even the universe—in his scheme of things.

'Men have compassionate natures'

When we say that K'ang cannot abandon the world because he feels love and compassion for other beings, we note that he is here firmly based on one of the most ancient and universally accepted theories of Chinese thought. The classical statement of this theory was made by Mencius, as follows:

> 'Mencius said, "All men have a mind which cannot bear [to see the sufferings of] others . . . When I say that all men have a mind which cannot bear [to see the sufferings] of others, my meaning may be illustrated thus:—even nowadays, if men suddenly see a child about to fall into a well, they will without exception experience a feeling of alarm and distress. [They will feel so,] not as a ground on which they may gain the favour of the child's parents, nor as a ground on which they may seek the praise of their neighbours and friends, nor from a dislike to the reputations of [having been unmoved by] such a thing. From this case we may perceive that the feeling of commiseration is essential to man . . ."'[7]

One wonders if the conviction of the rightness of this theory has not been one of Confucianism's staunchest bulwarks against the arguments of Buddhism, down through the ages. K'ang accepts the theory, but feels some need to give it additional verification. This he does through bringing in a metaphysical theory.

The 'compassionate mind', 'ether', 'spirit', 'jen', and 'ch'i'

The reason why all men have a 'compassionate mind' is that they are all formed from 'spiritual ch'i'. This ch'i is a concept even more ancient than Mencius's theory, and has played a great part in Chinese philosophy, especially in the Sung neo-Confucianism. *Ch'i*, says K'ang, is lightning (or electricity) which has 'awareness', or in other words, what is commonly called 'spirit'. All things arose from *ch'i*, and all things are moved by it. 'No creatures are without "lightning", no creatures are without spirit.' It is this 'aware-*ch'i*', then, which ensures the 'compassionate mind':'If there is perception and awareness, then there is attraction. Thus it is with the lodestone; how much more is it with man!'[8]

Pleasure (happiness), pain (suffering), and the Good

Naturally, in planning for an ideal world one has clearly in mind what it is that constitutes the Good for mankind. K'ang's views on this matter are similar to those of the Western utilitarians. He presents a psychological argument:

> 'The nerves of the brain contain the animus. Encountering material and immaterial [objects], there are then those which suit it, and those which do not suit it, those which please it, and those which do not please it. Those objects which please and suit the nerves of the brain then cause the spiritual soul pleasure; those [objects] which do not please and suit the nerves of the brain then cause the spiritual soul pain . . . Therefore, in human life there is only suiting and not suiting. What does not suit, is pain. What suits and suits again, is pleasure.'[9]

He analyses the laws and institutions of history, to show that they have all been established with the purpose of enabling men to attain happiness (pleasure) and to avoid suffering (pain). He observes that even the painful actions carried out by ascetics or self-sacrificing heroes is for the purpose of obtaining a greater pleasure through a lesser pain.[10] 'Therefore, under the firmament, all who have life only seek pleasure and shun suffering. There is no other Way.'[11]

His criterion for an ideal world is therefore obvious: 'The establishment of laws, and the creation of teachings [of the Way] which cause men to have happiness and to be [entirely] without suffering: [this] is the best [form] of the Good.'[12]

And on the more general moral question we have what I suppose will be called a pragmatic attitude:

'Now in universal principles originally there is no "good" or "evil". [Our concepts of] right and wrong are all according to what the sages have constituted. The Buddhist Law proscribes fornication; hence, that Confucius had a wife was a transgression against [this] proscription, and he should be cast down into hell. Confucius said that to be without posterity is the gravest unfiliality; hence, the two religious leaders, Buddha and Christ, likewise transgressed against the proscription [laid down by Confucius] . . . Thus we know that [what constitutes] "good" and "evil" is difficult to determine, and "right" and "wrong" [take their meaning] from the times. However, "right" and "wrong", "good" and "evil", all [take their meaning] from human life; universal principles likewise are determined from the [circumstances of] the times. As I figure it, whatever is injurious to man is wrong; whatever is not injurious to man is right.'[13]

The real conviction with which this criterion was held by K'ang is forcefully proved throughout *Ta T'ung Shu*. Only by holding to it unwaveringly could he have carried some of his ideals of One World out to their logical development. It must have been the beam which he cast into every dark corner of the future, as he examined it in his search for the Way. How else could we explain the unheard-of iconoclasm of his proposals—especially bearing in mind that they were the proposals of a *literatus* of late nineteenth-century China? One of the most truly admirable things about *Ta T'ung Shu*, to a contemporary mind, is the unflinchingly honest manner in which the author is faithful to his standard, lead him where it may. Is there to be absolute independence and freedom in sexual relations? But how about homosexuality—surely that is not permissible (one can hardly imagine the question even arising in the Confucian mind)! But, says K'ang, is it 'injurious to man', or is it not injurious to man? One cannot say it is actually any more injurious than normal sexual relations; very well, since there are some who prefer it, an ideal world of perfect freedom and independence cannot deny to those their right to practise it.[14] Such is an uncommon objectivity and integrity, even among social philosophers.

*Human nature: its goodness **and** perfectibility*

Naturally again, in planning for an ideal world one has accepted the idea of progress in history. And at the same time one has accepted the innate goodness of human nature. We know that in Christianity, which accepts the basic evil of human nature, Heaven is not on this earth. The Christian utopian is always confronted by this paradox: that no matter how much he may wish to bring about an ideal world, such is always a vain hope, for salvation admits a man to Heaven, but not to perfection on earth.

The Chinese view has been traditionally that defended by Mencius. As we might imagine, the philosopher who believed that all men have compassionate minds is the philosopher who says that man's nature is innately good: 'The tendency of man's nature to good is like the tendency of water to flow downwards. There are none but have this tendency to good, [just as] all water flows downwards.'[15]

Accepting this view, it is then possible to go on to a faith that there is a progress in history, and that eventually, the external conditions which warp the original goodness of men's natures having been made suitable, all men will become perfected and the world will reach a state of true excellence. The goodness—and potential perfectibility—of human nature, and the possibility of historical progress, are mutually dependent theories: the progress of civilization will enable social institutions to become perfect; while living in the environment of perfected social institutions will enable men to cultivate their basically good nature, and to perfect it. On the other hand, were human nature not perfectible, there would be little hope for the perfection of social institutions; while if there is no such thing as progress in civilization, then the conditions of man's environment will never permit him to cultivate his nature and to perfect it.

K'ang would definitely feel at one with the social philosophers and psychologists of the present day in the general conviction that 'bad' behaviour is resultant from the environment. In his chapter called 'Punishments Discarded', he explains very clearly this conviction by a series of examples that run along the following pattern:

'Now there are always reasons for men originally sinning to the point of incurring punishment. If during a man's life he has a body and has a family, then he cannot help but be in straits. It is natural. Being poor, he cannot bear it. Since he cannot bear it, then [he commits such] deeds as robbery, swindling, bribery, fraud . . . to the extreme crime of murder. We do not try to save him from the original cause of poverty, but treat him with severe punishments. [But] if clothing and food are inadequate, who can have considerations of shame, or fear the law?'[16]

Therefore, by removing the barriers which cause suffering, by channelling the competitive drive into constructive action, by giving every person a foundation of twenty years of physical security, moral training, and education, by arranging society so that every person has a place in which he is equal in standing and in material comfort with everyone else, and so on, there is no reason why human nature should not become perfected.

Theory of historical progress

For the faith that institutions and human nature can be perfected K'ang found a useful precedent in the ancient literature. Pending a really thorough study of his thought as a whole and in its development, it is premature to attempt a judgment as to the part actually played by his classical studies in K'ang's own philosophy. Leaving aside this complex question, we can at least point out that he used (and reformed) a theory of the movement of history through stages, the elements of which he found in the *Kung Yang Chuan*, the 'Li Yün' chapter of *Li Chi*, the writings of the Former Han scholar Tung Chung-shu (?179–104 B.C.), and the commentary on the *Kung Yang Chuan* by the Latter Han scholar Ho Hsiu (A.D. 129–182).

The theory is mentioned briefly in a single passage in *Ta T'ung Shu*:

'The sage-king Confucius, who was of godlike perception, in early [times] took thought [of this problem] (i.e. the problem of the Way of attaining happiness and doing away with suffering), and grieved over it. Therefore he set up the law of the Three Governments and the Three Ages: following [the Age of] Disorder, [the world] will change to [the Ages, first] of Increasing Peace-and-Equality, [and finally], of Complete Peace-and-Equality; following the Age of Little Peace-and-Happiness, [the world] will advance to [the Age of] One World.'[17]

The theory was expounded elsewhere by K'ang in his teaching and writing. The nature of his interpretation has been clearly explained by one of his pupils as follows:

'Confucius is like a great physician, and his teachings are like prescriptions. Just as the great physician never gives a single kind of medicine as a remedy for all diseases, so Confucius never gives a single form of teaching as the law of all ages. In the *Spring and Autumn*, he sets forth the principle of the Three Systems, and we meet this principle in all his writings. The Three Systems are represented by the Three Dynasties, Hsia, Yin and Chou, and he makes everything in three different forms . . . There is not a certain form, but the one is as good as the others. Hence the principles of the Three Dynasties are as in a cycle—the one succeeds the other, whenever the former principle does not work well. The fundamental concept is that all human civilization and social life are necessarily changed in order to reform the evil of the past and meet the need of the present. Any good thing must come to a period of decay and become an evil . . .

'A principle more important than the Three Systems is the Three Stages. In the first of these, the Disorderly Stage, primitive civilization is just arising from chaos, and the social mind is still very rude . . . In the second, the Advancing Peace Stage, there is a distinction only between all the civilized countries and the barbarians . . . In the third, the Extreme Peace State, there is no distinction at all . . . the whole world is as one unit, and the character of mankind is on the highest plane.

'The principle of the Three Stages, illustrated by the international relation [*sic*], is established in the *Spring and Autumn*. But we can find this principle in all Confucius's writings, whatever the subject.[18] For example, in politics, despotism, constitutionalism and anarchism are three stages; in religion, polytheism, monism [*sic*] and atheism are three stages. The three stages can be sub-divided into nine, eighty-one, and so on. It is simply the theory of progress, or evolution. But we must remember this principle in order to understand that the teachings of Confucius, although sometimes apparently inconsistent, are all fitted to different stages, and that we must not make the mistake of applying the theories of the low stage to the advanced stage . . . The principle of the Three Stages is the principle of progress; we must look for the golden age in the future; the Extreme Peace or the Great Similarity is the goal.'[19]

Now there seems to be a certain contradiction between the concepts of the Three Systems and the Three Stages. In the case of the former, we are told that of these three forms, 'the one is as good as the others'. In the case of the latter, there is obviously an evolution from disunity to unity, which is to say from bad to good. They thus do not seem to be equatable concepts. But even more difficult is the contradiction between the cyclical nature of the Three Systems and the ascending nature of the Three Stages. In the case of the former, we are told that 'any good thing must come to a period of decay and become an evil'. In the case of the latter, there is a steady improvement until perfection is attained.

The question then arises, what happens after the world reaches this utopian state? Will the inevitable workings of the cycle return it to the Stage of Disorder in accordance with the principle of the Three Systems? On this question, Liang Ch'i-ch'ao has categorically stated that in his teacher's view there was no reversion, and that he was thus diametrically opposed to Mencius's cyclical theory.[20] In *Ta T'ung Shu* the problem is recognized, and a solution proposed, in Part VIII (Chapters IX, X, XI, and XII). K'ang says:

> 'Now, the Way of Heaven is not peaceful. Not being peaceful, it is then disorderly. The Way of Man (i.e. human life) is affected by the afflictions of [this] disorder, and so [men] decide to cooperate, and seek with all their might for peace. But when they have won through to the time of peace, then the afflictions of peace also arise . . . This is our gravest anxiety for [the Age of] Complete Peace-and-Equality.'[21]

To prevent the 'afflictions of peace' (by which he means lack of continuing progress and eventual retrogression into disorder) from arising, he gives three methods. The first is called 'striving for excellence', the second is called 'encouraging knowledge', and the third is called 'encouraging *jen*'.[22] All three are really different aspects of the same method: to rechannel the competitive drive of men into constructive forms of competition. There will be no military, economic, or social competition; but men will compete to produce the best material goods, to invent new methods, to expand knowledge, and to manifest their *jen*. Through this co-operative kind of competition the world will not fear a stagnation of civilization or a retrogression into the disorderly stage, but will continue to progress.

Evolution of civilization: K'ang and 'Darwinism'

In thinking about K'ang's evolutionary views we are naturally led to wonder about the connection of these views with those of Darwin, who is mentioned by name in several places in the text.[23] There is no doubt that such a phrase as 'survival of the fittest' is taken from Darwin, and we may certainly conjecture that the evolutionary theory of the Western scholar added to the certainty with which K'ang believed in the progress of history. However, more than this, the text does not seem to show. There is no reason to believe, for example, that the Darwinian theories were important in leading K'ang's thought along the lines it took; and while he uses the new phrases from Darwin, he takes violent issue with what he understands to be one of the Darwinian principles:

'Nowadays the theory of natural selection is being proclaimed, and the idea of competition is being regarded as most rational . . . The hundred affairs, the ten thousand businesses are all founded upon competition. It is thought that talent and knowledge progress through competition, that implements and techniques are refined through competition, and that survival of the fittest is a Law of Nature . . . How can it be, that only [by] depraving men's mental processes and overthrowing men's persons, [men] learn how to fulfil the Way of Heaven, and to assist Nature! . . .

'Those who discuss [these matters] nowadays hate the calm of unity, and exalt the hubbub of competition. They think that with competition there is progress; without strife there is retrogression. This is for a fact suitable to the Age of Disorder; but it is most pernicious to the Way of One World of Complete Peace-and-Equality. Now with deceit and corruption confusing [men's] thinking processes like this, the ruination [of human nature] is complete; with misery and exhaustion, sickness and death like this, with pride and obsequiousness confusing men's character like this, the calamity is most severe. This is in direct opposition to our desire to lead men to peace and happiness.

'Hence those who advocate the theory of competition understand Nature but do not understand Man. There is no way to correct them, their stupidity is so enormous. Alas! This is truly a theory of the Age of Disorder!'[24]

And yet we know that the workings of competition are inescapable, so long as the private boundaries force men into mutually divided and opposing groups:

'However, if we do not free the Way of man from the selfishness of having the family and private enterprise, and yet we desire to do away with competition, how can it be done?'[25]

It cannot be done; therefore we must eliminate the conditions which produce competition, and rechannel the competitive drive into co-operative and constructive action.

'Ta T'ung Shu' and Western Communism

Ridding our minds of the present odious connotations of the word Communism, we can recall the communistic and anarchistic ideals of Western utopians from Plato onwards. We need not then be surprised to find similar ideals in our Chinese utopian. That K'ang had at least heard of Western communistic theories we are sure from the text. In a passage in Part VII, in which he discusses the futility of trying to cure the economic ills of agriculture by any other than the One World system, he says:

'For enabling the farmers to obtain equality in subsistence, we may perhaps advocate the methods of communism. But if we have the family, if we have the state, selfishness is then extreme. If we have the family, then the individual has wife and children dependent upon him; if we have the state, then the marshalling of troops and the levying of taxes daily increases. With such a polity, to hope to carry out communism is like "wishing to go southwards by turning the shafts northwards". Not to mention that it could not be carried out during the French Revolution, even America up to the present has likewise been completely unable to carry it out.'[26]

And in the following chapter, which deals with the futility of trying to cure the economic ills of industry by any system other than One World, he says:

'Now in the struggles of human affairs, "those who are unequal will cry out", which is a natural circumstance. Therefore in recent years there has been a springing up of struggles by labour unions to coerce the capitalists, in Europe and America. At present [such phenomena] are merely the germinating of the root, and the formation of labour unions will certainly increase in the future. One fears lest [this development] foment the disasters of "blood and iron". This struggle would not be between strong and weak states, but between poor and rich groups. A hundred years hence, it will certainly be this [problem] to which the whole world will be giving its attention. Therefore nowadays socialism is flourishing, communism is thriving. And in the future [this problem] will be the greatest subject of controversy . . .'[27]

It will be apparent that K'ang's notion of communism is very vague; we see that, according to the first-quoted paragraph, he thinks of it as a form of economic democracy which the French and American revolutions have tried but failed to bring about. He does understand that it is a movement which has arisen because of the struggling of the 'unequal' labouring and poor groups against the capitalist, rich group. (We will not fail to note, in passing, his prescience as to the importance of this struggle in the coming years).

But his mention of communism is no more than a passing comment, cited as another example in his discussion of the importance of the problem of unequal livelihood and the impossibility of solving the problem without using the Way of One World. In his view the basic barriers are not only private property but the State, and still more fundamentally, the family. We may safely conjecture that he knew nothing of the actual theories of Marxism, with its utopia via sanguinary class warfare. And we may safely conjecture also that he would have regarded the Marxian scheme as quite inadequate, taking into account only one of the great causes of human suffering.

One World: Government

In any utopian scheme there are bound to be certain aspects which seem more realistically attainable, and certain aspects which seem to be more in the realm of fantasy. Presumably the aspect of *Ta T'ung Shu* which will appeal to most contemporary readers as practically pertinent to the problems of our time is that which deals with the abolishment of the barrier of national states, and the formation of a united world under an overall government.

And certainly one of the most surprising things about this book is the way in which it anticipated the movement for such a world government. Few indeed were the people who would have seen, in the convening of the first Hague Conference at the turn of the century, the whole evolution of the political system into a single world government. And K'ang Yu-wei had this vision even before that time, his first draft of the discussion having been written down in 1884-5. It appears that to him must go the honour of being the first man to plan such a world government. Our wonder at this great leap of the imagination must be redoubled, when we think of the environment in which his thinking developed. One could scarcely think of a less likely place than the China of the late nineteenth century for the birth of a scheme for One World.

In his plan, unhampered as the theorist is by the innumerable and complex problems of the actual situation, our author has nothing to do with the half-way measures which have marked such primitive types in the evolution towards One World as the League of Nations and the United Nations. As a philosopher, he sought out the basic cause, and finding it in the existence of the boundary which is the State, he will abolish it. As we are well aware, that is in fact the crux of the matter, as the world today seems to grope towards unity. Until the concept of absolute State sovereignty is discarded, there will not exist the possibility of an actual world government.

Searching for a verification of his faith that history is progressing inevitably in the direction of this unity, K'ang cites example after example to prove his point. His study of history convinces him that there is this trend from many to one, from division to union, and from less democracy to more.[28] Some fourteen or fifteen years after he had come to this conclusion, the convening of the first Hague

Conference gave him a fresh feeling of optimism, and he now concluded that One World would materialize inevitably within two or three hundred years. Still later, he came to believe that complete political union will be achieved within one hundred years.[29]

When we remarked above that, as a theorist, he could be un-hampered by the innumerable and complex problems of the actual situation, it was not to say that K'ang's scheme ignored the world as it is, and outlined a completely arbitrary system. Indeed, as the reader will see from studying Part II, including the long chart, K'ang made a very detailed study of the world as it was and is, and developed his scheme for union with logical consistency. He re-marks a number of times that the evolution from the Age of Disorder to One World is a long and gradual process, and he provides for transitions from the one stage to the other, rather than for any sudden, unaccountable change.

Basic to the public government of One World is the public parliament. The most important feature of that government is that all its decisions will be made by the process of public discussion and voting. There will be no political rulers. Basic also is the autonomy in function of the local areas of the world; the public government is not a central government handing down decrees to all the world. Its actual work seems to be to carry on planning on a world-wide basis, and to ensure equality over all the world.

A unique conception is the division of the globe's surface into degrees. K'ang recognizes that there must be smaller working units in order to make government feasible; but he does not want to bring back the boundaries which were created by the existence of the old states. Hence he puts a grid on the earth, and has each of the resultant square-areas constitute an administrative unit. In the degree governments will reside the actual carrying on of most of the governmental functions, including the operation of the public insti-tutions. It is the degrees that will constitute the unit from which members will be elected to the public parliament. It will be up to the degrees and their residents to strive for the superiority of their area in the ways which are the goals of striving in One World—for constant betterment of the material conditions of life, for greater manifestations of *jen*. But no political sovereignty will attach to the degrees. The feeling one would have for one's native degree might, one supposes, be comparable to the feeling an American of today would have for his home state. Citizenship will be public citizenship; one will be free to live anywhere, and to move about as one likes. No boundaries of customs dues, entry or exit papers, or any other limitations will be imposed upon anyone.

'Ta T'ung Shu': A personal evaluation

One's general opinion of Ta T'ung Shu will depend, first of all, upon what one thinks of the value of 'utopias' as such. In the West there is a feeling that such schemes have had considerable practical importance. In fact, it is impossible to measure the influence of ideas upon social or individual conduct, so we cannot assert much very positively on this point. In China utopian thought has been almost completely negligible. One cannot point to any precedent in Chinese literature for Ta T'ung Shu. It may truly be characterized as a work of original genius. Whatever the influences borne in upon its author's mind from the West, there is not the slightest indication that he ever heard of any of the writings of the Western utopians or social philosophers, except possibly for those of Marx, and of Socrates, who is only mentioned by name in the book.

And furthermore, although he is not concerned to propose it as a thesis for demonstration, it is the present writer's opinion that the Ta T'ung Shu of K'ang Yu-wei is the most notable work of its kind which has yet been produced,[30] either in West or East. It is hoped, therefore, that the rendering of the text which is presented in the following Book will serve adequately both to acquaint the reader with the interesting and thought-provoking views of K'ang Yu-wei, and to bring K'ang to the attention of Western students in the full credit which is due for his remarkable work.

REFERENCES

[1] The fact that Ta T'ung Shu was written at different times has led to certain inconsistencies here and there, as well as to some repetitions. The public parliament is an example of the inconsistencies: it is stated in the Chart appended to Part II that the lower house will participate in such legislative functions as the election of the administrative officers of the

public government (19B), and that its members are elected according to the population of the various local areas; apparently K'ang has in mind a parliament like the American Congress, with one house elected on the basis of population and the other having an equal number of members from each degree. However, in Part VIII, the lower house is described as merely a recording office, without representatives (Chapter IV).

[2] Ch'ien Mu, in an otherwise able study of K'ang's thought, thus disparages the originality of *Ta T'ung Shu*. He also sees nothing but a simple borrowing from Chuang Tzu (in the completely pleasure-centred ideal of K'ang's thought), and from Mo Tzu (in the ideal of universal love). (See *History of Chinese Scholarship during the Last Three Hundred Years*, p. 664.) One is struck, in reading criticisms of *Ta T'ung Shu*, by the fact that so few of the critics seem actually to have studied the work!

[3] For the nine boundaries, see Book Two (Text), below, Part I, pp. 74-5.

[4] Text, p. 69.

[5] Text, p. 71.

[6] Text, pp. 65 ff.

[7] *Mencius*, II, B, 6.1, 3.4. (Legge's translation, in reference cited above, Chapter II, n. 28, p. 8.)

[8] Text, p. 65.

[9] Text, pp. 68-9.

[10] Text, pp. 70-1.

[11] Text, p. 71.

[12] Text, p. 71.

[13] Text, pp. 251 and 252.

[14] See Text, p. 252.

[15] *Mencius*, VI, A, 2.2.

[16] Text, pp. 247-8.

[17] Text, p. 72.

[18] In his *Confucius as a Reformer*, K'ang sets forth that Confucius was the actual author of all the Classics—i.e. the works considered genuine by the scholars of the 'new text school'.

[19] Chen Huan-chang, *The Economic Principles of Confucius and His School*, pp. 15 ff. Mr. Chen (whose Columbia University doctoral dissertation this is) was the founder of the National Confucian Association, and was active in trying to carry out K'ang Yu-wei's proposal to make Confucianism the state religion under the Republic. (See Hummel's

The Autobiography of a Chinese Historian, p. xiv, n. 1.) He states on p. xii of his work, 'My greatest indebtedness is to Kang [*sic*] Yu-wei, my former teacher, from whom I obtained a general view of Confucianism.'

[20] *Biography*, pp. 23–4.

[21] Text, p. 241.

[22] These are the titles of three chapters in Part VIII.

[23] See Chinese text, pp. 104 and 429.

[24] Text, pp. 214–16.

[25] Text, p. 216.

[26] Text, p. 212.

[27] Text, p. 213.

[28] See Text, Part II, throughout.

[29] Text, p. 89.

[30] It will not perhaps be out of place for the translator to mention that his expressed regard for the author's work as a whole by no means implies his agreement with any particular ideas; I have in mind specifically the racial views of the author. (Such a notice would seem unnecessary in a scholarly translation were it not for the fact that the problems dealt with in this work are so un-'academic' at the moment.)

BOOK TWO
TEXT

PART I

ENTERING THE WORLD
AND SEEING UNIVERSAL SUFFERING

Introduction:
Men Have Compassionate Natures

K'ANG YU-WEI [*ming* 有為 , also Tsu-i 祖詒 ; *tzu* Kuang-hsia 廣廈 ; *hao* Ch'ang-su 長素] was born into the world in the year in which the English [Crown began] to rule over India.[1] I was descended from Shao-nung (少農), my deceased father (君),[2] and my mother of the Lao (勞) [family].[3] [Since my birth] our earth has gone round the sun twenty-six times and some additional. [My birth was] hundreds and several tens of thousands of years after the congealing of the earth, fortunately long after the age of the great birds and beasts, and within the period when civilization had been developed. I live in the northern temperate zone; my country is the Central and Glorious (i.e. China), in the region to the south-west of the K'un Lun [Mountains], where the rivers approach the Pacific Ocean. I went to study in the capital city of the Hundred Yüeh (i.e. the south; used here to mean Kwangtung Province), on the shores of the Southern Sea,[4] called Yang Ch'eng (羊城 i.e. Canton). My native village, to the north of Hsi Ch'iao Mountain, was called Yin T'ang (銀塘). My family is traced from the son of King Wen of the Chou [dynasty],[5] named K'ang Shu (康叔), and they have been scholars for thirteen generations.

Now, I gathered up the five thousand years of Chinese culture [formed by] [Fu] Hsi (supposedly acceded 2852 B.C.), [Shen] Nung (supposedly acceded 2737 B.C.), and Huang Ti (supposedly acceded 2697 B.C.); [emperors] Yao (supposedly acceded 2356 B.C.), Shun (supposedly acceded 2255 B.C.), and Yü (supposedly acceded 2205 B.C.); T'ang (founder of Shang dynasty, supposedly acceded 1766 B.C.), King Wu (founder of Chou dynasty, acceded 1122 B.C.), the Duke of Chou (see above, n. 5), and Confucius (551–479 B.C.); and the Han (206 B.C.–A.D. 221), T'ang (618–907), Sung (960–1280), and Ming (1368–1644) [dynasties]; and I completely absorbed it. I also brought together [whatever] was fundamental and best[6] in the various wisdoms[7] of East and West in the [modern age], when the earth is [all linked together by] inter-communications, and the ten thousand states coexist; and I drank to the full of it. My spirit travelled beyond all the heavens, my imagination entered into the circulation of the blood.[8] At times I ascended White Cloud Mountain, the peak of the Mo Hsing Range (摩星嶺); how vast [the panorama] spread out[9] in the eight directions!

(Upon the outbreak of the troubles with France [in 1885]), Master K'ang fled from the military [preparations in Canton], and returned to his old home, Abiding Fragrance (延香) in his native village. My[10] grandfather handed this down. [There], divided by three ponds, was the Seven Cypresses Garden (七檜園); a several storied pavilion called Tranquillity (澹如)[11] overlooked the three ponds. Morning and evening I was enwrapped in books in this [pavilion]. Looking down, I read; looking up, I pondered. My purified spirit was separated from my body. On returning [home] to wife and children I was 'absorbed [in thought], as if dead'.[12]

However, [amid] the pledging of wine among the villagers, the mutual helpfulness of the neighbourhood women, the fondling of the children, and the [manifestations of] affection among family members, my ears heard all the sounds of quarrelling, my eyes saw all the aspects of distress. It might be the night-crying of a widow thinking of her husband. It might be the drawn-out wailing of a starving orphan child. It might be an old man without clothing, leaning on a staff under a tree. It might be a sick old woman without a coverlet, sleeping at night on the edge of a kitchen oven. It might be [one] crippled or with a serious infirmity,[13] holding an almsbowl, going about begging, crying aloud, with no home to which to return. Be they noble, or wealthy, then they are continually being involved in the civil strife of brothers and children and the quarrels of relatives. [All this] grief and misery is termed 'peace'; in reality, in every household in the world, the overflowing of jealousies and the clashing of wills at cross-purposes is more poisonous than yellow fog[14] and pervades the whole world. As for banditry and wars between states, those who are slain fill the cities, and the flowing of their blood congests the rivers. In ten thousand such years, with the great distress and misery [thus caused], alas! how painful [it is to contemplate]! The calamities which afflict human beings are severe; and there is no means to save them. Men are afraid of not having states; yet the harmfulness of having states is like this! And as for the boiling of sheep and the killing of oxen, the slaying of fowl and the butchering of swine: all the hosts of living beings are [constituted] of the same ether as I; [and yet] I slice open their guts, eat their meat, [use their skins] for sleeping on and dressing (?處) in.

Thus we see that the whole world is but a world of grief and misery, all the people of the whole world are but grieving and miserable people, and all the living beings of the whole world are but murdered[15] beings. The azure Heaven and the round[16] Earth are nothing but a great slaughter-yard, a great prison.

The sages have loved [suffering humanity]. They have gone into the sickrooms and jails, scratched a light and illuminated them. They have cooked rice and fed them. They have brought medicines and doctored them. We call them persons of *jen*.[17] They help for the moment. But how can [this] compensate for [all] the suffering?

Master K'ang was grieved and distressed, sighing and sobbing for days and months, ceaselessly [revolving this universal suffering] in his mind. [From] what subtle [cause] is this?

I myself am a body. Another body suffers; it has no connection with me, and yet I sympathize very minutely. Moving about I am distressed; sitting I reflect [on it]. If it is thus, why? Is it that there is perception, or not? Were I unperceptive and unaware, then, comfortable as the grass and trees, I would not know of [all] the killing; and what would I have to do with others? Do I indeed have perceptiveness? Then [since] the countless numbers of inter-state wars now [going on] among mankind on all the stars [is causing slaughter] which is incalculably greater than Pai Ch'i's slaughter of the 400,000 surrendered troops at Ch'ang P'ing,[18] or Hsiang Yü's slaughter of the 200,000 who surrendered at Hsin An,[19] how could I not feel sick at heart! Moreover, [at the time when] Bismarck burned France's Sedan, I was already more than ten years old, and there had been nothing which grieved me. [Then], when I saw a shadow-play, the corpses lying among the grass and trees and the burning of the houses frightened me. It was not that I had not been perceptive [theretofore]; the trouble was that I had not seen [suffering].

Now, as for seeing and perception: the forms and sounds of others are transmitted to my eyes and ears, and impinge upon my soul-*ch'i*.[20] Grief and sorrow attack my *yang*; darkness and depression enter my *yin*.[21] [From] what subtle [cause] is this? Is it what the Europeans call 'ether' (以太)? Is it what was anciently called the 'compassionate mind'?[22] Do all men have this compassionate mind—or do I alone have it? And why should I be deeply moved [by external causes]?[23]

Master K'ang then says: If [a thing be] external to myself, how can I have knowledge [of it], how can I feel affection [for it]? Since I have a body, then I share with coexisting bodies that which permeates the air[24] of Heaven, permeates the matter of Earth, permeats the breath of Man.[25] Can this be severed or can it not be severed? It can be severed—[but only as] the drawn knife can sever water. It cannot be severed, and so it is like the air's[26] filling space and being omnipresent; it is like the lightning's[27] going through the air and penetrating everywhere; it is like the water's encircling the land and being everywhere continuous; it is like the blood-vessels' serving the body throughout and penetrating every part of it. Sever the *ch'i*[28] of the mountain and it would fall; sever the blood-vessels of the body and it will die; sever the *ch'i* (气) of the earth and it would disintegrate. Hence, if men sever what constitutes their compassionate love, their human-ness will be annihilated. Those whose [human-ness] has been annihilated cease to be civilized, and return to barbarism. [Men can even] cease to be barbaric, and revert to their original animal nature!

The all-embracing Primal *Ch'i* created Heaven and Earth.[29] 'Heaven' is [composed of] a single soul-substance; 'Man' is likewise [composed of] a single soul-substance. Although [individual] forms may differ in size, still, they are [all but] parts of the all-embracing *ch'i* of the ultimate beginnings [of the universe].[30] Ladle out every drop from the great ocean, and there will be nothing different. Confucius said, 'The earth began from spiritual *ch'i*; the spiritual *ch'i* was wind and thunder; the wind and thunder flowed [into] form, and all things came forth to birth.'[31] Spirit is lightning[32] which has awareness. There is nothing into which the lightning-flash[32] cannot penetrate; [similarly], there is nothing which the spiritual *ch'i* cannot affect. Spirit [in] demons, spirit [in] emperors; giving birth to Heaven, giving birth to Earth; whole spirit, divided spirit; only [spirit] in the Beginnings, only [spirit] in man. How minute, how subtle, this stimulatingness of spirit! No creatures are without 'lightning', no creatures are without spirit.

Now spirit is 'aware-*ch'i*', the 'awareness' of the soul (*hun-chih*), vitality (*ching-shuang*), intelligence, shining virtue (*ming-te*). These several are differing names, but the same actuality. If there is perception and awareness, then there is attraction. Thus is it with the lodestone; how much more is it with man! Compassion is attraction (here we may call it empathy) in action. Therefore, of *jen* (i.e. compassion-attraction-empathy) and knowledge (i.e. awareness),[33] both are harboured within [us], but knowledge (i.e. awareness) is prior [in experience]. *Jen* and knowledge (i.e. intellectual knowledge, this time) are both used [in action], but *jen* is nobler.[34]

Master K'ang says, being that I am a man, I would be uncompassionate to flee from men, and not to share their griefs and miseries. And being that I was born into a family, and [by virtue of] receiving the nurture of others was able to have this life, I then have the responsibilities of a family member. Should I flee from this [responsibility] and abandon this family, my behaviour would be false. How could I bear to be so ungrateful? And why would it not be the same with the public debt we owe to one country and the world? Being that we are born into one country, have received the civilization of one country, and thereby have its knowledge, then we have the responsibilities of a citizen. If we flee from this [responsibility] and abandon this country, this country will perish and its people will be annihilated, and then civilization will be destroyed. This responsibility is [thus] likewise very great.

Being that I was born on the earth, then mankind in the ten thousand countries of the earth are all my brothers (literally, of the same womb) of different bodily types. Being that I have knowledge of them, then I have love (*ch'in*) for them. All that is finest and best of the former wisdom of India, Greece, Persia, Rome, and of present-day England, France, Germany, and America, I have lapped up and drunk, rested on, pillowed on; and my soul in dreams has fathomed it. With the most ancient and noted savants, famous scholars, and great men, I have likewise often joined hands, to sit on mats side by side, sleeves touching, sharing our soup; and I have come to love them. The values[35] and beauties of the dwellings, clothing, food, boats, vehicles, utensils, government, education, arts, and music of the ten thousand countries of the world I have daily received and utilized. Thereby my mind's eye and my soul-*ch'i* have been stimulated.[36] Do they progress?—then I progress with them; do they retrogress?—then I retrogress with them; are they happy?—then I am happy with them; do they suffer?—then I suffer with them. Verily, it is like there being nothing which the lightning (or electricity) does not penetrate, like there being nothing which the *ch'i* does not encompass.

Then extending it to the [other beings] produced by the earth— the savages, the grasses and trees, the scaly fish, the insects, the birds and beasts; all the ten thousand forms and the thousand classes of womb-born, moisture-born, egg-born, transformation-born—with all, likewise, have my ears and eyes met, [into] all has my soul-awareness penetrated, [to] all has my love-attraction (or empathy) been drawn. And how could I be indifferent [to them]? Be their appearance pleasing, I enjoy them; be they well-favoured, I delight in them; be their appearance distressing, be they ill-favoured, I likewise have [feelings of] distress and misery activated within me.

The jungle of the world: I shall also flee from it; I shall practise the Brahmins' [Way] of immuring oneself in a snowy cave so as to purify the soul (*ching-hun*). But if all men abandoned their families and immured themselves, then it would not be [more than] several decades before the civilizations of the whole earth would revert to a world overgrown by grasses and trees and [dominated by] the birds and beasts. Still less could I bear to bring [such a state] to pass!

How about the living creatures on Mars, Saturn, Jupiter, Uranus, Neptune? I have absolutely no connection [with them]; they are too distant and obscure to expect it. I wish to love (*jen*) them, [but] they are so far off I have no way to do it. The size of the fixed stars, the numerousness of the galactic clusters, the nebulae and the globular clusters, the aspect of all the heavens, my eyes themselves have seen, and my spirit has often roamed among (literally, with) them. Their states, men and women, codes of social behaviour (*li*), music, civilized pleasures, and their ways, [must be] vast and boundless. In the heavens as among men: although I have no way to see them; yet if they have creatures possessed of knowledge, then they will be no different in nature than we humans of [this], our earth.

In my roaming through the heavens I have imagined all the worlds of uttermost happiness; I have imagined all the worlds of uttermost suffering. The happy I have been happy with; the suffering I have [sought] to save. Being that I am a creature of all the heavens, would it be better if I could abandon the world and the heavens, cut [myself] off from my kind, flee from the social relationships (*lun*), and be happy all by myself? Those whose perceptiveness and awareness is small, their loving-mind is also small; those whose perceptiveness and awareness is great, their *jen*-mind is also great. Boundless love goes with boundless perceptiveness. The size and amount of love and perceptiveness are in ratio to each other.

AUTHOR'S NOTE: I have another book [on this subject], named *All the Heavens* (諸天).

EDITOR'S NOTE: The exposition of *All the Heavens* was block-carved in the winter of 1926, and was printed by the Chung Hwa [Book Store]. By the time of publication, the teacher had already died. This was a work with which the teacher amused himself in his late years. It amply shows the exalted nature of his great mind.

Master K'ang was not born in another heaven, but in this heaven; he was not born on another earth, but on this earth. Therefore he has an affinity with the human beings of this earth, and is intimate with [them] when he encounters [them]. He was not born as a furred or feathered, scaly or finny creature, but as a man. Therefore he is more intimate with the 'round-headed and square-footed', who are the same in appearance and nature. He is not a beyond-the-pale, cave[-dwelling] savage, but a man of a country with several thousand years of civilization; he is not a herd-boy or kitchen-maid, serf or illiterate, but a gentleman from a family with a tradition of literary studies for thirteen generations. Daily reading the writings of the ancients of several thousand years, he is thus intimate with the ancients. Because he looks at the several tens of nations of the earth, he thus is intimate with the people of the whole earth. Being able to think profoundly and look to the future, he thus is intimate with the people of the countless generations to come. To all that his perception and knowledge extends, he is unable to shut his eyes and keep it [from his concern], to cover his ears and stop them [from hearing about it].

Whereupon Master K'ang commenced first to examine antiquity, and then to study the present. Near at hand he observed China; far away he looked over the whole earth. [And he saw that] of the honoured, extending to emperors, of the base, extending to criminals; of the long-lived, extending to Chien P'eng,[37] of the short-lived, like those who die in childhood; of the withdrawn [from life], like the bonzes and Taoist [recluses]; of the gregarious like the birds: under all heaven, on all the earth, among all men, [among] all the creatures, there are none which are not grieved and distressed. Though it be shallow or deep, large or small, yet grief and distress will oppress them—thick and heavy, murky and evil. There are none who can escape it in the slightest.

All the former philosophers have sorrowfully, anxiously thought if there be a way to deliver them, to ferry them all across [the sea of suffering]. Each has exhausted the thinking of his mind in devising methods to help them. But with the unexpected, all-engulfing torrents [of troubles], men are never able to recover from the diseases in which they are sunk. [The methods of the philosophers] may be able to effect a little improvement, [but] there are none which completely cure. They may prop up the east, but the west falls down;[38] or [if] they support the head, the feet will ail.[39] Can it be that the principles of medicine are not yet refined [sufficiently]? Or that the methods of medicine are not yet adequate? I deplore [this lack of a remedy]. Or is it [merely] that the time has not yet arrived [when the world can be saved]?

Now, the awareness of living creatures [is like this]: the nerves of the brain contain the animus (*ling*). Encountering material and immaterial [objects], there are then those which suit it, and those which do not suit it, those which please (適) it, and those which do not please it. Those [objects] which please and suit the nerves of the brain then cause the spiritual soul pleasure; those [objects] which do not please and suit the nerves of the brain then cause the spiritual soul pain. It is especially so among humans: the nerves of the human brain being even more refined (蕋), and [the human] spiritual soul being even more pure, clearly the affectingness of the material and immaterial [objects] which enter into the [human] body['s aware-ness] is even more complex, subtle, and swift; and [those objects] which please or do not please it are even more clearly [perceived]. What pleases and suits it, it receives; what does not please or suit it, it rejects. Therefore, in human life there is only suiting and not suiting. What does not suit is pain. What suits and suits again is pleasure. Therefore, [the nature of] human life depends upon what men consider to be the Way; [what] depends upon man's Way is simply pain and pleasure. What is schemed for by men is simply to abolish pain so as to find pleasure. There is no other Way.[40]

To enjoy being in groups, and to hate solitude, to mutually assist and mutually help, is what gives pleasure to man's nature. Therefore the mutual intimacy, mutual love, mutual hospitality, and mutual succouring of fathers and sons, husbands and wives, elder and younger brothers—which is not altered by considerations of profit or loss, or of difficulties—are what give pleasure to man. Those who have no father or son, husband or wife, elder or younger brother, then have no one to be intimate with them, to love them, to take them in, or to succour them. If at times they have friends, then through considerations of profit or loss, or of difficul-ties, [their friends] will change their minds, and cannot be relied upon. We call them orphans and widows, widowers and childless. We term them 'impoverished', we pity them as 'defenceless'. This is the utmost pain of men. The sages, because of what gave pleasure to man's nature, and to accord with what is natural in matters human, then made the family law to control them. They said the father is merciful, the son filial; the elder brother is friendly, the younger brother respectful; the husband is upright, the wife complaisant.[41] This is likewise [what] best accords with man's nature. This method is simply [for the purpose of] enabling man to increase his happiness, and nothing else.

To form factions and compete for mastery, to follow the strong (or, through force) to protect oneself, cannot be avoided by human nature. Therefore we have the divisions of tribes and states, and the laws of government by rulers and ministers, so as to protect the happiness of men's homes and property. Were tribes non-existent, were states not relied upon [for protection], were there no rulers and ministers, and no governments, were [men] unsettled like the wild deer, then it would come to pass that men would be captured and enslaved, and would not be able to preserve their homes and property. Thus they would be sunk in limitless suffering, and there would be no way [for them] to find happiness. The sages, because of what man's nature cannot avoid, and to accord with what is natural in matters human and in the conditions of the times, on their behalf established states, tribes, rulers, ministers, and laws of government. This method is simply [for the purpose of] enabling man to avoid suffering, and nothing else.

Man, his knowledge great and his thinking profound, [able] to anticipate the future and to plan a long time [ahead], already having experienced happiness in life before, still more seeks eternal happiness after death; already having experienced pleasure in his bodily soul, still more seeks eternal pleasure in his spiritual soul. The sages, because of what man's nature enjoys and what gives pleasure to it, therefore devised the [Buddhist] Law of abandoning the world, the [Taoist] Way of purifying the spirit and nourishing the soul, and the methods for [attaining] immortality. Thereby [men] seek to be [re-]born into Heaven and to attain enlightment,[42] to escape the Wheel of Life (i.e. the Buddhist cycle of birth-life-death-rebirth), and [to arrive at] the limitless realm where their happiness will be exceedingly great and lasting—very much more so than the several decades of man's [mortal] existence.

In such cases men are following their [own] desires in carrying out painful actions. They abandon their beloved homes, cut themselves off from the honours and luxuries of human society, enter the mountains and sit with their face to the wall [in meditation], naked and barefooted beg their food, perhaps eating once a day, perhaps eating nine times in thirty days, plaiting grass [for clothing], tasting dung, sleeping in the snow, staring at the sun, food for tigers, food for hawks. They do not walk in this path [for the reason that they desire] to attain suffering. They have weighed the [relative] duration and intensity of pains and pleasures, and therefore willingly carry out [actions which produce] the lesser pain and the shorter pain, so as to gain the longer pleasure and the greater pleasure.

Regarding birth, old age, sickness, and death as painful,[43] they therefore will seek for what is not painful and for what is most pleasurable. This is to a still greater degree the seeking of happiness and the seeking to escape suffering.

Filial sons and loyal ministers, upright husbands and chaste wives, brave generals and morally disciplined scholars, have walked in the paths of danger and hardship, have followed the ways of peril and difficulty. They have eaten suffering as if it were sweet-meats. They have 'given up their lives without changing [their convictions]'.[44] They have 'died in defence of the Good Way'[45] . . . Thus, although [men] carry out painful actions, [they do so because] glory and fame lie therein, respect and recognition [are gained] thereby, and what gives them pleasure [is the result] of them. In this way, what causes them to suffer is changed into what makes them happy.[46]

Therefore, under the firmament, all who have life only seek pleasure and shun suffering. There is no other Way. Those who have detoured, gone a roundabout way (literally, borrowed their way), or taken many a wrong turn (literally, [gone] crooked and bent), who have carried out painful actions without hating to do so, are likewise only seeking pleasure [in the long run]. Even though men's natures have dissimilarities, yet we can definitely state that there is no such thing in the human career as seeking pain and rejecting pleasure. The establishment of laws and the creation of teachings [of the Way] which cause men to have happiness and to be [entirely] without suffering: [this] is the best [form] of the Good. [The establishment of laws, and the creation of teachings of the Way] which can cause men to have much happiness and little suffering: [this] is good, but not the perfect Good. [The establishment of laws, and the creation of teachings of the Way] which cause men to have much suffering and little happiness: [this is the not-Good].

(There follows a page in which the defects of religions and institutions are pointed out, in the light of the criteria set forth at the end of the last paragraph: austerities cannot be carried out by mankind as a whole; sexual abstinence cuts off posterity; mortification of the flesh for the sake of spiritual gain is not tolerable to most men; women have been abased and enslaved; the strong dominate and the weak are subservient; in states and families inequalities have thus been fostered.) Even if there be sages who establish the laws, they cannot but determine them according to the circumstances of their times, and the venerableness of customs. The general conditions which are in existence, and the oppressive institutions which have long endured, are accordingly taken as morally right. In this way, what were at first good laws of mutual assistance and protection end by causing suffering through their excessive oppressiveness and inequality. If this is the case, then we have the very opposite of the original idea of finding happiness and avoiding suffering.

India is like this, and China likewise has not escaped it. Europe and America are rather near to [the Age of] Increasing Peace and Equality; but in that their women are men's private possessions, they are far from [according with] universal principles, and as to the Way of finding happiness, they have likewise not attained it. The sage-king Confucius, who was of godlike perception, in early [times] took thought [of this problem], and grieved over it. Therefore he set up the law of the Three Governments (三統) and the Three Ages (三世): following [the Age of] Disorder, [the world] will change to [the Ages, first] of Increasing Peace-and-Equality, [and finally], of Complete Peace-and-Equality; following the Age of Little Peace-and-Happiness, [the world] will advance to [the Age of] One World. He said, '[When a Change] had run its course, then they altered.'[47] He said, '[The sages] observed their gathering together and their universal workings, so as to enact their codes and rules of correct social behaviour.'[48] For if those who deeply ponder how to keep to the Way do not understand the Changes, they will for ever follow the way of suffering.

Having been born in the Age of Disorder, my eyes have been struck by the way of suffering [of this Age], and I have thought if there be a way to save it. 'Bewildered, I have pondered.'[49] [The solution lies] only in following the Way of One World of Complete Peace-and-Equality. If we look at all the ways of saving the world through the ages, to discard the Way of One World and yet to hope to save men from suffering and to gain their greatest happiness, is next to impossible. The Way of One World is [the attainment of] utmost peace-and-equality, utmost justice, utmost *jen*, and the most perfect government. Even though there be [other] Ways, none can add to this.

(There follows an outline of the various forms of human suffering; the remainder of Part I is devoted to the elucidation of these forms in such detail that this occupies some sixty-five pages. It will be adequate for our understanding of the author's thought if we merely indicate the outline under whose headings this discussion is set forth):

CHAPTER 2. *Sufferings from living (seven in all)*

(*a*) Sufferings due to being born into the different states of existence.

(*b*) Sufferings due to premature death.

(*c*) Sufferings due to physical debilities.

(*d*) Sufferings due to being a savage.

(*e*) Sufferings due to [living] in frontier areas (i.e. outside of China).

(*f*) Sufferings due to slavery.

(*g*) Sufferings due to being a woman.

CHAPTER 3. *Sufferings from natural calamities (eight in all)*

(*a*) Sufferings due to flood, drought, and famine.

(*b*) Sufferings due to plagues of locusts.

(*c*) Sufferings due to fire.

(*d*) Sufferings due to inundations.

(*e*) Sufferings due to volcanoes (and earthquakes and landslides).

(*f*) Sufferings due to destruction of dwellings.

(*g*) Sufferings due to shipwreck (and trainwreck).

(*h*) Sufferings due to epidemics.

CHAPTER 4. *Sufferings from the accidents of human life (five in all)*

(*a*) Sufferings due to being a widower or widow.

(*b*) Sufferings due to being an orphan or childless.

(*c*) Sufferings due to being ill without medical care.

(*d*) Sufferings due to poverty.

(*e*) Sufferings due to low estate.

CHAPTER 5. *Sufferings from government (five in all)*

(*a*) Sufferings due to punishments and imprisonment.

(*b*) Sufferings due to harsh taxation.

(*c*) Sufferings due to military service.

(*d*) Sufferings due to the existence of the state.

(*e*) Sufferings due to the existence of the family.

CHAPTER 6. *Sufferings from human feelings (eight in all)*

(a) Sufferings due to stupidity.
(b) Sufferings due to hate.
(c) Sufferings due to love.
(d) Sufferings due to attachment.
(e) Sufferings due to toil.
(f) Sufferings due to lust.
(g) Sufferings due to tyranny.
(h) Sufferings due to caste or class.

CHAPTER 7. *Sufferings from those things which men most esteem*
(five in all)

(a) Sufferings due to wealth.
(b) Sufferings due to high station.
(c) Sufferings due to longevity.
(d) Sufferings due to being an emperor.
(e) Sufferings due to being a god, sage, immortal, or buddha.

All these many [kinds] are the sufferings of human life; while the sufferings of the feathered and furred, the scaly and finny [creatures] cannot be described. But if we look at the miseries of life, [we see that] the sources of all suffering lie only in nine boundaries (界).[50] What are the nine boundaries?

The first is called nation-boundaries: [this is] division by territorial frontiers and by tribes.

The second is called class-boundaries: [this is] division by noble and base, by pure and impure.

The third is called race-boundaries: [this is] division by yellow, white, brown, and black [skin types].

The fourth is called sex- (literally, form) boundaries: [this is] division by male and female.

The fifth is called family-boundaries: [this is] the private relationships of father and son, husband and wife, elder and younger brother.

The sixth is called occupation-boundaries: [this is] the private ownership of agriculture, industry, and commerce.

The seventh is called disorder-boundaries: [this is] the existence of unequal, unthorough, dissimilar, and unjust laws.

The eighth is called kind-boundaries: [this is] the existence of a separation between man, and the birds, beasts, insects, and fish.

The ninth is called suffering-boundaries: [this means], by suffering, giving rise to suffering. The perpetuation [of suffering] is inexhaustible and endless—beyond conception.

(The remedy for suffering lies, therefore, in abolishing these nine boundaries. The following nine parts of the book thus deal in detail with each of the boundaries, with the abolishment of each, and with the substitution of the One World of Complete Peace-and-Equality in their place.)

REFERENCES

[1] i.e. 1858, the year in which the East India Company came to an end, and the Crown took over the administration.

[2] Interlinear note, apparently added by the editor, gives the father's name, Ta-ch'u (達初), and *tzu*, Chih-mou (植謀). Shao-nung was his *hao*. He was also named Chih-hsiang (致祥).

[3] Interlinear note gives her name, Lien-chih (蓮枝).

[4] (南海濱); this may also mean: at the edge of Nan Hai [*hsien*], K'ang's place of birth.

[5] Posthumous title of the Duke of Chou (1184–1157 B.C.), famed in Chinese history as the virtual founder of the Chou dynasty, and the most important author of the *I Ching*. K'ang thus implies a distinction of family which could only be equalled by tracing the descent from Confucius himself.

[6] The Chinese is more expressive; literally, the heart and liver, the essential and splendid.

[7] 諸哲, being a broader term than 'philosophies'.

[8] i.e. my range of interest and investigation was unlimited.

[9] Correcting 驚 to 驚 (San Francisco text has it correctly).

[10] [*Sic*]; we go from first to third and then back to first person.

[11] See *P'ei Wen Yün Fu*.

[12] 慹然若非人 (From *Chuang Tzu*, 'T'ien Tzu Fang' 田子方, where 似 is used, rather than 若.)

[13] Correcting 㠠 to 庬.

[14] See *P'ei Wen Yün Fu*—none of whose references seem to cast much light on the term, however.

[15] 找殺 Thus put in the passive, to match the thought in the preceding sentence.

[16] Correcting 搏 博 as indicated; the San Francisco text has it correctly.

[17] On this word, see above, Book One, Chapter II, n. 31; and see also below, Book Two, Part VIII, Chapter XII.

[18] An episode of the period of Warring States (260 B.C.).

[19] An episode of the end of the Ch'in dynasty (206 B.C.).

[20] 魂氣 *Ch'i* is a term of great antiquity in Chinese thought, and like others of such key terms should best become familiar through context, as any translation will inevitably be either inadequate or misleading. In the present instance, our author himself equates *ch'i* with the European 'ether' (as he understands that term). (For discussion, see above, Book One, Chapter III.)

[21] *Yang* 陽 and *yin* 陰 are, of course, the two opposite, complementary, and ever-reproportioning forces or aspects of nature, exemplified by such contrasts as light and dark, hot and cold, dry and wet, positive and negative, male and female, etc.

[22] The Chinese word, originally a picture of the heart, includes both of the ideas which we express in English by mentioning two different organs—the heart and the mind.

[23] Taking 朕 to be 耶 .

[24] *Ch'i* again, but this time obviously in its everyday meaning.

[25] The three terms are capitalized, as they represent a triad in the traditional Chinese universe.

[26] 气 A variant of our term *ch'i*—actually its basic graph—and here also obviously used in the ordinary sense.

[27] See below, n. 32.

[28] 气 Here I take it the word is used in the 'ether' sense, rather than as meaning air.

[29] Compare *Mencius*, II, B, 2.11–15, where there is found the famous term 浩然之氣 (rendered by Legge as 'vast, flowing passion nature'), and the statement that the *ch'i* 'fills up the space between Heaven and Earth'. However, the *ch'i* to which K'ang is referring is a neo-Confucian *ch'i*; that is to say, the 'material' *ch'i* hypostasized by the great Sung philosophers of whom the chief representative is Chu Hsi (1130–1200).

[30] Although, as Bodde points out (in Fung-Bodde, *History of Chinese Philosophy*, vol. II, p. 685, n. 3), *yüan*—which I have rendered as beginnings—is used by Tung Chung-shu as a metaphysical concept; it appears to me that our author's *t'ai yüan* (太元) is more closely related to the well-known *t'ai chi* (太極), or so-called Supreme Ultimate, first found

in *I Ching* ('*Hsi Tz'u, shang*'繫辞上), and greatly expounded by the neo-Confucian thinkers. However, in the present context it does not seem necessary to capitalize it as a special term, if indeed it is one.

[31] A quotation from *Li Chi*, 'K'ung Tzu Hsien Chü'孔子閒居.

[32] It is also quite possible that this 電 means electricity. Fung-Bodde so take it (see above, reference cited in n. 29, pp. 685–6). Fung states therefore that K'ang is here drawing on the ideas of Western physics to supplement the traditional Chinese conception. In this case, the word which I have rendered as lightning and marked as n. 27, above, would also be electricity, as would the 'lightning' at the end of the present paragraph. I have found my own interpretation supported by the San Francisco text, which adds 光 after 電, and likewise has 電光 instead of 光電 in the second sentence. However, it must be admitted that the text in 不忍雜誌, which presumably was seen, at least, by K'ang, reads like the Chung Hwa edition. As for the 光電 in these latter two texts, it was not apparently a standard term at the time K'ang was writing; its present meaning is 'photo-electricity' (*Tz'u Hai*), but *Tz'u Yüan* (published originally in 1915) does not give the compound; nor is it found as an older expression in *P'ei Wen Yün Fu*. Whether it may have been used in some of the translations of Western scientific writings, or coined by a Chinese writer on science whose work K'ang had read, I do not know. If not, then I take it he uses the 光 as a simple adjective, and the 電 I would still interpret as lightning

[33] 智 I have rendered '*jen* and knowledge', because the author uses these as major topics later on in this book. He has used 知 rather than 智 just previously, in discussing awareness, rather than knowledge. However, in the context, it appears to me that he really *means* awareness here; knowledge could hardly be said to be prior in experience to *jen*, whereas awareness certainly is.

[34] My translation of the above two paragraphs differs importantly from Bodde's (see above, reference cited in n. 30).

[35] 神奇 San Francisco and 不忍雜誌 texts have 飛奇.

[36] 其 must be taken as 'my'.

[37] Generally referred to as 'the Chinese Methuselah'—a mythical character of great longevity.

[38] A proverb? It is reminiscent of the saying: 'Tearing down the east wall to fix the west wall'折東墙補西壁.

[39] A proverb? So it appears, but I have not been able to verify it.

⁴⁰ It is to be noted that the words rendered in the foregoing paragraph as 'pleasure' and 'pain' are the same Chinese characters which I have usually rendered as 'happiness' and 'suffering'. (See Fung-Bodde, reference cited in n. 29, p. 686, for another translation of this passage.)

⁴¹ The governing principles of the family relationships, in the Confucian tradition. The ten principles of social relationships are set forth in *Li Chi*, 'Li Yün', as follows: 'The father is merciful, the son filial; the elder brother is good (良), the younger brother submissive (弟); the husband is upright, the wife heedful; the adult is kind, the child obedient; the ruler is *jen*, the minister loyal. These ten are called the Principles (義) of man.'

⁴² Buddhist conceptions.

⁴³ The four basic forms of suffering in the Buddhist view; the first being what we must find a means of escaping—the very ultimate goal of Buddhism—and the latter three being, as he saw them incarnated, the immediate cause which impelled the Buddha to abandon his pleasant life as a prince, and to seek the Way to abolish suffering.

⁴⁴ *Shih Ching*, Cheng Odes, 'Kao ch'iu 羔 裘 .'

⁴⁵ *Lun Yü*, VIII, 13.1.

⁴⁶ Omitting 不 after 是 故 .

⁴⁷ *I Ching*, Appendix III, Section 2, Chapter II, 15. (See below, Part V, n. 3.)

⁴⁸ *I Ching*, Appendix III, Section 1, Chapter VIII, 39, and Chapter XII, 79 (in same reference). My rendering differs considerably from Legge's.

⁴⁹ *Shang Shu*, 'Ch'in Shih 秦 誓 .'

⁵⁰ Bodde translates this word as 'spheres' (in Fung-Bodde, reference cited in n. 29, pp. 687 ff.). This is perhaps not so indicative of our author's meaning, which is throughout an idea that sufferings are caused by a setting apart from each other, a demarcation—or, as he constantly describes it, a 'private' (the same character means 'selfish'), as versus a public order of things.

PART II

ABOLISHING NATIONAL BOUNDARIES
AND UNITING THE WORLD

CHAPTER I

The Evils of Having [Sovereign] States

THE *I* [*Ching*] says, '[After] Heaven had created the rude beginnings [of civilization], it was a natural concomitant that [the
system of] feudal lords should be constituted; but [this system]
did not bring about a peaceful [world].'[1] Since, in the time of the
rude beginnings, there were many states standing together, there
were then strong and weak coexistent. The large and small [states]
fought with each other, daily going to war and grinding down[2] the
people. This was most unpeaceful! Therefore the 'arising of difficulties in the beginning' follows after [the creation of civilization by]
the Creative and Receptive.[3] Alas, how dangerous! [Men] being
in these straits from the first, [their sufferings] could not be alleviated
by [all] the schemes of the ten thousand sages.

Now from [individual] people were formed family clans; accumulating family clans coalesced to form tribes; accumulating tribes
coalesced to form nations; accumulating nations coalesced to form
unified large states. Always this coalescing to become larger was
accomplished by numberless wars, and attained by unlimited grinding
down of the people. Finally the present Powers of the world were
formed. This process [of coalescing and forming fewer, larger units]
has all taken place among the ten thousand countries over [a period
of] several thousand years. The progression from dispersion to union
among men, and the principle [whereby] the world [is gradually]
proceeding from being partitioned off to being opened up, is a
spontaneous [working] of the Way of Heaven (or Nature) and
human affairs.

Even [those who] had arrived at sagely principles were able to transform [society] only in accordance with the [conditions] of the time, the place, and the nation in which they were born. Separated by mountains and seas, restricted by [the inadequacies of] boats and vehicles, [subject to] the limitations of human strength, [men] have been obstructed in making reforms, and have not been able to attain One World. Furthermore, the laws of empires have been piled on one another endlessly.[4] The ancients considered the China and the four barbarian [territories] of which they had heard to be the whole world. Today the globe is completely known, and when we look at that which was called 'The Central Nation' (i.e. China) and the four barbarian [territories], [we see that they] are then just one corner of Asia, and only one-eightieth part of the world. The Yeh-lang[5] did not know of the Han [empire], and thought themselves to be great; the Chinese forthwith made a laughing-stock of them. If the world were already united and joined into a single state, how would it not be the greatest possible! Yet [if] all the stars had been united, they would sneer at [this] petty little globe of 27,000 *li* as not amounting to a speck of dust. And would [that] not be [the same case as] the self-aggrandizement of the Yeh-lang?

Hence, the uniting of states will never be completed. [Since] there is no limit to the [possible] size of a state, then there is also no limit to the [feasibility] of uniting coexistent states. At the extreme of [this] amalgamation, it would extend to the star-clusters and nebulae, and still would be unlimited. [Since the possibility of] amalgamating states is unlimited, then warfare among states and the grinding down of living beings is likewise unlimited. In the international wars now going on among the people of Mars, how many millions of *li* of blood have flowed, how many billions of lives have been lost, I do not know.

Then my One World, my *jen*, can extend [only] to [this] earth. Can it deliver all the stars? [Since it cannot], then wars will never cease. I have pondered deeply how to rid all the stars and all the heavens of war, but could not [solve the problem]. Hence I am only going to consider how to do away with this calamity of war in the world in which I was born.

However, states having been established, patriotisms are born. Everyone looks to the advantage of his own state, and aggresses against other states. [Though a state] may not entirely succeed in seizing another state, yet it will not desist. At times a large state swallows up a small one; at times a strong state annexes a weak one; at times the large states form alliances and fight.[6] But the calamities of these wars—which have been caused by [this universal] quarrelling carried on for thousands and hundreds of years—reckoned according to their poisoning of the human race throughout the whole world for [these] several thousands of years, cannot be calculated, cannot be discussed.

I have observed the bearing of children. It is difficult and painful for the mother about to give birth. Sometimes [she] cries out for several days and nights without avail until giving birth. Sometimes the child dies in the mother's womb and mother and child both die. Sometimes the child issues forth prematurely and dies; sometimes the mother uses drugs and aborts it, and the child issues forth but likewise dies. Sometimes the umbilical [cord] is wrongly cut and [it] dies. Sometimes [the mother gives birth and then] nurtures [the child] for some days and yet it dies young—it may be for several months, several years, ten years or so, and yet it dies young. During these several months or years or ten years or so, [when] the child cries out in its days and nights of sickness, [the mother] carries it, pats it, and is unable to sleep, sometimes for months on end. [When it is] hungry she shares her food [with it]; [when it is] cold she shares her clothing. [Only] after [she] is just about through with the toil and trouble of helping and caring for [it] will [this] single person be fortunate enough to attain adulthood.

Coming now to the [matter of] the existence of states. [Having states], then there is quarrelling over land, quarrelling over cities, and the people are trained to be soldiers. [In] a single war those who die [will number in] the thousands and ten thousands. [They] may meet with arrows, stones, lances, cannon, poison gas. And then again, [they may be] disembowelled or decapitated, [their] blood splashed on the field, [their] limbs hung in the trees. Sometimes they are thrown into a river, dragging each other under. Sometimes a whole city is burned. Sometimes the corpses are strewn everywhere and dogs fight over them. Sometimes half [of the army] lies wounded, and then hunger and pestilence continue the deaths. . . . The difficulties of parents in bearing and nurturing [their children] are [so great], [and yet we then have] the inhuman afflictions of international war [to boot].[7] Alas! When selfishness and strife bring the people to such a pass, how can we but admit that it is due to the [fact of] there existing [sovereign] states?

(The remainder of this chapter (pp. 83–102) is devoted to a detailed recital of the wars of history and the cost of these wars in the butchery of human beings. The first part of this account surveys Chinese history, the second part Western history. Two conclusions are drawn from these lists of carnages: (1) 'The fewer the states the fewer the wars, the more the states the more the wars. Therefore, comparing the two, the oppressions received from a universal autocratic ruler are preferable to the wretchedness received from the calamity of wars among many contesting states.' (p. 91.)

(2) Therefore, the whole cause of this variety of human suffering is to be found in the existence of the 'boundary' of sovereign states.)

CHAPTER II

Wishing to Abolish the Evils of Having [Sovereign] States, it is Necessary to Begin by Disarmament and Doing Away with National Boundaries

THAT because of the existence of opposing states [there arise] such calamities of war, such grinding down of the people, has been most clearly demonstrated. If we exhaust the energies of the people in military training it is an unlimited waste; if the people are driven into being soldiers there is an unlimited loss of production. Even the Good and Upright[8] cannot help but be partial each to his own state. Hence what their wills are fixed upon, what they know and talk about, is always limited to [their own] state. [They] consider fighting for territory and killing other people to be an important duty; [they] consider destroying other states and butchering their people to be a great accomplishment. [They] engrave [these deeds] on tripods, carve [such exploits] on stone tablets, cast statues and write histories [of their victories]. [They] are called great by later generations throughout the world because they have [thus] conferred upon themselves posthumous titles of 'brilliant'. It is not realized that they are bloody butchers[9] and robbers of the people.[10] [By thus] cultivating the spirit of aggressiveness and selfishness [men are led] to rationalize and justify their narrow-mindedness and cruelty. In reality they are only [behaving] like a bunch of dogs rolling [on the ground in a fight], like savage beasts devouring one another, like bandits plundering [the people]. [The practice of] amassing being accepted as morally right, its violent evils become central in human nature: the original seed propagates itself, and [the desire to amass more] is turned over endlessly in the mind. Hence fighting and killing are endless also, and mankind throughout the world can never progress beyond the mind of the savage beast and the bandit. This being so, while [sovereign] states exist, to hope to bring about the perfection of human nature and to arrive at complete peace-and-equality is a self-contradictory proposal. It is like 'wishing to go northwards by turning the shafts southwards'.[11] Good men in antiquity were distressed about this, and likewise often discussed disarmament. [Disarmament] was first carried out [in China under the treaty of alliance between] Sung, Chin, and Ch'u,[12] while the various states of Greece also frequently undertook [to disarm themselves through treaties]. Nowadays disarmament conferences are being held ever more frequently, and such [conferences] aside, whenever individual states make treaties [with each other], these [treaties] are always based upon the principle of disarmament. Nevertheless, so long as the boundaries of states are not abolished, and the strong and the weak, the large and the small are mixed in together, wishing to plan for disarmament is [like] ordering tigers and wolves to be vegetarians—it must fail.

Therefore, the desire to bring about peace among men cannot [be accomplished] without disarmament; and the desire to bring about disarmament cannot [be accomplished] without abolishing [sovereign] states. For this reason [sovereign] states in times of disorder have no recourse but to take measures to protect themselves, [and yet such measures] in times of peace are the [very] road [leading to] the great calamities of fighting and killing. But men in [both] ancient and modern [times] continually have said that the countries of the world, like the Ways of men, cannot be few. This is a great falsehood. Now that we seek to save the human race from its miseries, to bring about the happiness and advantages of complete peace-and-equality, to seek the universal benefits of One World, we must begin with the destruction of state boundaries and the abolishment of nationalism (or, perhaps better, the *idea* of the state). This it is which Good men, Superior men,[13] should day and night with anxious minds wear out their tongues in planning for. Aside from destroying the boundaries of states, there is absolutely no way to save the people.

However, the state is the highest form of human organization. Outside of God (*t'ien-ti*) there is no superior law to govern it. Each state plans for its personal benefit. No universal law can restrain it, no empty theory can affect it. That the great power attacks and swallows up the small country, that the weak is the meat and the strong eats it, are natural matters to which [ideal] universal principles cannot apply. Hence even though Good men wish [to bring about] disarmament and [thereby to give] peace and happiness to humanity, [even though they] wish precipitately to abolish [sovereign] states and make the world a universal [state], it surely cannot be done.

Then, the hope of doing away with armaments, abolishing [sovereign] states, making the world one, [bringing about] complete unity (*ta t'ung*)—is this not [just] a vain desire in the longings of Good men? Yet viewing present conditions, [we see that] even though nationalism cannot precipitately be abolished and warfare cannot be eradicated [all at once], yet speaking in terms of universal principles, men's minds do behold this [coming about]. That to which the general state of affairs tends will in the future be attained. It is certain that One World eventually will be reached. It is just that it will take an age[14] and will be a complicated [task] to carry out. Confucius's Era of Complete Peace-and-Equality, the Buddha's Lotus World, Lieh Tzu's Mount Tan P'ing,[15] Darwin's Utopia,[16] are realities [of the future], and not empty imaginings.

[The Historical Evolution of] State Boundaries, from Division to Union, Presages One World

The progress of state boundaries from division to union is, then, a natural thing. Hence, [starting] from the time of Huang Ti, Yao, and Shun (legendary period), there were ten thousand states; coming to [the time of] T'ang (the founder of the Shang dynasty, supposedly about 1766 B.C.), there were three thousand states; [by the time of] King Wu (founder of the Chou dynasty, about 1122 B.C.), there were eighteen hundred states; [by] the Spring-and-Autumn [period] (722–484 B.C.), there were two hundred and some states;

[by] the Warring States [period] (403–221 B.C.), there were seven states, which Ch'in then united into one (in 221 B.C.). [This process of unification required] altogether two thousand years.

Ma-tai[17] destroyed a thousand and some states to form Persia. India before the Buddha's time also [comprised] more than a thousand states. King Asoka then united them (c. 274–c. 236 B.C.). They were again united by King Harsha[18] (606–647) and under the Moslem religion; and the English [later] continued to govern them [under a single rule]. The twelve states of Greece lasted for two thousand years and were then united by Macedonia. [They were later] also governed [under a single rule] by Rome. Rome controlled all the states of Europe and Africa.

With regard to Europe, [during] the thousand years of feudalism, there were three hundred thousand German lords, one hundred and ten thousand French [lords], and more than ten thousand Austrian and English [lords]. Today they have all been subordinated to the rule of the kings [of these states]. The twenty-five confederated German states have also been united into one. Italy has united its eleven states into one.

Russia has embraced Albania; France has taken Annam and Tunisia; England has swallowed Burma; Japan has joined Kaoli (Korea) and the Liu Ch'ius [to itself]; all Africa has now been carved up like a melon. The remaining small states, Siam and Afghanistan, because [they are] 'border entrenchments' are merely buffer states. As [in the cases of] Egypt becoming attached to England and Morocco becoming attached to France, they cannot long remain independent.

The parts becoming joined thus being due to natural selection, the swallowing up by the strong and large and the extermination of the weak and small may then be considered to presage One World. But [the way in which] Germany and America have established large states through [uniting their small] federated states is a better method of uniting states. [They have] caused all these small and weak states to forget that they have been destroyed [to form the united state]. Some day America will take in [all the states of] the American continents, and Germany will take in all the [states of] Europe. This will hasten the world along the road to One World.[19]

[The Historical Evolution of] Democracy,[20] *from Less to More, Presages One World*

The progress of democracy from less to more is a natural principle. Hence after the United States had been established a great revolution in laws took place, and other countries followed this. Thereupon constitutions were set up everywhere, republican[ism] flourished, communist theories appeared, and labour parties were started up every day. Now when states are autocracies, it is natural that they are self-centred, and it is difficult to unite them [with other states]. But if they are democracies, then federation is easy. This is because people only seek profit and benefit for themselves, and so when Good men advocate the pleasures and profits of One World it naturally accords with men's minds. The general conditions having been initiated, men will hope for it just as [naturally as] water flows downwards. Hence the arising of democracy, the flourishing of constitutions, the talk about unions (? labour unions) and communism, all are the first signs (literally, sounds) of One World. As for constitutional monarchy, [since the monarch] is already powerless, it is just the same as a democratic [form of government]. Some day monarchy will certainly be abolished and discarded, and [all states] will only belong to the One World [government].

There are Three Types of Unions of States

Now if we wish to bring about One World, first we will initiate it by disarmament, next we will bind [the world] together with alliances of [all] the states, and then we will guide [the whole world] by means of a universal legislature. Proceeding in [this] order, it is certain that one day One World will be attained. Now alliances of states are of three types. There is the type in which equals are allied; there is the type in which each state carries on its own internal government but the overall administration is united under the overall government; there is the type in which the names and boundaries of the states have been abolished, and there are formed independent (i.e. locally self-governing) districts and prefectures, united however under [the control of] the universal government. These threes type each derive naturally from the conditions of the times, and we cannot force union [on the world] all at once.

(There follow three equally short sections explaining the three types of alliances of states given above. These three correspond to the three stages of evolution towards One World.)

There are Six Difficulties in Uniting States

(In sum, the six difficulties in the way of union are:

1. Conflicting self-interests of states.

2. Unwillingness of states to surrender their sovereignty.

3. Even after the establishment of a strong union, the unwillingness of member states to submit to laws of the overall government which conflict with their individual interests.

4. Disparity between large and small states, raising problems of proportional representation in the legislature.

5. Problems of reaching agreement on legislation in view of the number of states whose opinions are to be harmonized.

6. Even after the union has been in effect for some time and is firmly based, the possibility of some serious difference arising which would lead to a rupture, as in the case of the American Civil War.)

(These six kinds of difficulties are each illustrated from American history. Once again it is pointed out that any quick and easy transformation from the conditions of the present to the ideal One World is impossible:

'Going from winter's cold to summer's heat, we must pass through spring's warmth before we can arrive; going from the level plain to the mountain peak, we must pass by the foothill slopes before we can ascend . . . Thus, given the conditions of the present, we must [start by forming] alliances, disarming, and establishing a universal legislature, and after [these have been accomplished] we will be able gradually to attain One World.')

Allying of States begins with Small Unions, begins with Small Assimilations

[Regarding the way in which] union will begin, will the ten thousand states suddenly unite, or will they each form small unions and later on large unions? Certainly they will begin with small unions. The small type of union will start with the alliance of two or three states whose strength is equal and whose interests are mutual. After that the large states of the world will form the unlimited type of union for mutual support. Nowadays the right of control over a state's affairs rests with the citizens, and advantages and disadvantages are obvious. It is not like antiquity, when in the time of the Warring States (403–221 B.C.) [this] right rested with the ruler and his ministers. And [things] cannot be changed about through the discussions of one or two men, or for the advantage or disadvantage of one or two men. Thus we [must have] equal strength, equal power, mutual support, and parity [among the uniting states]. No one state will have the power to be able to unite [all the others]. Thus, [take] a powerful [state] like Russia, in which autocracy is extremely far advanced. Yet, the rights of the people having become clear, within several decades if it has not become a republic, then it will certainly become a constitutional monarchy.

> AUTHOR'S NOTE: I wrote this in the tenth year of the Kuang Hsü [period] (1884); it was not twenty years until Russia enacted a constitution.[21]

When the form of government has been changed to democracy then mutual aggressions [among states] will automatically be eased.[22] And [there is another point]: [take] Russia's attack on Turkey (the Crimean War, 1854–6). First two states, England and France, formed an alliance and opposed her. Then five states, England, France, Germany (Prussia), Austria, and Italy (Sardinia), joined forces to oppose her. Russia was then unable to fulfil its intentions. [With this example to go by], how should there again be the fear of [another] Ch'in [state arising and] swallowing up the six states[23] and unifying the world [by force]?

When alliances of [states having] the same form [of government] and the same strength have been formed, [this process of unification] will be carried on further by alliances of [states] of the same continent, of the same religion, and of the same race. Take the case of the American continents. It is proper that the Americans themselves should rule them, and not permit the people of other continents to interfere with them. Should Europe and Asia, with their large populations and strong states interfere with them, then the states of the Americas, all of which were originally republics, would certainly unite in a great alliance, and set up a single public government.[24] This would form one-half of the globe into a united-states. The

American continents being united their power would be unmatched. Hence Europe and Asia might also follow the plan of allying [the states of their] continents so as to oppose their [power], thus forming great confederacies. Australia will, in time, establish itself as an [independent] state. England will not be able to control it from afar, and so it will follow the example of America in separating [from England] and [proclaiming its] independence. Or it might also attach itself to another state as its ally. .

The states of [either] half of the globe being united, this pattern and system will be hardly any different from the complete unity of the whole world. It is just that there will still exist two half-globes at the same time. Since it was possible to unite [each] half-globe, then why should it be difficult to unite the whole globe [after that]?

Therefore, within this next hundred years all the weak and small states will certainly be entirely annihilated, all monarchical and autocratic forms [of government] will certainly be completely swept away, republican constitutions will certainly be enacted everywhere, democracy[25] and equality will certainly be burning brightly. The peoples of civilized nations will be increasing in knowledge and the inferior races[26] will be gradually diminishing. After that, what conditions in general will tend to, and what men's hearts[27] will incline towards, will certainly be to go on to complete unity of the whole earth. [The progress of mankind towards] Complete Peace-and-Equality throughout the world is like the rushing of water through a gully: nothing can check it.

The weak and small states which will certainly be annihilated within a hundred years are Sweden, Denmark, Holland, and Switzerland, which will be united with Germany, all the small [states] of eastern Europe, which may be united with Russia, and Asia's Afghanistan, Korea, Siam, Egypt, and Morocco (sic).

AUTHOR'S NOTE: I wrote this in the tenth year of the Kuang Hsü [period] (1884); it was not twenty years until Korea was lost.[28]

Spain and Portugal will first be united with France, and then [? all three] will be united with England. The transformation of Spain into a democracy is perhaps not distant. The conservatism of Persia and Turkey imperils their existence.[29] It is difficult to gauge [how

long it will take], but given the firmness with which Moslem
nations have preserved their religion during several hundred years
of intercourse [with other nations]—[which intercourse] has not
been able to change them in the slightest—then we can judge the
difficulty of completely reforming them within the next hundred
years. During this next hundred years, when the strong influences
and potent ideas of the [other] nations are everywhere pervasive and
compulsive, whether [the Moslem nations] will be able to preserve
themselves we cannot tell. It may be that being of the same religion
they will unite with India to form a single great central Asian state.
India, Persia, and Turkey all are Moslem states, but men of ability
are most numerous in India, and new learning flourishes [there].
Although it is ruled by England, should England undergo internal
changes (? a revolution) or engage in a war with Germany and be
defeated, then India would be able to become independent. In that
event it would be most likely that [India] would [form] a united
state together with Persia and Turkey. Hence, of [all] the states
of Asia, it may be that only China and Japan will survive [as separate
states]! [And then] should monarchy fall in Japan and it be
transformed into republic, the [independent] situation of [that]
state would also be endangered. Perhaps China will become united
with Japan and India!

The states of South America are divided in their religions, and
their governments are immature [because their] republican
[governments] were initiated in haste. [Hence] the Europeans
will certainly find a pretext to encroach upon them. But the
Americans will [just as] certainly strongly resist them, and this
would of course be a great incitement to war! The South Americans
being attacked by other [states] would certainly unite into a single
state under the leadership of Brazil; or they might unite in a grand
alliance led by (or unified with) North America. Since the five
states of Central America have already in recent [years] talked
of forming a union, this cannot be far off.[30]

*The Russian Disarmament Conference[31] has laid the Foundations for One
World*

(In this section, added to the original draft at some later date, our
author declares that the first step towards the alliance of all the

world's states has been taken with the international peace conference called by the Russian Czar (i.e. the First Hague Peace Conference of 1898). He points out that there are many ways in which the world is actually becoming ever more united, such as postal unions, international copyrights, tendencies of more conservative nations such as Persia and Turkey and Siam to enter into international intercourse, the spread of democracy and decline of autocracy, etc. Again he tells us that the whole trend of affairs and inclination of men throughout the world is towards eventual unification under a single parliamentary government. One World will materialize inevitably within two or three hundred years. A note at the end of the section, apparently appended still later, remarks that 'flying ships' are becoming more and more common, and [? hence] the boundaries between states are being increasingly broken down. Complete [political] union will come about within one hundred years.)

CHAPTER III

Founding of a Public Parliament is the First [Step towards] One World

ITEM: The strength of the various states being the same, and their form of government naturally [having become] the same, then the [first] form of government of the allied states [of the world] will not be set up as a presidency, but will be formed [merely] of parliamentary representatives. Therefore we cannot call [this first stage] a public government, but a public parliament. Furthermore, the powers of the individual states [at this time] will [still] be very great, and the public government—[which is merely the parliament] —will simply consist of a body of permanent delegates meeting in regular sessions. [This] body will be somewhat like the Swiss [legislature], but cannot be like [that of] America. The local divisions will be extremely far apart, [so that in this respect] it will not be like the Swiss [system] either.

Item: Those who will manage the administration and deliberate on affairs in the public parliament and government must first be elected and delegated by the individual states. Each state might have one person, or perhaps several persons, or it might be that the number of delegates will be according to the size of the state, as in the German system. But for fear of the large states gaining strength this [latter] system might not be feasible. This is what the second- and third-rate states would say.

Item: The powers of the individual states being very great, the public government [of this time] will not be able to institute [the office of] president, nor will it be able to set up [the office of] prime minister. It will merely have a parliamentary chairman, publicly elected from among the delegates by majority vote. [He] will be like the overall commander of an allied army. However, [this] parliamentary chairman will also be without [superior] authority, and will only be ranked as one among the members. Whenever both sides [in a debate] are even, the decision will be made by simple majority. Soon after [this stage] the structure of the public government will be definitely determined. Confucius said: 'There appears a flight of dragons without a leader (literally, heads). Good fortune ... When the Creative, the great, undergoes changes in all the nines, the world is set in order.'[32]

The Universal Parliament will deliberate only upon [Matters Relating to] the Universalization of International Intercourse

During the time when the powers of the individual states are [still] very great, the universal parliament will deliberate only upon the main outlines of the intercourse of the states. Other affairs of government will be under the jurisdiction of the states themselves. In general it will be like the parliament of the German individual-states international intercourse union.[33]

1. The parliament will determine the public law of the states. All [laws regarding] intercourse between states or nationals of the various states will be drawn up on the basis of presently existing international law. [The parliament] must seek to refine [these laws], always having universal peace as the main objective. Each member of parliament [may] make proposals at any time. Upon the sanction of the individual states [the laws drawn up by the parliament] will go into effect throughout the world.

2. Problems arising from relations between states will be decided according to public law. After parliament has deliberated and

reached a decision by majority [vote], the individual states cannot but follow [this decision].

3. All import and export duties should gradually be equalized. There may not be restrictions upon [the trade] of other states so as to enable one state to form a monopoly.

4. In all designations [used by] individual states for measuring and weighing length, size, and weight, [the parliament] should urge uniformity so as to avoid confusion and troublesome computations which [cause] a waste of people's mental energy.

5. [The public parliament] should seek energetically for a new system [to replace] the spoken and written languages of the various states. Uniformity should be brought about so as to facilitate intercourse and to avoid the incalculable amount of studying [that must be devoted to languages] throughout the world [at the present time]. Studying the useless languages of the various states is both a waste of time and a waste of mental energy. Should [language] be standardized it would increase people's useful years and be a universally beneficial [form of] learning; its benefits would be inexhaustible.

Now spoken and written languages are purely artificial (literally, proceed merely from man's doing). They must have form; but if we take what is simple and convenient for [world-wide] intercommunication it will be adequate. [Language] is not like mathematics or law or philosophy, which are fixed and must be [pursued according to their inherent nature]. Thus by excising complexities and crudities we can arrive at a single way of expressing important ideas. But so long as individual states coexist and the boundaries between states have not been abolished, then in the education [of its youth] every state will continue to use its own national language so as to inculcate patriotism as the foundation of the national existence. Hence I am afraid that we shall not be able to discard [these national languages] all at once. But a universal spoken and written language should be determined upon, and the people of every nation caused to study this one kind to use in [international] communication. Then people would study only two kinds [of languages]: the language of their own state, and the universal language. [Thereby] we can save boundless time and mental energy, which can be devoted to other, useful studies according to [the needs of] the times. This is what is described [by the saying]: 'Not doing what is neither beneficial nor harmful, is beneficial.' Furthermore, it would transform useless years into useful years, transform wasted mental energy into productive mental energy. If we take all the people of the world and [try to] figure out the surplus of time and mental energy [which would be derived therefrom], the amount is incalculable. [When people can] take [this surplus] and devote it to original scholarship and the invention of new implements and [works of] art, how can we estimate the rapidity with which civilization will advance!

And when boundaries between states have been abolished, when boundaries between races have been abolished, then national and racial languages will also be abandoned. Such writing will then remain in use [only] by archaeologists, as nowadays with Greek and Latin, and the *chuan* and *li* styles of ancient Chinese, and the Pali and Sanscrit of India. (The Chinese language has become highly refined, and it will not be easy to discard it.) (*Parentheses in text.*)

> EDITOR'S NOTE: The last two phrases are not in the original manuscript. I imagine they were added at the time the blocks were cut.

6. When an individual state acts in an unpublic (i.e. selfish), unpeaceful, uncivilized manner, the universal parliament may transmit a letter of censure, ordering it to reform.

7. When an individual state violates [the code] of civilization and the public peace and happiness, and disobeys the public law of the nations (i.e. international law), the public parliament may use the public joint military forces [composed of troops] of the individual states to repress it. Should it still be recalcitrant, then the joint [forces] will attack and subjugate its national territory and change over its government.

8. The public parliament having a budget of expenditures, it should be supplied [with funds] by the individual states according to their ability. Each state should give according to the amount determined for [the particular] year.

9. The public parliament should have a public territory. Those persons coming to live in the public territory will consent to shed their nationality and to become citizens of the public government of the world.

10. When an individual small state wishes to belong under the protection of the public parliament, [since] its territory and people all belong to the public parliament, [the latter] will depute persons to set up a small government [within the territory].

11. The fortified frontier areas of the various states will all belong to the public government, [which] will depute persons to take charge [of them].

12. All the seas outside of the thirty *li* limit of the individual states will belong under the control of the public government. These seas will become territories of the public government. All undeveloped islands will be public territories, and their inhabitants public citizens. All who fish in [these] waters, all whose boats pass through the public seas, will pay duties [to the public government].

13. The members of the public parliament elected by the various states will be changed once each year. But [the members] may not be called great ministers because, when they enter the public government, they then relinquish official status in their own states. For even though a person of a certain state is deputed by that state, yet he actually [takes part in] planning for the whole world's benefit. This is the same thing as in the case of a member of a national parliament who, [although] elected by his home district, yet is not responsible [merely] to that district.

> NOTE: This idea cannot be carried out during the present monarchical interim. It will be carried out only after republics have become numerous. As they gradually become numerous it will have to be carried out.

14. Members of the public parliament from the various states may remain in the public territory as public citizens or return to their own states. It will be entirely up to them.

15. The seas being public territories, the public parliament may have six naval vessels, which will be split up [here and there among] the various states to provide against inter-state wars. Should there be any [state] which dares to resist, it will then be regarded by all the states of the world as a public enemy. The public government may annihilate this state, take its territory as public territory, and take its people as public citizens. The number of warships and naval

personnel may be increased at any time [upon due] deliberation [of the public parliament].

16. The universal parliament will have disarmament as its main objective. The number of troops, armaments, armament factories, and warships possessed by each state must be reported to the public government. [Whenever] there is discussion of increasing [these] beyond what is needed by a state for its own defence, the public parliament may intervene. What is excessive, it may prohibit. It will at the same time yearly consider ways of reducing armaments. [Suppose there are] two states having a common boundary, both of which are increasing their armaments by way of precaution against attack. The public government, having public territories and public citizens, should train public troops to act as guardians of the dual boundary. By avoiding the mutual precautions against war of the two states, the number of their troops can daily be reduced.

17. Dependencies and self-governing areas of the various states which wish to come under the public government will be made public territories. [Since they] belong to the public parliament, [it] will depute small governments to rule them.

18. Citizens of the public territories, no matter of what race or nation, will be uniformly equal.

19. Individual states may not separately conclude treaties with one another, [or make] secret covenants.

20. People of the various states may become citizens of any state as they choose, and may not be restricted or prohibited on account of national[34] differences.

CHAPTER IV

Establishing a Public Government to Govern All Nations is the Middle [Step towards] One World

IF we have been able to set up the public parliament and enact [these] various laws, before many decades have passed the alliance of [all] the states will certainly be completed, the laws of the allied states will certainly be firmly established, the mind of the individual state to injure others and benefit itself will certainly be lessened, cases of individual states oppressing others for their own benefit will certainly be few. Public territories having been set up, public citizens will become more numerous every day, and there will certainly be countless self-governing territories which will put themselves under the public government. The power of the large states must daily become more divided and weak. Democratic organizations will certainly thrive still more within every state, and the governmental authority within each state will certainly dwindle. It will be like the American federation: the legislatures of the individual states must gradually bring about a centralization of authority, such as [exists in] Washington. Thus, even those states which are hereditary monarchies must be like the individual states of the German confederation, [while] states having a democratic form of government will be like the states of America and the cantons of Switzerland. Even though there be strong and large states, they will not be able to create disorder or swallow up [other states]. When we have reached this time, then the public government of the world will be completely constituted, the foundations of the One World government will be firm, and the overall authority of the overall public government will be in effect.

Outline of the Public Government

1. Yearly reduction of troops of every state. Every year [the public government] must order all the states to equalize [their armaments]. They will be reduced and again reduced until they are non-existent. If we plan that each year the states will reduce by ten thousand [men], before the passing of a few decades we can bring about that every state is [totally] without troops.

Now when the states fight with each other there is a terribly heavy expenditure on military taxation. Should we be able to abolish armies there would be six great benefits, and the military expenditures of all the states would be transferred for use in increasing the [number of] public schools, hospitals, and institutions for the aged and the poor; in opening up mountainous and forested [areas for human habitation]; in repairing roads; in building ships; in inventing implements which will benefit civilization; in assisting in projects for the happiness of mankind. How can such benefits be calculated!

In the first place, having reduced military expenditures, we can lighten all taxes and spare the people of all the world from bearing [this] burden. This will be benevolence (*jen*) incalculable.

In the second place, the countless soldiers of the world will be shifted [into useful pursuits] and taught to be scholars, farmers, artisans, and merchants. The benefits this would add to the world are beyond our comprehension.

In the third place, when the people of the world are not permitted to be soldiers, they can [then] be free of [the horrors of] being killed or wounded in battle, of the inhumanity of ten thousand decaying bones [for the sake of] a single general's acquiring glory. The whole globe will be a very happy world, when there are no battlefields over which to condole.

In the fourth place, when among the people of the world there is no inhumanity of warfare, no calamity of soldiers pillaging and burning, no knowledge as to what things shields and spears, guns and cannon are, no acquaintance with the sufferings of slaughter, burning, pestilence, and homelessness, the preservation of human lives in all the states will be incalculable, and the preservation of the implements of peaceful production will [likewise] be incalculable.

In the fifth place, cannon and [other] weapons are completely wasted and useless. When we shift over from the work of [producing implements with which] to kill men and produce the implements of civilization, when we shift over from calculating the killing of men to calculating for the benefit of the world, this will also be benevolence and benefit incalculable.

In the sixth place, past or present, there has never been a benevolent, righteous, merciful, and compassionate government to compare with this. Surely, being like this, it can then save the world and bring contentment to the people.

2. Troops of the individual states having been [thus] gradually done away with entirely, the public troops can [also] gradually be dispensed with. Eventually, when there are no states, there will be no soldiers [either].

3. [In cases where] monarchs [rule over states] which have had a constitution for a long time, their great powers have been completely pared away. [Such a monarch] is but a contented, rich, and honoured individual, and nothing more. Even though the titles of

emperor, empress, and the like are hereditary, [they may] be changed to 'honourable', or perhaps to 'excellency', or we might wait until the [present monarch] has passed away to discard them, or [in case the monarch] is without an heir, [the title] can be abandoned. Any [of these methods] is possible. Moreover, when [the world] has reached this time, the principle of equality will be very obvious; all men will see that such titles as emperor and monarch are other names for the militarists, bloody butchers (see footnote 10), and men of violence[35] of antiquity, and will naturally loathe them, hate them, and not wish to have these titles.

4. (National languages must be abolished as being one of the major barriers which perpetuates disunity in the world.)[36]

5. The earth will be divided into ten 'continents'. Europe will be one continent by itself. China and Japan, Korea, Annam, Siam, and Burma will be one continent, called the East Asian continent. The South Seas [islands] will be dependencies [of that continent]. The Siberian area will be one continent, called the North Asian continent. From the Caspian Sea eastward, Central Asia and India will be one continent, called the West Asian continent. South, North, and Central America will each be one continent. Australia will be one continent by itself. Africa will be one continent. Altogether [making] ten continents. For each continent there will be set up a supervisory government. [This supervisory government] will have the old (i.e. former) states within the continent publicly elect persons to fill its [offices]. Should the [old] states already have been annihilated it will be all right if no supervisory government is set up.

6. So as to [carry on] self-government [within] naturally demarcated localities, every old large state will be divided into several tens of small political divisions. So as to [carry on] local self-government a small government will be constituted [in each locality].[37] All will abolish their [old] state names, and be called such-and-such a 'boundary'. The continents will generally have several tens of boundaries.[38]

7. The world globe will be divided north and south into one hundred degrees—fifty degrees each, north and south of the Equator. [The globe] will also [be divided] east and west into one hundred

degrees. Each degree will be divided into ten-minute [demarca-
tions], [so that] there will actually be a hundred minutes [in each
degree] (i.e. each degree will be divided into ten minutes measuring
north and south, as well as ten minutes measuring east and west).
Each minute will be divided into ten *li* (Chinese miles) [each way],
[so that] there will actually be a hundred *li* [in each minute]. For
each degree, each minute, and each *li* the boundaries will be established and a map drawn of it [so as] to trace out its likeness. All
persons will be called persons of such-and-such a degree, and it may
be [so] written in the registers.

Then, below the *li*, we come to the *liang* (量). Each *li* will be
divided into ten *liang* [each way]; each *liang* will be divided into
ten *yin* (100 feet, Chinese measure) [each way]; each *yin* will
be divided into ten *chang* (10 feet, Chinese measure) [each way];
each *chang* will be divided into ten *ch'ih* (10 inches, Chinese measure)
[each way]; each *ch'ih* will be divided into ten *ts'un* (1 inch,
Chinese measure) [each way].[39] Ancient weights and capacities were
all based on the *ts'un*; the weight and size of metals was calculated
[according to the *ts'un*].

The whole earth will [measure] altogether 10,000 square degrees,
1,000,000 square minutes, 100,000,000 square *li*, 10,000,000,000 square
liang, 1,000,000,000,000 square *yin*, 100,000,000,000,000 square *chang*,
10,000,000,000,000,000 square *ch'ih*, and 1,000,000,000,000,000,000
square *ts'un*.[40] Each degree will be approximately double [the size]
of the present degree.[41] Altogether they will constitute the major
boundaries; all [things] will be differentiated according to the
degrees. Should the time come when the whole earth is populated,
there will already be no strife between separate states (because such
will not exist), no separation of 'yin and yang'. Each self-government
will then exercise control over [one square] degree.[42]

8. The beginning of the World Era: all [dating] will be according
to the One World period; private dating by religious leaders or
monarchs will not be permitted, in the interests of unification.
Earlier times will always be reckoned as such-and-such a year before
One World.

9. Measurements, capacities, and weights will be the same for the
whole world. It will not be permitted to have different systems and
different names.[43]

10. (A decimal system will be used for all measurements; all other systems will be abandoned. The reason is that the decimal system is easiest, and will save much time and energy.)

11. Spoken and written language should be the same for the whole world. It will not be permitted to have different words and writing. As a means of studying the languages of each locality a 'global ten-thousand sounds room' should be constructed. [That is], a one-hundred-*chang* room will be constructed, round in shape to simulate the earth, and suspended in the air. For every ten *chang*, natives of that part of the earth will be summoned, several per degree. Where there are linguistic differences they will be summoned; where there are no differences one person will suffice. Having brought together [representatives of] the peoples of the whole world, whether civilized or uncivilized, we will [then] have philosophers who understand music and language join together to study their [languages]. [These philosophers] will select what is the lightest, clearest, roundest, and easiest for the tongue, as the sounds [of the new world language]. [They] will also select from the world's high and low, clear and turbid sounds those which are most easily understood, and form an alphabet from them. For all material things [names] will be written according to the division and union of their original constituents.[44] For immaterial things the easiest among the old names [used by] the world's nations will be selected. If the Chinese [language] were to be adopted, with the addition of an alphabet, to form the [new world] language, the energy expended would be slight, and much would be gained. [For], calculating the easiness of languages, China has one term for one thing, one character for one term, one sound for one character. India and Europe have several terms for one thing, several 'characters' for one term, and several sounds for one 'character'. Therefore, in simplicity of language China exceeds India, Europe, and America by several times. Thus, the same book or letter[45] can be written several times as fast in Chinese as in [the languages of] Europe, America, or India. And if we figure it out [so far as the development of language for] the handling of affairs or for conversation [is concerned], the age of the Chinese people is also several times greater than that of the Indians, Europeans, or Americans. Only China is still not provided [with terms] for various new things, and

should adopt the new European and American terms to rectify this.

However, the vowels of French and Italian are the clearest, being quite like the Peking [dialect] but surpassing it. Now when we wish to construct the sounds of the [new world] language we must take those which are purest and most elevated, which are suitable to singing and harmonizing, which are sufficiently beautiful and clear to gratify the soul. Generally speaking, if most of the sounds of the [new] alphabet are widely taken from [the languages prevailing] between the fortieth and fiftieth degrees, then they will be most pure and elevated. If we adopt the Chinese terms for things, but give the sounds by means of an alphabet, and write them with a simple new script, then [the new world language] will be extremely simple and fast. The beasts are near the earth, therefore their sounds are turbid; the birds are near the sky, therefore their sounds are clear. Now the sounds of the people near the equator are turbid and near to [the sounds of] the beasts; the sounds of the people near the arctic seas are clear and warbling[46] like [the sounds of] the birds. Therefore, in the phonetic system [of the new world language] we should take our examples from the [sounds of the languages prevailing] in the fortieth to fiftieth degrees. . . . The system of the [new] language having been decided upon, if we make up books and send them to the schools, then after several decades the whole world will use the new language. As for the old languages of the various nations, they will be preserved in museums, where they can serve in the researches of antiquarians.

12. (In this section of seven and a half pages the author goes into details of his proposals for calendrical reforms and other time measurements of the One World Era. He displays a good acquaintance with modern knowledge in this field, as well as his customary originality. He discusses the problems of the lunar calendar handed down from antiquity, and the solar calendar derived from the later realization that the earth revolves about the sun. [He suggests that the proper term for the year in Chinese should be *nien* or *ch'i*, rather than *sui*, since the latter was used when it was thought the stars revolved above the earth.] He notes that different months have at different times and in different places been designated as the first month, and that in truth any day can just as well be the first day of

the year. The solstices and equinoxes may be used to determine this day; the vernal equinox is most suitable, since it is the same everywhere on earth, and on account of its obvious connection with ideas of new and renewed life. The four seasons will be called the four 'journeys', as the earth travels from equinox to solstice to equinox to solstice, and back to spring equinox.

(The lunar calendar was the most natural way for the ancients to calculate time; however, this involves difficulties because of the noncorrespondence of the earth and moon in their movements. The solar calendar is more accurate, even though it also presents the awkward problem of months of varying numbers of days. In the One World Era it will supplant the lunar calendar; however, among the common people of China who have used the latter since ages past, it may continue to be used for some time, since the sudden change would be very confusing. The solution may be to use the ancient Moslem dual lunar-solar calendar for a time.

(As in all measurements, the day will be divided according to the handy decimal system, rather than by twelves. There will be ten hours with subdivisions of ten, and smaller divisions of ten in the subdivisions. This is not original, as he notes the *Tso Chuan* speaks of it. The exception to the decimal system will be the week, which will remain seven days, this being sanctioned by universal usage throughout history, and the fact that it is suited to human nature—to rest a day after five days being too soon, and after ten days too long.

(There will be time-towers in every city and along the main roads. These will have models of the sun and earth, with four faces each giving graphic representation of the various aspects of time, even to the relationship of the earth and the more important stars. There will also be small timepieces for carrying on the person and placing in a room. Thereby, the lunar calendar can be discarded without confusing the common people, and the various improvements and benefits of the new time system can be brought into effect.

13. (This section deals with the matter of determining the date from which the One World Era will begin. Three ways by which various peoples have established their dating systems are discussed; usually at first the date is based on the local ruler's reign, later it is according to the reign of an emperor, and eventually it is from a

religious leader. This sequence is illustrated from Chinese and foreign history, and the confusions of the first two methods are noted. Dating from a religious leader is better, for 'It is always better when men give obedience to the morality of a religious leader than when they give obedience to the power of a monarch'. Besides that, monarchy will cease to exist on earth within a hundred years. However, the difficulty with dating from religious leaders is that there are many religions, and the followers of each will not defer to the others. 'Man and man, each has his own right to self-determination, his principle of independence. We cannot determine the matter by majority vote.'

(But when the world is unified, all things will be the same everywhere, including religion. The universal belief will be what is called 'serving Heaven' (*feng t'ien*).[47] Better than dating according to that belief, however, will be according to the One World itself. How to decide on the precise date to commence the Era is a problem, since unity will not suddenly be achieved at any given time. The suggestion is made that a most appropriate year to start from would be the year in which the first great step was taken on the road to One World—the First Hague Conference—which happens also to mark the beginning of the twentieth century in the Western calendar, corresponding to the Chinese *keng-tzu* year [and, as he says, *keng* 庚 equals 更 ; and *tzu* 子 equals 始].[48] Let us begin the One World Era from the spring equinox of that year. Dates in all the histories will be revised accordingly.)

Progress towards One World will not be even; we will [proceed] from conferences and alliances at first, and [eventually] arrive at One World. In the Era of Complete Peace-and-Equality there will be very many changes, and we cannot [specify] one law [for that time]. Now [I] shall divide [the evolution towards One World] according to a Chart of the Three Eras. Although the governmental forms are numerous, in a general way they will not be other than these:

CHART OF THE THREE AGES [IN THE EVOLUTION] OF UNITING THE NATIONS INTO ONE WORLD

	1. The Age of Disorder at the Time the First Foundations of One World are Laid.	The Age of Increasing Peace-and-Equality, When One World Is Gradually Coming into Being.	The Age of Complete Peace-and-Equality, When One World has been Achieved.
2.	The old states are allied.	New public states are created.	There are no states, [only] the world.
3.	Governments of the individual states hold all power. International public conferences are held; every state sends delegates to deliberate [on international questions].	The public government is first established, with members [of parliament], and administrative officers to govern the various states.	The whole earth is [under] the public government. There are administrative officers to carry out governmental [functions]; there are members [of parliament] who deliberate [on legislation.] There are no national boundaries.
4.	There are public (i.e. international) conferences; there is no public government.	[Portions of] the national territory [of individual states] and some of the islands in the seas will be taken from [the states] and [placed under] the public government.	The world and all the earth will be entirely [under] the public government.
5.	The lands belong to the states; the seas are [under] no government.	The seas are territories of the public government, and the small islands likewise.	The whole earth, land, and sea is all public territory.
6.	Individual states join as they see fit in international conferences.	Individual states may as they see fit join the public states. It is not permitted to form a single state by the union of two; it is only permitted to make several states by dividing one.[1]	All [the former] states are under the public government; [their old] state names are abolished, [and they no longer exist as states].

CHART OF THE THREE AGES [IN THE EVOLUTION] OF UNITING THE NATIONS INTO ONE WORLD—continued

7.	The people are under the old states.	The people gradually throw off the authority of the old states and come under the united public government.	The old states do not exist. The people are all citizens of the world, under the authority of the public parliament.
8.	The international conferences have chairmen, but no president.	The public government has a chairman; it has no president, much less a monarch. And it will not be permitted for the monarch of any state to serve as a chairman. Or perhaps there will [not even] be a chairman.	The public government has only members and[2] administrative officers; there is no chairman,[3] and no president, much less a monarch. Important matters are decided by majority vote.
9.	All the states have monarchs or presidents [who] each have independent powers.	Most of the states have presidents, [although] a few may have monarchs, but [all are] under the control of the public government.	There are no individual states or territories; there are only [local] presidents, who are, however, under the control of the public government.
10.	The individual states [exercise] complete sovereignty and autonomy; the international conferences are only [empowered] to discuss [problems].[4]	The individual states [exercise] limited sovereignty and autonomy; important matters belong [under the jurisdiction of] the public government.	There are no more states; all [important decisions] are [made] in public election by the people. [The peoples of the world] are autonomous, but all under the [ultimate] control of the public government.
11.	There is no public government; there are only international conferences which utilize the services of people and officials of the individual states [on a permanent basis].	The public government may utilize the services of people and officials of individual states at its own convenience.	There are no states. The people are united under one public government, and universally bear responsibility for its affairs.

12. There are international congresses; there are no territories [belonging to] a public government.

There is a public government. It builds cities, stations officials, constructs ships, establishes storehouses, buys and uses land of individual states—all only upon the consent of the individual states. Its regulations will be determined as the times require.

The public government may in any place whatsoever build cities, station officials, construct ships, establish warehouses.

13. [Jurisdiction] of the international conferences does not extend to the internal affairs of the individual states. Therefore in its internal affairs[5] each state [exercises] unlimited powers.

Even though [jurisdiction] of the public government does not extend to the internal affairs of individual states, yet in the important governmental functions of military forces, taxation, postal service, telegraphic communications, and law, [the states] will all be limited in their powers [by the public government].

There are no states; but the small governments of the various localities and the public government are all limited in their powers. [This] will be determined as the times require.

14. International conferences are responsible for keeping the peace and safeguarding the individual states.

The public government is responsible for protecting individual states, for pacifying their internal disturbances, and for settling their external quarrels.

There are no states. The public government rules over all the degrees.

15. The laws [made by] international conferences, being public law, are superior to the laws of the individual states.

The laws of the public government are above the laws of individual states; the latter cannot contravene the former.

The whole world is, all alike, under public law.

16. Individual states obey the laws and decisions of the international conferences.

The laws [made by] the [public] parliament certify the laws [made by] the individual states.[6]

All [the world] is under the law of the public government.

CHART OF THE THREE AGES [IN THE EVOLUTION] OF UNITING THE NATIONS INTO ONE WORLD—*continued*

17.	Individual states [form] treaties of alliance.	Individual states are half under treaties and half under constitutional law.	There are no states. There is only constitutional law.
18.	Individual states can make treaties; individual states can terminate or conclude mutual alliances.	Individual states are not permitted to terminate or make treaties; individual states are not permitted to terminate or form mutual alliances.	[Since] there are no states, we can say there are no treaties; [since] there are no states, we can say there are no alliances.
19.	International conferences have no power to limit or restrict individual states.	The public government has the power to limit and restrict individual states.	Although there is a public government, the autonomy of the various boundaries —the various degrees—will not be limited or restricted.
20.	The governmental authority of allied governments extends to individual states; it does not extend to the people.	The authority of the public government extends to individual states and gradually to the people.	There are no individual states, divisions of territory, or divisions of people. There is only the Union and the governing of it.
21.	Individual states are sovereign; they do not come under the [authority of] the international conferences.	The powers of individual states are all seen to proceed from the public government.	There are no states. All [authority] proceeds from the public government.
22.	Those [states] which do not take part in the international conferences, but dispute with [their decisions], cannot become members of [these] conferences.	Those [states] which rebel against the public government and dispute [its decisions] are the worst of criminals.	All persons being public citizens of the public government, there are none who dispute [its decisions].

23. Those among the states which do not participate in the international conferences are expelled, and do not share in the rights and privileges of international law.

Those among the states which take up arms against the public government are regarded as rebels.

All persons who oppose the public government, scheme to seize territory, create disturbances, assume the title of emperor or ruler and desire to return [to the system of] hereditary nobility—all are [regarded as] rebels and the worst of criminals.

24. The individual states have their own laws, originating outside of [any] international government; [such] international governments do not have much authority.

Laws of the individual states cannot originate outside of the public government; the public government has unlimited authority.

There are no laws of individual states; all [law-making authority] proceeds from the public government. The public government in turn distributes authority to the individual boundaries, individual degrees.

1B. The power to make laws resides in the individual states and does not belong to the international conferences. The international conferences only deliberate on international law.

Although the power to make laws belongs to the individual states, the power [to make] public law for the whole earth belongs to the upper and lower houses of the public government.

The individual localities also have [the power] to make laws, and govern themselves; but the [power to make] laws for the whole earth belongs to the upper and lower houses of the public government, which makes the laws [according to its] public discussions.

2B. International conferences deliberate on important cases involving international law which are brought up by the individual states. The individual states may at any time bring up cases [involving] facts and principles of government to the international conferences for discussion.

There is the public government and the public parliament to deliberate on cases of undecided and divergent laws of the individual states, including cases in which [the laws] are defective or erroneous.

[The public government] deliberates upon and determines the laws, and [sees to it that] they are put into effect everywhere. When there are changes in governmental affairs [anywhere] in the world, [the problems involved] can be brought up yearly and deliberated upon.

CHART OF THE THREE AGES [IN THE EVOLUTION] OF UNITING THE NATIONS INTO ONE WORLD—*continued*

3B.	The rules [drawn up by] international conferences are deliberated upon and decided by the members of the individual state parliaments; the monarch or president of each state signs and promulgates them.	The laws [drawn up by] the public government are signed by all the members of parliament and political leaders of the individual states; [when signed] by the majority they are promulgated. Or perhaps the assent of the monarch or president is awaited before promulgating them.	The laws [drawn up by] the public government are signed by all of the political leaders (i.e. ? heads of ministries and the like); [when signed] by the majority, they are promulgated.
4B.	There being a two-thirds [majority] of the international conference [delegates in favour of] changing a law, it can be changed. There being a two-thirds [majority] in the individual state's government [in favour of] changing a public law, it can be changed.	There being a two-thirds [majority] of the legislature of an individual state [in favour of] changing a public law, it can be changed. There being a two-thirds [majority] in the public parliament [in favour of] changing a public law, it can be changed.	There are no individual states, only the public parliament and the public institutions[7] of the various localities. The members of parliament will make laws according to the majority [vote].
5B.	International conferences meet once every few years, or, should there be an important matter on which various states have requested a conference, then a conference is held.	The [public] parliament meets once every year. Whenever more than half of the individual states request a meeting, then a meeting is held.	The [public] parliament is constantly in session throughout the year. When there are public elections, it does not meet, [but the members] disperse, each to his own locality. [Thus] there are [times] of meeting and [times] of dispersal.
6B.	There are [international] congresses, but they do not have upper and lower houses. [Promulgation of their laws] waits upon the signatures of the home governments.	There are upper and lower houses [in the public parliament]. Both houses must pass a bill before it is enacted: if [both houses] do not pass it, it is not enacted. Perhaps the signatures of the individual states [must] be awaited before it can be enacted.	The same, only [since] there are no states, there is nothing to wait for; [a bill] having been discussed and passed is forthwith enacted.

7B. Delegates sent by the governments [of participating states] must be officials of the governments.	The upper house [of the public parliament] is composed of government officials; the lower house is composed of [members] publicly elected half from officials and half from the people [at large].	The members of parliament are all publicly elected from among the people; all are citizens, [and citizens only].
8B. Representatives must be [persons who have been] deputed by the governments of the individual states. They may hold dual offices.	As members of [the public] parliament the [states] must use persons who are resident nationals; they may not use nationals of other states to fill [these offices].	As members of [the public] parliament, each locality publicly elects persons who have long resided in that locality.
9B. The government of each state sends one person to act as its representative. Large states may [send] three persons. China's [sending] one person is like the German system (?). [The matter is decided upon as the situation requires.	Members of the upper house are elected by the [individual state] governments or parliaments; there are two persons from each state. Members of the lower house are publicly elected by the people [of the states]; the number [of members] is according to the size of the population.	There being no states, members of the upper house are elected by boundary, by degree; members of the lower house are sent according to the size of the population [of each locality].
10B. Representatives represent their own states.	Members of the upper house represent their own states; members of the lower house represent the world.	Members of [the public] parliament represent only the people of the world [and not any particular region].
11B. Delegates to the international conferences do not have limited terms.	Members of parliament from the various states are elected either once every year, or once every three years. This will be decided as the times require.	Members of parliament are elected either once every three years, or once every year. This will be decided as the times require.
12B. International conferences may have a chairman.	The public parliament does not have a chairman; [all matters] are decided according to majority [vote].	The public parliament does not have a chairman; [bills] are passed or rejected according to majority [vote].

CHART OF THE THREE AGES [IN THE EVOLUTION] OF UNITING THE NATIONS INTO ONE WORLD—*continued*

13B. Chairman and secretary are both chosen by public decision, according to majority vote.	Same.	There is no parliamentary chairman; all [decisions] are by public vote, according to the majority.
14B. Representatives are paid by their own states.	Members of parliament receive salaries from the public government.	Same.
15B. Qualifications of representatives are [determined] by their own governments; if guilty of malfeasance, they are tried by their own governments.	Qualifications of members of parliament are [determined] by the public parliament itself; if [a member] is guilty of malfeasance, he is tried by the public parliament.	Same.
16B. Representatives are subject to suit in their own states.	[Members of the public parliament] are not subject to suit in their own states.	[Members of the public parliament] are not subject to suit off the floor of the legislature.
Whenever guilty of a crime, unless recalled by his own state, a representative may not be punished by [the government] of the place where he is.	A member of parliament being guilty of a crime, his own state cannot recall and punish him. All [punishment] is by public deliberation of the public parliament.	A member of parliament having erred, may not be punished by the legal officials. [All punishment] is by public deliberation of the public parliament.
17B. A representative being guilty, he is punished by his own state.	A member of parliament being guilty, the public parliament may punish the crime without having to await the consent of his own state. There must be a two-thirds [vote] of the members before this may be carried out.	Same.

18B.	In case of something happening to a representative from an individual state, whether he makes mistakes or becomes ill, the government of that state delegates another member to fill his place.	In case of something happening to a member from an individual state, such as illness, that state elects someone to fill his place. The [state] parliament elects members to the upper house; the people [at large] elect members to the lower house. Or, when the [state] parliament is adjourned, the government will appoint a temporary delegate.	In case of something happening to a member from any state (sic: we should assume 'locality' is meant), such as illness, the citizens of that locality again hold elections.
19B.	International conferences have representatives from the various states; they do not have administrative officials.	The administrative officials of the public government are all publicly elected by the members of parliament from the various states. Each [official must] have the joint support of at least three states. If there still be many states in the world, then it will require the joint support of five states. If there are Great Powers, they may, as in the example of the German Confederation, be permitted to have many members, or they may use one person (?).	The administrative officials of the public government are publicly elected by the upper and lower [houses] of parliament.
	The representatives all being delegated by the individual states, only the great ministers of the individual states can take the floor and represent the views of their own states.	Both the great ministers and members of parliament may take the floor and represent the views of their own states.	Persons of honour from the whole world may take the floor and represent their views.

CHART OF THE THREE AGES [IN THE EVOLUTION] OF UNITING THE NATIONS INTO ONE WORLD—continued

2OB.	The international conferences have no officials.	The public government has officials. All are subject to appointment and dismissal, demotion and promotion, by the chairman of the [public] government. However, their official rights and privileges in their own states are not [thereby] prejudiced.	The officials of the public government are all subject to demotion or promotion by the chairman of the [public] government. There being no states, there are likewise no [official] rights and privileges of their own states.
1C.	The international conference having important business, it can tell the postal and telegraphic facilities of the individual states to act with despatch; but it does not have the power to command them.	The public government having important business, the postal and telegraphic facilities of the individual states will all obey its commands, or [those of] the official appointed as superintendent. [If] a large state does not consent, [the public government] will let it delay for a while.	Postal and telegraphic [facilities] are all under the public government.
2C.	Postal services and telegraphic facilities all intercommunicate; [but] there are large states and out-of-the-way localities which do not take part, [and] are outside of [these international networks].	The postal services and telegraphic communications of all the states are uniformly interwoven.	There being no state boundaries, postal services and telegraphic communications are all under one [control].
3C.	Each state sets up its own postal service and telegraph lines and takes the fees for itself.	The public government has the expense of setting up postal services and telegraph [lines]; hence the public government takes [the fees] for itself.	The fees from the postal service and telegraphic [facilities] all belong to the public government.

4c. Railways, canals, frontier defences and highways of the individual states cannot completely inter-communicate.	Railways, frontier defences, and roads can completely intercommunicate.	There being no states, all communications are uniform.
There cannot be complete intercommunication with small boats [by means of] the internal rivers and canals.	There can be intercommunication with small boats [by means of] the internal rivers and canals.	There being no states, all communications are uniform.
5c. There are no international railways.	There are public railways to facilitate inter-communication. When they cross over a state, they can always buy land [for the line]; but this does not impair the sovereignty of the state.	There are no private railways of individual states; all are public railways.
The regulations and legal forms of the various states' railways are not uniform.	The legal forms and regulations of the various states' railways gradually become uniform.	The regulations and legal forms of the railways have become uniform.
There is no [international] authority to examine and fix the transportation of the railways.	The public government has the authority to examine and fix railway transportation prices. It orders fair transportation prices on rock, coal, mineral ores, lumber, rice, fertilizers, and essential agricultural and industrial products.	Same. In time of famine, [the public government] can set the very lowest transportation prices.
	[Thereby] the whole earth is greatly benefited—strong states which do not follow [these orders] aside.	

CHART OF THE THREE AGES [IN THE EVOLUTION] OF UNITING THE NATIONS INTO ONE WORLD—*continued*

6c. [Each state] protects its own trade and transportation.	The public government protects the trade of the individual states.	There being no state boundaries, there is no need for protection.
7c. Individual states may cast their own metal coins and make their own paper money.	The coinage and paper currency of the various states has become uniform.	There are no states. Coins [are cast] by the public mint; paper money [is printed] by the public printery.
8c. Measures and weights are not standard; but the international conferences can deliberate on this [problem].	Most measures and weights are standard; the public government selects the best ones to follow, and the individual states gradually [come to] follow them.	Measures and weights are completely standardized.
9c. Copyrights and patents for new books and articles are gradually becoming effective everywhere.	Copyrights and patents for new books and articles are effective everywhere.	Same.
10c.8 Copyright protection is gradually becoming effective everywhere.	Copyright protection is effective everywhere.	Same.
11c. There is increasing discussion about putting the health and anti-epidemic [measures] of individual states into effect everywhere, but [as yet] no uniformity.	The health and anti-epidemic [measures] of the individual states are uniform.	There are no state boundaries; anti-epidemic [measures] are uniform [throughout the world].
12c. People of the various states must [undergo] investigations when they travel.	People of the various states need not [undergo] investigations when travelling.	There are no state boundaries and no investigations.

13c. Banks are not to be found every-where.	Banks are to be found everywhere.	Banks are under the public [government.]⁹
14c. There being no public government, the individual [states] do not pay revenues to the public [government].	There is a public government, which has the high seas as its territory for levying taxes, and taxes the ships [which sail thereon]. [Should this] amount be insufficient, then the public government divides the burden [among the individual states]. [Should] there be Great Powers which do not pay [their share] for a while, [the public government] permits this.	All revenues belong to the public government.
15c. The individual states can collect customs duties.	Shipping revenues belong to the public government	All shipping revenues belong to the public government.
16c. Each [state] takes for itself its internal revenues.	The public government deliberates on and determines the revenues to be collected by the individual states, and puts [these laws] into general effect. And it [also] deliberates on cases concerning reduction of [taxes], and unjustly levied taxes.	Each locality levies its own taxes, but shares them with the public government.
17c. Customs duties and tariffs are being unified and put into general effect. Despite the boundaries, they are being put into general effect. Large states which do not assent [are permitted] to delay.	Customs duties and tariffs are uniform.	There are no states, no [customs] duties, and no tariffs.

CHART OF THE THREE AGES [IN THE EVOLUTION] OF UNITING THE NATIONS INTO ONE WORLD—continued

	Imports and exports are taxed.	Imports and exports are taxed.	Imports and exports are not taxed.
18c.	Imports and exports are taxed.	Imports and exports are taxed.	Imports and exports are not taxed.
19c.	[The expenses of] quelling disturbances among the various states are laid to the public debt.	The promotion of public commerce, and care for the people, are laid to the public debt.	Publicly caring for the people, publicly sustaining them, and publicly transporting them are laid to the public debt. It is all the same, whether or not there be [this public] debt; everyone being publicly employed, everything [comes from and goes to] the public.
20c.	The fiscal accounts of the individual states are not audited by international [organizations].	The fiscal accounts [of the individual states] are subject to public audit and periodic inspection.	Fiscal accounts are examined by the public government.
21c.	Annual budgets are made by the individual states themselves.	The annual budgets [of the individual states] are always reported to the public government.	The annual budgets of [every locality] in the world are all under [the control of] the public government.
22c.	International conferences are not provided with information as to the populations of the individual states.	Populations of the individual states are always truthfully reported [to the public government].	There are no states. The population of each locality is assessed and reported [to the public government].
1D.	The international conferences have disarmament as their main objective. The individual states gradually join the disarmament conferences.	The public government hears and decides the litigation of the individual states, and prohibits their going to war. The individual states always obey the public government, and do not dare to go to war.	There are no states. Armaments have been discarded.

2D. The international conference [having agreed on] disarmament, should there be [a state] which does not obey, the various states may join in attacking it.	[Should] an individual state not obey the disarmament [order] of the public government, [the latter] can use its troops and attack it; or it may combine the forces of individual states and attack it.	There being no states, there is no obeying or not obeying, no troops, and no attacking.
3D. The international conferences have disarmament conferences. For the passage of their joint police forces they can borrow the use of the railroads of the various states for a low cost and on short notice.	The public government [may do] the same.[10]	There being no states, there are no troops, and there is no borrowing of [rail-] roads.[10]
4D. Each state is allowed to run its own army.	Augmenting of armies is prohibited.	Individual state armies have been entirely done away with; [armies] have been transformed into police.
Same, for navy.	Same, for navies.	Same, into naval police.
Same, for warships.	Same, for warships.	Same, into police ships.
Same, for weapons.	Same, for weapons.	Same, into implements of agriculture and industry.
Same, for poisons.	Same, for poisons.	Poisons and methods of burning [as used in warfare] are absolutely prohibited and may not be transmitted [to the knowledge of future generations].

CHART OF THE THREE AGES [IN THE EVOLUTION] OF UNITING THE NATIONS INTO ONE WORLD—*continued*

5D. The people of the various states are always subject to military service for their state.	The public government has done away with compulsory military service in the states. It is only permitted to solicit recruits.	Compulsory military service is completely abolished among the people of the earth. However, everyone must serve one year[11] in the various [public] institutions, after reaching the age of twenty.[12]
The people of the various states are always subject to the expenses of [supporting] military forces.	The public government has abolished the bearing of military expenditures by the people; but they bear the expenses of public care[13] [for all the people].	Half of the taxes collected by the public government from the people are expended in public care.
The military forces of the various states belong under the control of those states.	Even though the military forces of the individual states belong under the control of those states, the public government has the duty of supervising them, with the main objective of daily reducing them.	There are no states; military forces have been abolished.
The soldiers and officers of each state are always used by the state itself.	The soldiers and officers of the various states are all at the disposal of the public government.	There are no states, no soldiers, and no officers—only police.
6D. Each state may have a navy and warships. The international conferences are permitted to deliberate over [questions regarding] them.	Navies and warships gradually come under the public government.	The public government has abolished navies; only passenger, mail, and commercial vessels exist.
Commercial vessels of the various states can become naval units.	Commercial vessels of the individual states belong to the public government, which sets forth the laws [regulating them].	There being no states, commercial vessels all belong to the public government, which compiles and administers their laws.

7D. The ruler of each state has the power to control his state's military forces.	The public government gradually does away with the power of rulers to control their military forces.	There being no states and no rulers, there are likewise no military forces and no power over same.
8D. Walled cities, mountain passes, strategic posts, and forts are all under the control of the individual state.	The public government is able gradually to abolish walled cities, [military strongholds guarding] mountain passes, strategic posts, and forts. Great Powers which do not consent to this all at once [will be permitted] to delay for a while.	With universal peace, and no states, all walled cities, [military strongholds guarding] mountain passes, strategic posts, and forts will be entirely abolished.
9D. There are no international troops.	There are international troops.	International troops are abolished.
Same, for warships.	Same, for warships.	Same, for warships.
Same, for armaments.	Same, for armaments.	Same, for armaments.
10D. There are battles between the troops of the various states, with killing and wounding.	The states have abolished war. Even if there is a war, it is permitted to tie up and wound men, but not to kill them.	There are no states; military forces have been completely abolished.
11D. The people are all forbidden to store up weapons.	The people do not store up weapons.	All weapons have been destroyed.

CHART OF THE THREE AGES [IN THE EVOLUTION] OF UNITING THE NATIONS INTO ONE WORLD—*continued*

12D. In cases of international litigation, it is up to international conferences to decide them. There are no judges constituted [to judge] international litigation.	There are judges of the public government who hear international litigation but do not act in civil litigation. All litigations involving private or public parties are under the jurisdiction of their own state. Only litigation involving nationals of two states, or persons of one state but concerning land, will be heard by [the judges of the public government].	The public government has judges. There being no states and no international litigation, they only hear plaints of the people of the various boundaries and localities.
1E. In deciding maritime cases, two states may publicly discuss and decide [the matter]. [The decision] may be changed by the international conference (or, the decision may be carried to the international conference).	The judges of the public government hear maritime cases, [as] all authority over the high seas belongs to the public government.[14]	The whole earth is under the public government, without distinction as to land or sea.
2E. All cases of international litigation are sent to the international conferences for consideration.	The public government can delegate officials to go to the various states and judge litigation.	There are no states; in important cases the same procedure is followed as in column two.
3E. The people do not dare to bring charges to the [international] conferences against their rulers or presidents.	The people may bring charges to the public parliament against their rulers and presidents.	The people may bring charges to the public parliament against their superiors.

4E. International conferences can judge cases [involving] the various states, but cannot try cases [involving] the rulers of the states.	The public parliament can judge cases [involving] the individual states; if a ruler has committed a crime it can also try him. However, without a two-thirds [majority] it cannot render a decision. In dealing with [a ruler's] crimes, it can dishonour him, reduce his powers, or even remove him from office. This will be decided upon according to the requirements of the times and circumstances. The ruler may also appeal for a new verdict.	The upper house may try cases for the whole world; it may deal with any case of a crime committed by a person of rank or authority.
5E. The principles used in adjudicating cases are not entirely the same. The international conferences have not codified contractual and criminal law, commercial law, law of evidence, law of punishment, and procedural law.	The principles used in adjudicating cases are generally the same. The public government deliberates and fixes the contractual law, criminal law, commercial law, law of evidence, law of punishment, and procedural law. Generally speaking, the various states follow the same [practices] in considering [cases].	There being no state boundaries, jurisprudence is all the same [everywhere]. There being no state boundaries, laws may at any time be discussed and determined, and carried into effect universally.
6E. A person who has not committed a crime may not have his freedom taken from him. Law cases are not dealt with promptly. There are no juries and no lawyers.	Even having committed a crime, [a person] is still reckoned to be free. The necessary investigations and trials in law cases must be [carried out] promptly. The accused has the right to use witnesses and lawyers.	People do not commit crimes. There is no litigation, no judges, nor lawyers. There are only public discussers.
7E. Crimes can be punished by fines. Serious crimes [entail] severe punishments.	Heavy fines are not levied. Serious crimes do not entail severe punishments.	There are no punishments, only disgrace. The people do not commit crimes, [so] there is no punishment.

CHART OF THE THREE AGES [IN THE EVOLUTION] OF UNITING THE NATIONS INTO ONE WORLD—continued

8E.	The body of a criminal can be killed, but cannot twice receive disgrace.	There is no capital punishment, thus there is no suffering [it even] one time.	Punishments have been discarded.[15] All men are happy and there is no suffering.
9E.	There are capital crimes under the law.	There are no capital crimes constituted. There will only be [provision for] life imprisonment.	Punishments have all been discarded. There is only [the punishment] of disgrace.
1F.	The people of individual states are protected by one law. But when living abroad and carrying on their business, they are restricted from holding office and participating in government (i.e. voting). Or it may be that they cannot live abroad and carry on their business.	There is no difference in the rights of citizens in the various states. The people of all the states can live together wherever they wish, doing business, holding office, participating in government. All are protected without distinction.	All are One World citizens. There are no boundaries to rights and privileges, and no distinctions.
2F.	The rights and privileges of the people are limited by their own states and by the various foreign states.	The people have the rights and privileges [inherent under] the public government. [These] may not be limited by their own states or foreign states.	There being no states, rights and privileges and freedom are only limited by the public laws.
3F.	[People] are not at liberty to transfer their residence from their own state to other states.	[People] are free to transfer their residence among the various states.	There being no state boundaries, people may transfer their residence [anywhere].
4F.	People of the various states do not have special rights or concessions in [other] states. When a criminal flees from one state to another, he is not necessarily extradited.	There is mutual extradition.[16]	There are public criminals [only].[17]

5F.	States succour their own poor, and also at times [the poor] of foreign states.	The public government succours the poor without distinction between their own state and foreign states.	The poor are cared for by the public government [in the institutions for the poor].[18]
6F.	States treat their own sick, and sometimes [the sick] of other states.	Those in foreign states who are sick are treated the same as [in their own state].	The sick are cared for by the public hospitals.[19]
7F.	States inter their own deceased, and sometimes [the deceased] of other states.	The state's deceased, and the deceased of a foreign state, are uniformly interred.	The deceased are interred by the [public] institutions for those who have enjoyed their allotted span.[20]
	The people all have private [real] property. If it is taken for official [use], it must be paid for.	Without great cause, the private [real] property of the people cannot be taken.	The people do not have private [real] property.
8F.	The persons, houses, documents, and property of the people may not be taken without cause. Material evidence is required before even the officials may search or arrest.	Manners and customs are being perfected. At times there are cases when [it is necessary] to search and arrest.	The public morals have become perfected; there is no searching or arresting.
9F.	The people do not have the right of complete independence of person.	The people all have the right of independence of person; without it absolutely cannot be helped, [this independence] may not be encroached upon.	The people are all in possession of independence of person; naturally, there being no crime, there is no encroaching upon [this independence].
	People's rights and privileges are limited.	People's rights and privileges are not limited.	Rights and privileges are all free [of limitations].

CHART OF THE THREE AGES [IN THE EVOLUTION] OF UNITING THE NATIONS INTO ONE WORLD—*continued*

10F.	Rights and privileges of the people of the various states are not equal.	The people of the various states gradually become equal; but the races are still unequal.	There are no state boundaries and no racial boundaries; [all] people are equal.
	The people are subject to taxation by the state.	The people bear [the burden of] taxation by the state.	The people are all cared for by the public; they do not bear [the burden of taxation by the state].21
	The people do not have complete civil rights.	A person, having committed a crime, is deprived of his civil rights.	The people do not commit crimes; they all have civil rights.
	[? The state] being in [? financial] straits, the people are besought to contribute.	[? The state ? The public government] does not ask the people to contribute.	All peoples are equal.22
11F.	Citizens are regarded differently on account of race, servitude, and female [sex].	Citizens may not be regarded differently on account of race or bodily form.	Citizens are not regarded differently on account of female [sex] or bodily form.
12F.	If a slave of state 'A' flees to another state, he is then [no longer] a slave.	All the states absolutely forbid slavery.	There are no states. Mankind is equal. There are no slaves.
13F.	Various states have slaves, but are gradually freeing them.	Various states forbid slavery, but do not forbid persons from being servants.	The people of all the [former] states are equal; there are no servants.
14F.	The states are all free to have their own religions; the international conferences do not decide them.	There is public discussion of religious ideas and the honouring of Heaven; but choosing the strong points of all the sages which 'match Heaven' will constitute the New Religion.	All the former philosophies, and all the new principles, are universally honoured. [Men] will not honour one religion alone, but will take from among all their principles.

15F. [People] revere Heaven; they revere the spirits still more.	None of the spirits are revered, but only Heaven.	Heaven is likewise not revered. [Men] only revere the former philosophers and the spirit of every man (i.e. the human soul).
16F. There being only single states, [their people] are 'the little people'.	There being a great union (ta t'ung) [the people] are 'the great people'.	All men are [citizens of] the universal One World; they are thus 'Heaven's people'.[23]
17F. The various states have the rank and power of 'emperor' or 'monarch'.	The rank of 'emperor' or 'monarch' is gradually done away with, and changed to 'president' or 'chairman'.	There are no ranks of 'emperor' or 'president'. The people are equal. There is only the parliamentary chairman.
There are the separate [classes of] hereditary nobles, commoners, and slaves.	There are no slaves, but while hereditary nobility is gradually being abolished, it has not yet completely [disappeared].	There are no hereditary nobles. [All men] are absolutely equal.

REFERENCES TO CHART

[1] While this seems at first glance to encourage the divisive tendency rather than the union which we desire, its purpose is clear enough: to prevent acquisitive wars. Although the author has perhaps nowhere in the book clearly enough emphasized it, his One World is just as definitely based on local autonomy as it is on world union. (See, for example, under column three in the chart, nos. 10, 19, 24, 1B, 16C; also Chapter IV, above, *Outline of the Public Government*, item 6.) It is opposed, in this fundamental sense, to the Fascist scheme.

[2] Taking 無 to be 有, which is the only way it makes sense. (It is correctly given in the San Francisco edition.)

[3] The author has contradicted himself on this matter in the chart. The 'chairman' (if that be anything like an appropriate rendering of this title) is *not* to be with us according to items 8, 12B, and 13B; he *is* to be with us, according to items 20B and 17F.

[4] 但有集議 . One is tempted to translate: 'the international conferences are merely debating societies'. However, although grammatically closer to the Chinese, the term is too strongly contemptuous for the author's meaning.

[5] Taking 法 to be 治.

[6] Or, more plainly, the laws of the individual states must be certified by the laws of the public parliament.

[7] See below, Part VI, Chapter I, section 4 ff.

[8] There seems to be no clear distinction between this item and the foregoing, except that the latter is more inclusive.

[9] See below, Part VIII, Chapter IX.

[10] These two items are included in the San Francisco edition, but not the Chung Hwa edition.

[11] The 'one year' is in the San Francisco edition, but not the Chung Hwa edition.

[12] See below, Part VI, Chapter IX, no. 3.

[13] Referring to the system of public institutions (for which, see below, Part VI, beginning at Chapter I, section 4).

[14] See above, items 4 and 5.

[15] See below, Part VIII, Chapter XIV.

[16] The San Francisco edition has here: 'The people of each of the states can receive the special rights and concessions in all the states. Criminals of the various states are mutually extradited.'

[17] The San Francisco edition has here: 'The people of the earth, in whatever locality they may be, their rights and privileges are identical. There are no state criminals, but [only] public (i.e. world) criminals.'

[18] See below, Part VI, Chapter VII.

[19] See below, Part VI, Chapter VIII.

[20] See below, Part VI, Chapter X.

[21] Compare above, item 19C.

[22] Something of a *non sequitur*. But the whole item is unclear.

[23] See above, Book One, Chapter II, n. 28.

REFERENCES

[1] *I Ching, chun* hexagram 屯. The present translation of this excerpt, while departing from the oracular mood of the original text, brings out the meaning which our author has given to it. (For two English versions of this passage, see James Legge, *The Yi Ching*, being vol. xvi, *The Sacred Books of the East*, 2nd edition, Oxford, 1899, pp. 215–16; and Richard Wilhelm, *The I Ching or Book of Changes*, rendered into English by Cary Baynes, 2 vols., New York, The Bollingen Series, XIX, Pantheon Books, 1950, vol. ii, pp. 33–4.)

[2] The Chinese expression—'mudding and charcoaling' (塗炭)—is quite as vivid, though impossible in English.

[3] Again referring to *I Ching, chun* hexagram: 屯 剛柔始交而難生 剛 refers to the *ch'ien* hexagram, 柔 to the *k'un*, as used by our author. (I have taken Wilhelm's renderings of these hexagram names.)

[4] An uncertain translation for 帝網重重層累無盡   , accomplished by taking 糸罔 for 網.

[5] Yeh-lang was an independent country in Han times, occupying territory in the region south and east of the Yangtze, and west of the Wu River—i.e. the borderlands of Kueichow and Yunnan provinces. (According to Yanouchi and Wada, *Historical Atlas of the Orient*, 箭內 亘(編)和田清(補)東洋讀史地圖, Tokyo, 1941: map no. 7.)

[6] Following the San Francisco edition (Part II, p. 2, 1.8), which has 阝巳 instead of the 巳 of the Chung Hwa edition (the latter even so being misprinted 己).

[7] 如彼...如此.

[8] 仁人義士.

[9] 屠伯 (from a particularly bloody period during the Han dynasty. *Tz'u Hai* refers to 漢書嚴延年傳   ).

[10] 民賊 Mencius said, 'Those who nowadays serve their sovereigns say, "We can for our sovereign enlarge the limits of the cultivated ground, and fill his treasuries and arsenals." Such persons are nowadays called "good ministers", but anciently they were called "robbers of the people" . . .' (James Legge's rendering, in *The Four Books: The Works of Mencius*, VI, B, 9.1).

[11] A stock phrase, used a number of times in this book.

[12] The text mentions the names of ministers of each of these states. The

alliance of states lasted from 546 to 506 B.C. (For the story of its formation, see James Legge's *The Chinese Classics*, 1st edition, Hong Kong, 1861–72; 2nd edition, Oxford, 1893–5, vol. v, Part II, *The Ch'un Ts'ew, with the Tso Chuen*, Duke Seang, 27th Year, pp. 528–35. A brief summary of the history of the alliance will be found in T'ung Shu-yeh (童書業), *Ch'un Ch'iu History* (春秋史); see also, in English, Evan Morgan, 'A League of Nations in Ancient China', in *Journal of the North China Branch, Royal Asiatic Society*, New Series, vol. LVII, 1926, pp. 50–6.)

13 仁人君子 Despite my remarks concerning the defensibility of using the Chinese term itself (see above, p. 36, n. 31), many times *jen* obviously means just what the English 'good' means, and many times it obviously means 'love' in the broadest, most altruistic sense. As for *chün tzu*, it would again be possible to cite whole pages of opinions defending the greater accuracy of this or that translation; however, we should certainly not arrive at any happy solution to the problem. I have adopted another translator's dodge in the face of this problem, and have capitalized the terms when using a standard, if unsatisfactory, rendering.

14 年歲.

15 甗瓶山 See *Lieh Tzu*, 'T'ang Wen 湯問.' (This section is not included in the English translation of Lionel Giles: *Taoist Teachings from the Book of Lieh Tzu*, 'The Wisdom of the East Series', London, John Murray, 2nd edition, 1947.)

16 [*Sic*] I am unable to suggest the derivation of the author's confusion here.

17 馬代 Media seems to be intended, although another and quite different transliteration is now used for that name.

18 色臘 So transliterated by Hsüan Chuang (玄奘) in his famous *Account of the Western Regions* (西域記).

19 A very free rendering for what would be most awkward if given more faithfully.

20 民權 The Chinese term, 'people's authority', is perhaps more precisely expressive of the author's meaning.

21 As a matter of fact, it would be a little more than twenty years. The Russian constitution was finally granted by Nicholas II in October of 1905. (Incidentally this furnishes us with a definite date for at least a touching-up of the manuscript by our author.)

22 A free rendering of what would be most ungraceful in literal translation.

[23] In 221 B.C. the state of Ch'in finally succeeded in vanquishing its rivals, bringing the period of the Warring States to an end and unifying the whole of China for the first time under a centralized monarchy which was not feudal in organization. (This kind of unification is obviously at quite the opposite pole to the unification envisaged by K'ang Yu-wei.)

[24] 公政府 This term is used throughout the book as part of the political vocabulary of One World. I have rendered it literally, since the distinction between the 'private' world of the past and the 'public' world of the future is basic to our author's theories. The emphasis in this overall world government is on its being 'public' even more than on its being 'universal'.

[25] I have ventured arbitrarily to change the compound from 民黨 to 民權, on the perhaps shaky grounds of the latter's seeming a more likely companion to the following compound.

[26] See Part IV below.

[27] Again the Chinese *hsin* is too inclusive for the translator, who must choose between the cerebral and the emotional, or else combine the two in the barbaric rendering 'mind-heart'.

[28] Japan became dominant in Korea after the Sino-Japanese War was terminated by the Treaty of Shimonoseki (1895). She was drawn into the Russo-Japanese War (1904–5) because of her determination to exercise control over the peninsula. She formally annexed Korea in 1909.

[29] 其亡其亡 from *I Ching*, *p'i* hexagram 否 .

[30] There was sentiment for a confederation among the Central American states all during the nineteenth century, following the separation from Mexico in 1823. The five states were originally, in fact, constituted as the United Provinces of Central America. The union was beset with inner conflicts, however, and was constantly falling apart and being patched up again.

[31] i.e. The First Hague Conference. (It happened that agreement on disarmament or limitation of armaments was not accomplished by this conference.)

[32] *I Ching*, *ch'ien* hexagram 乾. (I have corrected mispunctuation of the text.) Legge explains (see his translation, cited in n. 1 above, p. 60), 'Force would have given place to submission, and haughtiness to humility; and the result would be good fortune'. This is also mentioned in the *Tso Chuan* (see Legge's translation, cited in n. 12 above, p. 731). The 'flight of dragons without heads' is the abandonment of control by 'superior

men' (dragons), and indicates the transformation to the opposite hexa-gram, the Receptive (*k'un* 坤), as is likewise indicated by the second phrase—'the nines' referring to the undivided lines of the hexagram, which all change to divided lines. I have used the Wilhelm-Baynes rendering (see work cited in n. 1 above, vol. II, pp. 7, 16).

33 各邦萬國交通 I have not ventured to translate this more precisely, although it would seem to refer to the *Zollparlament* (customs parliament) set up by Bismarck in July of 1867.

34 民族 The term is vague, though perhaps not as vague as it is in English. It connotes 'racial', in the sense of a 'people', as we speak loosely of the 'Chinese race'. It is significant and reflective of some of the serious troubles of our times, that we have no clear definitions for such carelessly bandied terms as 'race' and 'nation' and 'people'.

35 強梁 From a passage in *Tao Te Ching*, Chapter XLII, rendered by Waley as follows: 'Show me a man of violence that came to a good end, and I will take him for my teacher.' (Arthur Waley, *The Way and Its Power*, London, Allen & Unwin, 1934, p. 195.)

36 See below, no. 11, as well as pp. 93-4, no. 5, above.

37 See below, Part VIII, Chapter VIII.

38 See below, Part VIII, Chapter III.

39 Compare below, Part VIII, Chapter I. As we shall see in that chapter, mathematics is not our author's forte. However, the system outlined here is consistent, provided we allow the author to assign arbitrary values to these names of measurements. (For this reason, the values I have given in the brackets should not be taken as true for this system; in fact, they obviously cannot be.) The reader will note that the ten-measurement is in each case a *square* measure, although the text does not make this clear.

40 These astronomical figures are expressed by the following single characters, of which only the first two are common: 萬兆陔壞澗載. 恆沙.

41 Since our author's system is devised on a purely arbitrary, decimal basis, it seems that his values for the measuring units will fail to accommo-date to the actual shape of the earth, with its gradual flattening towards the poles, and its bulging middle. However, he recognizes this in his discussion in Part VIII, Chapter I, and allows for it.

42 See below, Part VIII, Chapter III.

43 See above, p. 93, no. 4.

44 Here the author seems to be thinking in terms of Chinese characters,

with their 'significs' and 'phonetics'. However, the method of combining parts is of course common in our scientific terminology derived from Greek and Latin.

[45] Taking 扎 to be 札.

[46] Taking 轉 to be 囀

[47] But compare below, Part X, pp. 274–6, as well as the Chart of Part II, items 14F and 15F.

[48] 更 始 would mean, 'to change and commence'.

PART III

ABOLISHING CLASS BOUNDARIES AND EQUALIZING [ALL] PEOPLE

O F the sufferings of mankind due to inequality, none compare to [those which stem from] a baseless [distinction by] classes. There are three important kinds [of inferior classes]: the first is inferior races; the second is slaves; the third is women.

Now, the practice of inequality is not only contrary to the universal principles of nature (*t'ien*) but is actually detrimental to the progress of man. By looking at India we can learn this.

(There follows here a description of the caste system of India and its stultifying effects upon the individual. Caste and slavery have existed in Egypt, Babylon, Greece, the Far East, and Europe in the Middle Ages. In Europe these class divisions were responsible for the thousand-year period of darkness and cultural stagnation. The great revolution of modern times is the abolition of this system, as the principle of equality is recognized more clearly day by day.)

Japan was formerly feudalistic, having its Imperial House, its nobility, its feudatory lords, its knights, and its commoners. It rather resembled the [Chinese society of] the Ch'un Ch'iu period (722–481 B.C.). Since the Restoration (1868) there has been a clean sweep, and therefore Japan has been able rapidly to become strong. At present, Egypt, Turkey, Persia, and Russia have their royalty, their great priests, their hereditary nobility, their commoners, and their slaves, [comprising their] five classes. Hence, the Turks are weak; and Russia, even though outwardly strong, is internally inert.

The people of America have attained equality. There is no monarch, but a president. Since Washington established the Constitution, hereditary nobility has been regarded as seditious [*sic*]. Although there are great priests, they cannot hold office or interfere in public affairs. [When] Lincoln freed the negro slaves, a war was fought over it, strongly contested and with much bloodshed. As a result [of this war whereby the slaves were freed], all of America's people are ordinary citizens, and have attained equality. Even though negroes are [still] not treated equally. [America] is still the harbinger of the Era of Increasing Peace-and-Equality. Therefore [America] is most tranquil, strong, prosperous, and happy.

China, during the Ch'un Ch'iu period and before, had a feudal, hereditary nobility. The lords inherited their states, and the lesser nobles also inherited their fiefs.[1] ... At that time, even though it was not as bad as India, it was quite like medieval Europe and pre-Restoration Japan. Confucius originated the idea of equality. [He] made clear the unity [of the Empire] so as to do away with feudalism, and derided the [institution of] hereditary nobility so as to do away with heredity of office. [He transmitted the ancient] assigned-field system[2] [so as] to do away with slavery, and wrote (作)[3] the constitution of the Ch'un Ch'iu so as to put a limit to the monarch's powers. [He] did not exalt himself [to] his followers, and [he] rejected [the authority] of great priests. Hereby caste was completely swept out from Chinese institutions. Everyone became a commoner; anyone could [rise] from common status to be ennobled, to be a minister of state, to be a teacher or scholar; anyone could aspire to official advancement, could 'show his stuff'.[4] The evils of caste did not exist. Verily this was the remarkable accomplishment of Confucius, and he did it two thousand years before [it was done] in Europe. [That] China has been stronger and more flourishing than India is entirely due to this.

However, even though the prince's authority be exercised with principle, yet we have not done away with autocratic rule; even though Kuang Wu[5] had employed the ideas of the Confucian teachings and manumitted the slaves,[6] yet an endless [number] have been given over [to be slaves in] the households of the wealthy since Ming [times]. And [persons bearing] the name of prostitute, beggar, or boat-dweller,[7] are still not able to be fully equal citizens; while the restrictions on women have not been relaxed. [These] three [types of inequality] not having been amended, the ideal of equality has not yet been fully realized, and ignorance and weakness follow thereupon. However, the freedom of males has been attained. But a single step remains to be taken.[8] It actually will be possible to reach the Way with one [more] reform.

The coming to birth of all men proceeds from Heaven. All are brothers. [All] are truly equal. How can [men] falsely be divided [according] to standing in society, and be weighed [in the balance] and be cast out? Moreover, speaking of it according to the general trend of affairs, wherever there is much class gradation and men are not equal, the people will inevitably be ignorant and miserable, the state will inevitably be weak and disorderly,[9] [as] India is. Wherever class gradations have been completely swept away and men are equal, the people will inevitably be intelligent and happy, the state will inevitably be prosperous and orderly, as America is. The [relative amount] of ignorance and intelligence, misery and happiness, strength and weakness, prosperity and decline of other peoples and states can all be seen to be caused by the percentage of equality and inequality [existing among] those peoples. How great is the significance of equality! Hence it is that Confucius, in regard to the world (t'ien-hsia) did not speak of governing, but spoke of equality; and in the Ch'un Ch'iu, [in discussing] the progress of the Three Eras, [he] particularly spoke of it in terms of 'increasing equality' and 'complete equality'.

Nowadays slavery is almost entirely discarded. To China belongs the credit for having first abolished it, under Emperor Kuang Wu; while Confucius was the first to propound the idea of having no slaves. After Lincoln freed the negroes in America, the emancipation of slaves throughout the world soon followed. The slavery that still remains in China is all the more shameful, because, while in America at least the slaves were of a different race than their masters, in China both are of the same descent. Therefore, speaking of it in the light of the universal principles of nature, men all have the right to self-determination and independence; they should be equal, and should not have slaves. Speaking of it in the light of human affairs, [since, if] they are equal, then [people] are intelligent and happy, prosperous and strong; [but if] they are not equal, then [people] are ignorant and miserable, decadent and weak; [therefore] it is impossible to have slavery [and yet promote the welfare of a nation]. Speaking of it in the light of the genealogy of the Chinese people, then [since] we are all sprung from the same forebear, we are all kinsmen and brothers, and cannot bear to have slaves [from among our own people]. Above, it is to break the holy laws of Confucius; below, it is to shame the loving hearts of Kuang Wu and Lincoln. Hence, since China carried out the emancipation of slaves before other nations had done so, that China now has not done it is most shameful.

(Examining into the history of slavery in China, we find that there never was much of it. Although there was some use of captives of war as slaves, and some buying and selling of persons, yet, since every man had his land under the well-field system, slavery did not fit into the economy. Confucius did not countenance slaves as a class in society, and thus we find no mention of slavery in the Six Classics. Liu Hsin [a minister of the usurper Wang Mang—A.D. 9–23] revised the penal code to include various types of slaves, falsely attributing this law to Chou Kung [the universally revered younger brother of the founder of the Chou dynasty]. But Emperor Kuang Wu, [returning the Han dynasty to the throne], emancipated the slaves with several edicts, returning them to the status of commoners. In truth, China was the first to abolish slavery, under Confucianism.

(Slavery became common under the Mongols, but this was not due to its being a Chinese institution. Under the Ming, many people were forced into slavery for economic reasons. The true teachings of Confucius had been forgotten, and Liu Hsin's foisting of the slave laws on to Chou Kung was accepted. Still, of the eighteen provinces, in only two—Kwangtung and Chekiang—was slavery much practised. The Ch'ing have some slave laws; these are counter both to universal principles and to the holy laws of Confucius . . .)

Now man is [a being] to which Heaven has given birth; people are what a state possesses. No single family or person is private. Laws freeing the slaves would certainly be proper. (Still, hasty action would arouse the resentment of slave-owners, so emancipation should be carried out with due consideration for all concerned. Besides the manumission of the slaves, the outcasts—boat-dwellers, singing girls, beggars, *yamen* lictors and actors—should be given status in society. As for the first group, there is no essential difference between their occupation and farming; as for the second, their occupation is music, a refined one; as for the third, they should be gathered into institutions, and trained to do useful work; as for the fourth, their bad actions are due to the fact that they have no chance to earn advancement honestly; as for the fifth, their occupation is actually a very beneficial one, giving both pleasure and instruction, so they should certainly not be outcast.)

India's race and caste laws are the worst. Therefore, its many . . . races and castes should be scoured out and expunged, and all be made equal. [They should] first encourage the opening of occupations [to all]; and then universal intermarriage should be fostered. [This] transforming [process] having gone on for a long time, equality will become customary, and after that we may hope for complete unity. Egypt, Turkey, and Persia still have their castes. These should all uniformly be eradicated so as to bring about the transformation to complete equality.

The nations having swept away slavery and perfectly equalized their peoples, yet hereditary nobility will not have been abolished, the great priests will still be reverenced, and imperial families will still exist. [However], after several hundred years, people's rights will have been thriving every day, and every day more countries will have been becoming democracies. [They] will inevitably follow the example of America: hereditary nobility will be abolished and prohibited, and regarded as seditious. Natural philosophy daily becomes better understood, the [traditional] religions daily become fewer and weaker, [while] the New Religion[10] is daily advancing. The great priests [of the traditional religions] will become fewer day by day, and [their authority] will daily wane. It is certain that eventually there will come about the transformation to complete equality. The countries [of the world] having entirely altered into democratic presidencies, [they] will then have neither emperors nor monarchs. When there are no imperial families, equality will no longer be awaited, it will then have been attained. The rights and personal independence of [all] men and women will be attained by this time. Mankind throughout the world will be perfectly equal. Then the efficacy of Complete Equality will gradually be manifested!

REFERENCES

[1] Literally, 'their families'.

[2] 授田制 Under the first three dynasties land-ownership was a 'public' rather than a private matter. That is, fields were assigned by the state (i.e. the suzerain) to a man upon his coming of age; and they reverted to the state upon his decease. It was only with the first Ch'in

emperor (216 B.C.) that private ownership of land became permissible. (For a good, detailed account of the 'well-field system', of which this assigned-field arrangement was a part, see Chen Huan-chang, *The Economic Principles of Confucius and His School*, vol. II, Chapter XXVI, pp. 497–533.)

[3] For another possible interpretation of 作 (but definitely not one K'ang Yu-wei had in mind), see Fung-Bodde, *History of Chinese Philosophy*, vol. I, p. 62, n. I.

[4] 發揚踏 (correcting 踏) 厲 . A phrase from the *Li Chi*, impossible to translate, but well expressed in our colloquialism.

[5] First Emperor of the Latter or Eastern Han dynasty (reigned A.D. 25–58).

[6] 頻免為良人.

[7] There is a large boat-population in Canton and other south-coast cities.

[8] 但一間未達耳 .

[9] Reading 妄 for 忘.

[10] See above, Part II; Chart, item 14F, column 2.

PART IV

ABOLISHING RACIAL BOUNDARIES AND
AMALGAMATING THE RACES

THERE is a saying that among the nations of the world, having all the small boundaries is the most obstructive great boundary. The more small boundaries that are set up, the greater the advance towards the baneful [effects] of the great boundaries. Therefore, if we have family boundaries in order to protect people, and state boundaries in order to protect citizens, it will be more difficult for One World of Complete Peace-and-Equality to evolve. In China, for example, there are established the boundaries of the province, the prefecture, the department, the district, the section, the village, the clan, and the household. And [so] we have [developed] to the extreme our partiality for a certain province, a certain prefecture, a certain department, a certain district, a certain section, a certain village, a certain clan, and a certain household, as well as our hatred of other provinces, other prefectures, [other departments],[1] other districts, other sections, other villages, other clans, and other households. Thus, [although] the attainment of happiness for human life is to be found in complete unity (ta t'ung), yet in the beginnings of human life self-protection was found in many divisions. This is a circumstance which could not be helped. [Supposing] that family boundaries and state boundaries were now abolished, there would still remain one uncommonly great boundary to obstruct the way to One World of Complete Peace-and-Equality, [which is], then, the racial boundary. This is the most difficult [of all the boundaries to abolish].

The states having been joined together we shall already have our One World, [politically speaking]. But the amalgamation of races will be difficult. When civilizations are equal, when they are the same in their [social] aspects, when [peoples] have become intermingled, [receiving] the same education and the same upbringing so that there is no natural division of the people into high and low, then equality [among men] will be near at hand, and the change will certainly be natural and easy. For example, the Romans, Teutons, and Slavs of Europe will quite naturally become completely unified, and will certainly be easily amalgamated. And the Chinese, Mongols, and Japanese of Asia, once they have been brought to equality in their civilizations, their wisdom and intelligence being entirely similar, and their physical appearance likewise being the same, then it will be extremely easy to amalgamate and smelt [them]. Those which will be the most difficult to amalgamate and smelt are the races of men which are completely different in colour. At present there are in the world the white race, the yellow race, the brown race, and the black race. Their surface colours are completely different, and their spiritual constitutions are very dissimilar. How can they be smelted?

The silver-coloured race is spread out over the globe, while the gold-coloured race is still more numerous. These two kinds—the yellow and the white—have occupied the whole world. The strength of the white race is assuredly superior, while the yellow race is more numerous and also wiser. But it is an indestructible principle that when [two kinds] join in union they are smelted. I have seen my countrymen who have been a long time in England or Australia and sometimes those living in this country who have skilfully selected their food and drink, who have been able to adopt those Western methods which are conducive to good health: their faces were as if dyed a deep red, like the Europeans. Suppose they went about a great deal in the sun, absorbing its rays, travelling and dwelling in places swept by the wind, drinking in the air; [suppose that] in addition there were two or three generations of interracial propagation, a certain amount of moving of southerners to the north, and a removing of mountain people to the littoral. Within a hundred years the people of the yellow race all would gradually become white, and in addition these races would have been able naturally to join and smelt. Therefore, before One World has been perfected, the yellow people will already have changed completely into white people. These two races having amalgamated into one colour, nothing will distinguish them. Only the two races, brown and black, being so distant [in colour] from the white people, will be really difficult to amalgamate.

Now, throughout the whole of the earth the various kinds of men have propagated themselves, and there have been numberless racial groups. But in accordance with the principle of the survival of the fittest they have successively been destroyed. Taking those which have survived up to the present, we have the white race of Europe, the yellow race of Asia, the black race of Africa, and the brown race of the Pacific and South Sea islands. And of this number there are at present those which are stronger and weaker, and those which are best suited to their environment. Discussing [the matter] according to the theory of natural evolution by survival of the fittest, our China's southern [regions] were anciently the territory of the three Miao (aborigine tribes); but [these regions] were developed by the intelligent posterity of our Yellow Emperor race. The various other kinds [of tribes] which still exist in Hunan, Kwangtung, Kwangsi, Yunnan, and Kweichow, [such as] the Miao (苗), the Tsung (猔), the T'ung (狪), the T'ung (獞), the Chung (狆), the Yung (猣), and so forth, also were the original inhabitants [of those regions] in ancient times; but now they have fled to dwell in the mountain fastnesses, are scattered, and almost extinct.

The American Indian aborigines have by now all been pushed out [of their original lands] by the whites; those who are left do not amount to a million [persons]. The Australian aborigines numbered several millions a hundred years ago; today they are only ten thousand. The Hawaiian islanders are likewise scattered now, and [only] a few tens of thousands are left. And the aborigines of India of several thousand years ago were also destroyed by the Aryans. Deducing from these [examples], even though there are at present a hundred million black people in Africa, after a thousand and several hundred years they will all have been annihilated by the white people; if not, then whites and blacks will have mixed and will be amalgamated into white people. This is [a process of] natural evolution which cannot be escaped.

At the present time the Powers fight with each other, [but] it is certain that after a thousand and several hundred years we shall gradually enter the bounds of One World. But all the peoples of the black and brown races, having gone through these thousand and several hundred years of selection of strong and weak, will be decimated. Alas! I fear they will not be able to transmit their kind to the new Era of One World; or should [some] remain [of these] races, the survivors will not be many.

The races of India are all black in colour. [Their] appearance is fierce and ugly because their land is hot. The descendants of the English living there all turn a yellowish-blue (*sic*) colour, and therefore [the English] dread to live there. The dwellings of poor Indians are mean and cramped, filthy and stinking. Therefore every year several tens of thousands [of them] die of epidemics. So how can they multiply their kind? After a thousand and several hundred years the English residents will be increasing daily, while the Indians will probably become scattered and will gradually decline. Thus, when the One World Era is attained, there will remain only the white race and the yellow race. The black people and the brown race will probably all be swept from the earth. Remaining will be only a few people of India, and they will mostly be moved away in the four directions, while their racial colour will be somewhat changed.

That mankind should be equal, that mankind should be completely unified in the One World Era of Complete Peace-and-Equality: this is of course a universal principle. But the inequality of creatures is a fact. Whenever we speak of equality, it is necessary that creatures have the capacity to be equal in abilities, knowledge, appearance, and bodily characteristics before equality can be effected. If not, then even though it be enforced by state laws, constrained by a ruler's power, and led by universal principles, it still cannot be effected. Were we to do obeisance to dogs or horses, men would certainly [think us] mad. Those who eat chickens and pigs are not dealt with according to the law of a life for a life. [Thus we recognize that] the inequality of creatures is of long standing.

However, it is likewise so among men. Thus, with the noble intention of liberating the black slaves, Lincoln [activated] hosts of troops[2] and shed blood to bring this about; and yet to this day the people of America do not admit to the equality of negroes. They do not permit negroes to eat with them or to sit with them; they do not permit negroes to enter first class on ships and trains; they do not permit negroes to enter hotels; negroes who have been elected as petty officials are still kept down by the Americans. Negroes of [outstanding] learning and character have been honoured by the president, and the Americans do not still laugh at them. But the negroes' bodies smell badly, and so it is difficult for the racial barrier to be levelled. Not only [is it the case that] book-learning among those who are inferior cannot be equal, and so book-learning and talent are prevented from emerging; but because their appearance and colour is dissimilar, they are still kept down by all [the white Americans].

Thus, in the One World Era, the talents and appearance of the white and yellow people not being very disparate, they can be equalized. [But] the appearance of the negroes—with their iron faces, silver teeth, slanting jaws like a pig, front view like an ox, full breasts and long hair, their hands and feet dark black, stupid like sheep or swine—brings fear to [one who] beholds them. This [being so], to hope that refined white women will share a mutual love with them, will [consider them to be] equals, will eat with them, is likewise difficult. Hence, [although] we wish for the equality and unity of mankind, how can it be attained?

If we wish to join mankind in equality and unity we must begin by [making] the appearance and bodily characteristics of mankind alike. If appearance and bodily characteristics are not alike, then manners and occupations and love cannot of course be the same. Now, if we wish to amalgamate appearances and bodily characteristics which are completely dissimilar, and change them and make them the same, [and if we] set aside the method of intercourse between men and women, there is no way by which to change them. [But] with the refined beauty of white women and the monstrous ugliness of negro men, to hope for intercourse between them which will transform the race is [to hope for something] which will never be desired by human nature. Nowadays in America there are such cases, and it is not long before [the offspring] are completely changed into whites. Nevertheless,[3] there is almost no hope of making the appearance and bodily characteristics of [all] the negroes the same as the whites. If there is no way to change their forms, if the sifting out is not completed, then there will be no way for the world ever to attain to One World.

Men's appearance and colour and bodily characteristics are due in part to race, in part to adaptation to environment, in part to weather, in part to food and drink, daily behaviour, housing, and exercise. [These factors] are mixed together, combined, and then [the various characteristics] are produced. (The changes which are brought about by these factors can be noted in the case of the American Indians, who were originally of the same stock as the Chinese. Examples of the argument are adduced. The case of a Chinese child taken to live with a white family in Canada is mentioned—whether an actual or hypothetical case is not clear. By the age of seventeen or eighteen the child is ruddy complexioned and strong like the whites, because he has also eaten meat, has been out in the sunshine and fresh air, has gotten lots of exercise, etc. The Chinese will come to resemble the Westerners in appearance by another hundred years through adopting these healthful practices, and especially since intermarriage will certainly become a common occurrence.

(Seeing various examples of changes in people's appearance upon their moving about to live in different places, we know that colour is conditioned by climate. People who live in the same climatic zones of the world have the same colour): People of the frigid zone are white; people of the temperate zone are yellow; people of the tropical zone are black. The nearer they are to the equator, the blacker they are. Those in the frigid zone, continental [areas], are yellow in appearance; those in the deserts are black. Those who are in the temperate zone, coastal areas, are yellow, approaching white; those in the temperate zone, inland areas, are yellow, approaching black. Those in the tropical zone, near the sea, are brownish-yellow; those in the tropical zone, land and desert [areas], are pure black. This is the general outline [of the influence of climate on human coloration].

Human races being the product of adaptation to environment and of climate, it is thus possible to change appearance and colour by changing locale. Should we take the brown and black people and move them to the coastal regions of the fortieth and fiftieth parallels, or to the continental regions of the thirtieth and fortieth parallels, the races will change with the passing of the generations, and their appearance and colour will certainly be altered . . . (The improvement of these races will be hastened by intermarriage with the yellow and white people. We may think that because of the ugliness of these darker people the lighter ones will not desire to unite with them; however, experience shows us that whites and yellows who have lived among the dark-skinned peoples soon lose this idea, and no longer consider them ugly. Therefore we can know that there will some day be countless intermarriages between the light and dark races.) And so, if we wish to bring all the races of man into complete unity, [the means lie[4] first in moving them and settling them [in more favourable regions], then in mixed marriages to smelt them, and finally in nurturing them with [suitable] food and drink and exercise. These three [methods] being effected so as to select out [the inferior strains] and transform [the races into the white colour], there will not be many [unamalgamated people] left over. If in the One World Era the methods of selecting out the bad races, encouraging migration [to more favourable regions], and [encouraging] mixed marriages are used, it will be very easy to bring about complete union [of the races].

The Method of Migration

Throughout India, Africa, and the Central and Southern Seas—which territories are near the equator—human roots institutions, compassionating children institutions,[4] and the various [levels of] schools will not be established. [People] will wait until they have grown up before going to live there. In order to put a stop to the source of propagating the black race of the tropical zone, the negroes [who have dwelt] there from of old will all be moved to Canada and to the thirtieth and fortieth degrees south of Brazil in South America.[5] For one thing, this will fill the empty [lands], and for another it will transform their appearance and colour. Perhaps their best [people] might be moved to the [regions] at the fortieth, fiftieth, and sixtieth parallels by the Baltic Sea, the North Sea, and the Black Sea. It will be necessary to use the power of the One World public government to transfer them. Those of them that are wealthy and able to move will be encouraged to do so; those of them that are poor and unable to move will be helped to move. We must bring about that they do not remain from generation to generation in these tropical regions to transmit to successive generations this bad race.

The Method of Mixed Marriages

Their localities having been transferred, [the brown and black people] will then live mixed in with yellow and white people.

Thereupon rules will be formulated to encourage mixed marriages. All [yellow and white] men who can mate with brown and black women, and all [yellow and white] women who can mate with brown and black men will have conferred on them the decoration of 'person of *jen*',[6] and will [be treated with] a special kind of etiquette. Then there will be many who will intermarry, and the races will easily be transformed. The name of the decoration will be 'race reformer'.

It may be said: by taking people of the superior races and crossing them with people of the inferior races, might we not expect it to cause the superior race to revert and become inferior? [I] say, no harm will be done. Reckoning a thousand and several hundred years hence, there will not be many brown and black people left. Throughout the whole world there will only be the yellow and white peoples. Taking it that there are numberless [persons of the] good yellow and white races; if they contract mixed marriages with one or two persons of the bad brown and black races, then the one or two of the inferior races are few, and forthwith there are the numberless [persons] of the good races to rectify and redress this . . .

The Method of Improving Food

(The kinds of foods eaten, and the preparing of them, influence the bodily shape and colour and odour. When we can bring about that the people of the coloured races eat the same foods, properly cooked, as the yellow and white races, then they will eventually become yellow or white themselves. We should not let the example of the negroes in America cause us to doubt this; they have had countless generations of their old ways handed down before they began to live like the whites, and we cannot expect their bodily odour to be changed in a few short generations. But after many generations they will assuredly be changed and be as sweet as the white and yellow races.)

Race Reformism

(The brown peoples, although inferior in appearance and intelligence, can yet be changed and smelted into yellow and white without too much difficulty by the methods above described. This should be possible within two or three hundred years. The black peoples, however, are a really difficult problem, owing to their extreme ugliness and stupidity. Promoting mixed marriages with them is next to impossible. The only solution is to remove them wholesale to Canada, Sweden, and Norway, to occupy the empty lands there. This, plus improving their food and clothing, will result in their becoming brown after two or three hundred years. Thence, they could continue to merge into lighter shades, through these methods as well as the mixed marriages encouraged with the browns. Thus, in from seven hundred to a thousand years, the blackest African negroes will be transformed into white persons. By the time we have our One World, the people of all the earth will be of the same colour, the same appearance, the same size, and the same intelligence. This will be complete union—*ta t'ung*—of human races.

(Those brown and black people whose natural dispositions are too evil, or who have diseases, will be given drugs to make them sterile . . .)

Chart of Mankind's Progress

(This is a chart covering nearly three pages, summarizing political and social conditions in each of the Three Eras. It is not reproduced here, as it neither adds to nor clarifies the material already presented or to be presented in the following Parts.)

REFERENCES

[1] Text inadvertently omits this member of the series here.

[2] Taking 靡兵 to mean 靡費兵.

[3] I have switched the 然 and the 然則 in these two sentences, as they would otherwise seem to contradict the meaning intended.

[4] For these two public institutions, see below, Part VI, Chapters II and III.

[5] As a matter of fact, only the smallest, southernmost portion of Brazil lies below 30° south. (It will be recalled that K'ang Yu-wei took an active part in sponsoring a plan to develop Chinese emigration to Brazil, in 1897 [see Book One, Chapter I, p. 17].)

[6] See below, Part VIII, Chapter XII.

PART V

ABOLISHING SEX BOUNDARIES AND
PRESERVING INDEPENDENCE

Women

IN the world, when there are cases of injustice and inequality in which there are only one or two persons being unduly repressed, and one or two persons being unduly favoured, there are many who will go to law for them and help them. If ten million persons have been unduly repressed, then we cannot express [how many] have gone to law for them and helped them, in times past and present.

[But] with regard to the ten and some thousands of years of past history, [taking] all the nations of the whole earth together, [their] incalculable, inconceivable numbers of people have all alike had human form, have all alike had human intelligence; moreover, all men have had [particular] persons with whom they were most intimate, whom they loved the most: [their women]. Yet [men] have callously and unscrupulously repressed them, restrained them, deceived them, shut them up, imprisoned them, bound them, caused them to be unable to be independent, to be unable to hold public office, to be unable to be officials, to be unable to be citizens, to be unable to enjoy [participation in] public meetings; still worse, [men have caused them] to be unable to study, to be unable to hold discussions, to be unable to advance their names, to be unable to have free social intercourse, to be unable to enjoy entertainments, to be unable to go out sightseeing, to be unable to leave the house; still worse, [men have] carved (*sic*) and bound their waists, veiled their faces, compressed their feet, tattooed their bodies, universally oppressing the guiltless, universally punishing the innocent. These are worse than the worst immoralities. And yet throughout the world, past and present, for thousands of years, those whom we call Good men, Righteous men, have been accustomed to the sight of [such things], have sat and looked and considered them to be matters of course, have not demanded justice for them, have not helped them. This is the most appalling, unjust, and unequal thing, the most inexplicable theory under heaven.

I now have a thing to do: to cry out the natural grievances of the incalculable numbers of women of the past. I now have a great wish: to save the eight hundred million women of my own time from drowning in [the sea of] suffering. I now have a great desire: to bring the incalculable, inconceivable numbers of women of the future the happiness of equality, complete unity, and independence.

Now, because in nature there are odd and even, *yin* and *yang*, there are then male and female birds and animals. [This principle] extending to humans, we have men and women. This is assuredly an essential extension of natural principles, and something which the forms of creatures cannot be without. Having become human beings, their (i.e. men's and women's) intelligence and wisdom is the same, their disposition and temperament is the same, their morality and immorality is the same, their bodies, heads, hands, and feet are the same, their ears, eyes, mouths, and noses are the same, their ability to walk, sit, and manipulate is the same, their ability to see, hear, speak, or be silent is the same, their ability to drink, eat, and dress is the same, their ability to go about, see things, to do or to stop [doing] is the same, their ability to handle affairs and to use reason is the same. Women are not different from men; men are not different from women. For this reason women are equal with men in their ability to handle the occupations of agriculture, industry, business, and commerce.

In the country villages today, there are none among the farmers' wives who do not help with the tilling. In various countries women are already being much used in industry and commerce. Women are equal with men in their ability to study for official positions. There have already been many women writers in China. And so far as holding office and managing affairs is concerned, those who have [done so] with clarity, decisiveness, and real sagacity according to the historical biographies are innumerable. Therefore, speaking of it according to universal principles, women should [be considered as] exactly the same as men. As proved by results, women should [be considered as] exactly the same as men. This is the utmost universality in natural principles, and the utmost equality in human principles. In the whole universe there is no change [from this principle]; if we call the spirits to witness there will be no question [about this principle]; if we await the sages of the farthest future there will yet be no doubt [of this principle]; if we abide the public opinion [of mankind] in the farthest future [this principle] will not be perverted. Men, even though they possess the greatest talent for dialectics and the most selfish of minds, cannot deceive [us about] it, or alter[1] it.

Now, within the world, from past to present, the way in which women have been treated is alarming, appalling, lamentable, [such as] to make one weep. How can I describe this inequity? I cannot absolve men [of their responsibility] for the innumerable sufferings [of women] in the past.

1. [Women have been] unable to serve as officials. (Examining the histories of all nations, we find that there are no women who have served as high officials. Now if this were due to a natural stupidity of women as compared to men, it would be reasonable. But we know it is not, as we can think of examples of women of great ability, and men of little or none. Confucius never expressed the idea that women should be excluded from holding office. But while there have been men of no talent who have held office, not a single woman has done so; how could it be possible that this is due to there not having been a single able woman? It is a great pity when persons of high ability are confined to low positions. We feel this when we think of the men of history who have unjustly been prevented from attaining the positions to which their abilities entitled them. But how about the countless women, of whom not even a single one has had her chance?

(The most unfortunate thing for a nation, which should seek out its best talent, is this repression of the worthy. The unreasonableness of keeping women from office is further demonstrated by the fact that women have performed ably as rulers, both in Europe and in China. If they are capable of being empresses, how is it possible that they should be incapable of being officials? But the repression of women is rooted in law and custom, and women are kept outside the pale. How can this exclusion of eight hundred million persons from humanity be considered natural or right? From the point of view of the individual nation, to throw away the talents of half of the population is surely a stupid policy. In America some progress has been made in admitting women to serve in the professions, but it is still far from adequate. Preventing the worthy from receiving their due is against the will of God and universal principles.)

2. [Women have been] unable to [participate in] the state examinations.

(This point is discussed with the same sort of reasoning and the same conclusions as the first.)

3. [Women have been] unable to serve as members of parliament.

(Same sort of reasoning, with the major point being that women are as much entitled to be full citizens as men, including suffrage and eligibility for office by election.)

4. [Women have been] unable to be [full] citizens.

(Similar argument; one noteworthy point made in this and the above item, is that women themselves should not abdicate their duty to take a full and equal share in public affairs, merely because it has always been customary that they be excluded; thus the responsibility for their exclusion rests in part on themselves.)

5. [Women have been] unable to participate in public affairs.

(The same reasoning as in the preceding items is carried further, in pointing out the injustice and harmfulness of excluding women from participating in local affairs, especially in China, but also in the West.)

6. [Women have been] unable to be independent.

(Despite the fact that men and women are equal by natural right, women have long been subjected to men. They have lost their independence in three aspects: (1) they always follow their husbands, giving up their independence to accept the husband's status; (2) they give up their own family name and take their husband's, thus losing their identity; (3) they give up being able to care for their own kin, since their duty after marriage is to the husband's kin. So far does the loss of independence extend, that a wife must obey her son after her husband's death. All this is a sin and a crime against natural human rights.)

7. [Women have been] unable to be free. All human beings have bodies given by Heaven; and so all human beings have the right of freedom given by Heaven. Therefore, as human beings, all [persons] so far as studying is concerned may freely study, so far as talking is concerned may freely talk, so far as going about and sightseeing

is concerned may freely go, so far as entertaining is concerned may freely [take their] pleasure, so far as going out or coming in is concerned may freely act, so far as sexual relations are concerned may freely determine [their choice]. These are universal rights and privileges of all human beings. Those who forbid [them to] others are said to usurp the rights of others, and to oppose natural principles. Nowadays the women of Europe and America are generally free in studying, talking, entertaining, travelling about, and sightseeing, choosing their husbands or getting divorces. In other things they still do not rank [with men]. As for all the nations of Asia and Africa, they all bind and restrict their [women]. Although their standards may be [relatively] higher or lower, yet in that they restrict [women] they are the same.

[Women] are Unable to Marry Freely

(This chapter discusses the sufferings of women due to their frequently being compelled to marry men unsuitable to them, and all the evils of this marriage system in which matches are arranged for reasons of expediency. This situation is summed up by the saying: 'Marry a chicken, follow a chicken; marry a dog, follow a dog.' It is a system in which women are imprisoned and punished, and treated like slaves and playthings.)

Why I Say [Women] are Prisoners

(While the women of Europe and America are quite free to come and go as they like, the women of China are restricted by custom to the women's quarters of the home, and cannot go out to see the world, to study, to exercise, or to meet people. The women of India and Turkey are in even worse case, with their rigid customs of the veil, seclusion, and self-imprisonment in widowhood. These customs are not only unnatural and inhuman, but also physically harmful to the race.)

Why I Say [Women] are Punished

(The custom of piercing the ears or nose for rings is just like the ancient punishments of cutting off feet, ears, or nose, which were too barbaric to be carried on. However, the worst punishment is the Chinese custom of binding women's feet. It is really amusing, but very shameful, that China should call itself a civilized, cultured nation, and yet carry on this practice. The author mentions the enthusiastic response to his own efforts to abolish this custom through establishment of the Anti-Footbinding Society [1883], and his memorial to the Throne [1898].)

Why I Say [Women] are Slaves

(Women's work is precisely that of slaves: the menial household duties of cooking, serving, washing, mending, etc. And women in Chinese families are completely subject to the will of their husbands, male relatives, and the elder females. They must serve them and give them the same respect as slaves would have to give. Their status in the family from childhood on is that of servants, while their brothers are given respect. Even in the higher class of homes, there is distinction.)

Why I Say [Women] are Private

(Women are not allowed to use their talents and abilities for the benefit of society, but are restricted in their usefulness to one home. They must only take what the husband gives. This is contrary to their rights and responsibilities as human beings.)

Why I Say [Women] are Playthings

(Women are regarded by men only from the point of view of their beauty and sexual desirability. Their dignity as human beings is ignored. Although all human beings are born of Heaven, and there should be no such thing as valuable and base, still women are regarded by men as toys.)

[Women] Cannot Become Scholars

(Book-learning is essential for us, and especially essential for women, since they are the mentors of children. It is also a prerequisite for becoming independent, for self-advancement, and for women's attaining equality with men. However, as it exists, women are denied the opportunity for learning, even in families in which the men are scholars. Thus the talents of women have been wasted throughout history. Even though in Europe and America there has been progress, still women usually only study such polite subjects as French and music, and after reaching the marriageable age, give up their jobs. After that they occupy themselves with novels and games, rather than with serious studies. So women's learning has still not been really opened up, and women's rights have not been fully attained. This is a violation of human rights; it is enslavement, imprisonment and lowering of women to the status of playthings. All the philosophers and all the religions of history have not given women their rights.

(This is the way of savages, and not according to universal principles. And even the so-called Good men have not helped to alleviate this situation. Now, when we consider the earliest societies, it is certain that it was women, and not men, who discovered and originated all of the arts and crafts of civilization. This is because the men were hunters, who had no time to sit at home, thinking, and finding new methods of doing things. So it must have been the women, who stayed at home, who originated such techniques as cooking, agriculture, house-building, weaving, silk-making, cloth-weaving—and including the fine arts, music and writing—while men were still brutes who spent all their time and energies in the hunt. We can see the same principle in history, when we think of strong and weak countries, such as the Mongol Empire as compared with the Six Dynasties and the Southern Sung): 'Civilization is always [highly developed] in weak states, and not in strong countries.' (It is a shame that in our day, when the world is moving towards civilization generally, women, who originated the basic arts of civilization, are still subordinated just because of men's greater strength.)

(This has been defended on the grounds that women are smaller than men, and therefore inferior. However, taken on this basis, then there would be no accounting for the superiority of certain men in history who were very small; nor would we be able to account for the present rise of Japan, whose people are all dwarf-size. Another assumption is that women's brains are smaller than men's, and that they are therefore inferior. However, examinations of human brains at the Tokyo University medical department has proved that there is no difference except that men's brains are slightly heavier. There is a view that the brains of men are such that the more they are used, the wiser they get, and the more distinguished the men look; while in the case of women much use of the brain exhausts it, and they become ugly. But this is just speculation, and not to be believed without more verification. Physically, women do have the monthly menstrual loss of blood, which makes them unfit for such work as military service. But equality among human beings does not lie in this matter. It is an individual matter. If we could examine their talents, I think we would find that countless numbers of women are superior to men. All this restriction of women, and discrimination against them, is contrary both to nature and to the best interests of mankind.

(These repressions and restrictions of women are rooted in the remote past, and were made hard and fast by custom and religion. In the progress of civilization and thought, there has been some amelioration of this situation. Now the strict guarding of women's chastity and the separation of men and women is based on the desire to keep clear the line of descent of the family through the sons who will carry on the family name. In the Age of Little Peace-and-Happiness, the clan and religious systems all derive from this necessity to establish and preserve the family. Without the family, everyone would indulge his own desires. Without it we would return to the ways of the ancient savages, in which men and women mate indiscriminately, there is no way to establish the family, religion, or culture, and people are like animals. Furthermore, it was necessary to establish the family to protect the children. The life of savages, with its constant demand for men to fight and hunt, automatically creates a condition in which men are strong and women weak; when religions and governments were started, it was thus the men who already had the power. Moreover, through being used to repression for so long, women came to acquiesce in it, and to consider it right.

(In ancient times descent of name and rank and property was matrilinear, as we can see from looking at many savage peoples today. The reason was because of the indiscriminate mating of men and women; therefore, a child knew its mother, but not its father. In time this situation changed, as the matrilinear system did not serve the development of society as well as the patrilinear. The patrilinear system thus enabled civilization to progress, but at the same time it was the cause of the inferior status of women.

(. . . In the next several pages the author goes over much the same ground previously covered, in demonstrating the inequalities and repressions of women. His main point is the thesis that the fundamental cause of this double standard [enforced by mores and law] is the family system, which has as its most vital principle the protection of the male descent. Basically, the thing which is guarded against is the promiscuity of women, which would confuse and pollute the purity of the family [male] line.

(The logical extension of this principle is to be seen in the custom of widows not remarrying, or in the most extreme form in the Indian customs of suttee or self-incarceration of the widow.)

Those who do not serve two husbands are then virtuous women and unusually constant. We cannot but respect the way in which they have denied themselves sexual dissipation. This is like the Buddha's abandoning his family to follow the path of self-mortification, and [is as noble as the conduct of those] who, in Ming times, [took to] mending pots and begging, out of patriotic loyalty. [Such acts] are naturally sufficient to inspire a custom and give rise to beautiful behaviour. But if within the world we were to cause everyone to leave their families and become Buddhas, then inside of fifty years mankind would become extinct, and throughout the world there would be [only] the birds and beasts. Should there be a national revolution, and should everyone [adopt] the plan of remaining faithful by mending pots and begging, then China would not be inherited by the Chinese, and all the vastness of the Divine Land (i.e. China) would for ever be a colony of a different race. How could we do such a thing!

The Sung Confucians were very high-principled. They sought to surpass the sage (i.e. Confucius). They succeeded in causing countless numbers of widows to grieve in wretched alleys, harassed by cold and hunger, their pent-up resentment filling heaven—but [these Confucians] thought it a beautiful custom. Now goodness in the doctrines of government lies in causing the people to enjoy their happiness and benefit from their profits, in nourishing their desires and giving them what they seek. The Shih [Ching], in speaking of government, says: 'Within, no resentful women.'[2] How can we consider it to be good government when pent-up resentment fills heaven and cold and hunger pervade the earth! Now, in the principles of government, there is also such a thing as sacrificing an individual for the good of the group. Suppose we sacrifice the people of a state in order to establish the state; this is then because we consider the state to be important, and therefore the lives of the people are [comparatively] unimportant. In the interest of establishing the state this really cannot be helped. But when we are speaking [in terms] of the universal principles of the world we will still condemn its unfairness.

Aside from this, all governmental doctrines without exception seek with all their strength things that will make happy and will benefit man. Therefore, the sole criterion for distinguishing the [relative] advancement or decadence of civilizations and the [relative] enlightenment or barbarism of governments is [the degree of] suffering or happiness [of their people]. Those which cause their people happiness and profit, their civilization must be advanced and their government must be enlightened; those which cause their people suffering and resentment, their civilization must be decadent and their government must be barbarous. This is a universal saying of the world; it is likewise a universal principle of experience.

(The author here makes a convincing argument as to the evil of the custom that widows must remain forever single. This practice results in practically no benefits, a great deal of harm, and untold suffering. It is unnatural as well as immoral. It was not laid down by the sages, but was fostered by stupid scholars, and hardened into custom as time passed.

(A psychological point is made: in China the customs of propriety regarding women are all aimed at preventing sexual misconduct. However, when men of the middle and lower classes attend the theatre, they become dissolute in word and deed. In the West, where men and women mingle freely, touching hands and shoulders, there is no misconduct, and everyone behaves himself. This is certainly not because there are no coarse men in the West, nor is Western culture as strict as Chinese. No, the reason is because what is commonly seen is not considered precious—familiarity breeds, if not contempt, at least unconcern. It is the very strictness of the separation of the sexes that arouses men's concupiscence . . .

(After further discussion of the evils of inequality, we come to the following material):

Anciently, in the Age of Disorder, the family system was formulated so as to put in order the social relations; hence there was no help for it but that [women] were pitilessly and unjustly repressed. In the present age of Increasing Peace-and-Equality, so as to bring about the advancement of all mankind and the perfection of civilization, we must change this [repressive system]. The Age of Disorder and the Age of Equality are as opposite as winter and summer, to which furs and linens are respectively suited. The *I* [*Ching*] says: '[When a Change]· had run its course, then they altered. Having altered, [the new Change] was universal. Being universal, [their reigns] were long-enduring.'[3] The present is the age when affairs have run their course, the day when moral principles, human minds, the conditions of states, and the [old] era of the earth should all be altered, [and the new conditions] be made universal. The taking of slight differences in the body as cause for the unbounded punishments of imprisonment and slavery—this is also a thing that Good men should with all their hearts help to rectify.[4] In the present [age] we should vigorously reform the ancient evils, completely change our depraved customs. Men should do away with hereditary nobility, and they should not use force to oppress others. To rescue women [from their old subjection] is just like rescuing [humanity] from the custom of selling slaves. It is the same thing as sending troops to rescue the weak.[5]

The regulating [of this inequality] will be divided into three Eras, [so that] the deliverance [of women] will be in a sequence: [1] Imprisonment and slavery, punishment and restriction will first be relinquished. With this we will get rid of Disorder. [2] The prohibitions against social intercourse, entertaining, [freely] going out and coming in, and going about sightseeing will be discarded, as in European and American custom. This is called Increasing Equality. [3] The prohibitions against holding office, voting, being a member of parliament, and holding [the full rights of] citizenship [will be abolished, and women] will be permitted to go by the same rules as men. This is called Complete Equality. This is the teaching handed down by Confucius. In truth, the thousand sages have had the same mind to sweep away the age-old abuses [suffered by] women, to establish their equality, to bring about complete unity. After that, we shall be able to avoid all [the sufferings which have been borne] throughout the countless years by countless women. The laws [for emancipation of women] will be as follows:

Item: At present it is impossible suddenly to attain Complete Equality. We should first establish girls' schools, whose organization will be just the same as boys' schools. Girls graduating from colleges and professional schools will receive degrees such as the Chinese *chü-jen* and *chin-shih* or the foreign bachelor and doctor, and will hold them for life.

Item: Having completed their studies, they may by election or examination become officials or teachers. We shall ask only as to their abilities and will not lay any restrictions on them. In those countries which have an elected president, [women] will also be permitted to be this [official]. There will be no difference between [women] and men.

Item: Those women who desire to act as public officers and assume the responsibilities of affairs of state will be permitted to fill vacancies [in such positions]. Those whose abilities and learning are sufficient to [qualify them] as members of parliament may be elected [to such office]. Whenever there are international conferences [women] will always be permitted to be delegates. In the deliberations of international conferences there will be no difference between [women] and men.

Item: In the eyes of the law women must be permitted the status of independent persons. All restrictions as to their obeying their husbands will be abolished.

Item: The European and American custom of taking the husband's surname will be entirely prohibited and changed; [women] will be restored to their own surname.

Item: In getting married, women will be entirely independent, and will themselves choose their mates. We will not have the parents or the close relatives in the superior generation[6] serve as the selectors of the son-in-law. We will only retain an age-limit of twenty, when they will have completed their studies, and will then be free. Before twenty they are still under the restraint of the parents.

Item: Countries should establish the office of marriage agent, selecting those who are talented and advanced in years to fill it. [These persons] will at the same time serve as teachers. Men and women who are getting married will inform the marriage agent. [The couple] will themselves draw up the [marriage] pledges, and will receive their certificate. Only they must be twenty years old before they may get a certificate. Early marriages of those who have not yet come of age should be entirely prohibited.

Item: Women will be entirely independent in going out and coming in, in social intercourse, in going about and sightseeing, in entertaining. However, there will still be the limitation that [only] when they have completed their studies by the age of twenty will they have these rights. Before twenty they are still under the restraint of their parents or close relatives in the superior generation. But going about and sightseeing, social intercourse, and entertaining have to do with nurturing the body and improving the understanding, and do not have to do with corrupting morals; [so] parents need not be too strict. The rules of propriety of the Age of Disorder [intended] to guard against going and coming between the inner and outer [apartments] (i.e. the women's and men's quarters) will be completely done away with.

Item: Women having become independent persons. we should strictly forbid the old customs of binding the feet, compressing the waist, piercing the ears, nose, and lips to hang ornaments, and of veiling the face and covering the body with a long cloth, or adding a band (? 加領) between the eyebrows. [Violations of these prohibitions] will be punished by defamation or fines. [Such customs as] baring the shoulders and unclothing the body, and dancing with men in the Western style (literally, 'rubbing together') are barbarous, and arouse lewd thoughts. All [such customs] will be strictly prohibited.

Item: Women already sharing with men [the status of] independence, whenever walking or sitting or entertaining, there will be no question[7] as to rank or virtue or age or occupation; there will be no necessity to adhere to placement or precedence (literally, right and left, preceding and following), or to the rule of pairing off of ladies with gentlemen. All [these social distinctions] are too conservative of barriers [between human beings], easily lead to contempt [for the socially 'inferior'] and to lewd thoughts. They should be reformed.

Item: Clothing and ornaments should be the same for women and men. Throughout the world [both] in antiquity and at present, men and women have worn differing apparel: for one thing, so as to guard against [sexual promiscuity] by means of differentiation in dress, and for another, so as to afford [men] pleasure by means of differentiation in the beautiful clothing [of women]. Now, if men and women are not differentiated (or, separated), then it is difficult to prevent lewdness. Anciently, women were considered to be the private possessions of men, and it was essential to prevent lewdness. Hence it was impossible that their clothing should not be differentiated. All entertainers must differentiate [themselves by] their clothing. They may be arrayed in the five colours, [but the purpose is] only to provide pleasure. Thus, men who are actors must also wear rouge [as if they were women]. Women, being the private possessions of men, were but men's playthings. Therefore they pierced their ears, bound their feet, compressed their waists, blackened their teeth, shaved their eyebrows, applied mascara, wore rouge, used face powder, [adopted] odd coiffures, walked mincingly. They did not grudge to harm their [own] bodies in order to provide a man one day of pleasure. It was still more the case in the matter of clothing: how could it have been that there should not be different modes [of dress] for the purpose of contributing [to their function as] playthings [of men]? Thus it is that men still [dress] plainly, while women still [dress] gaily. The whole idea is to manifest [women's function as] a plaything.

When human morality has [reached the perfection it will attain] in One World, there will be few distinctions which would give rise to barriers [between human beings]. While monarchical states, [both] past and present, have differentiated nobles from plebeians by the [relative] elegance of their dress, [yet] in America the sort of clothing worn by the people's leaders and by the common people [themselves] is identical. We have not yet heard [that this practice] is disadvantageous to good government; [while] its benefit is to show the equality [of all the people]. If [this] is alright for rulers and subjects, how much more so for men and women!

Regulations should be made for clothing, the clothing of men and women to be uniformly the same. In the Era of Complete Peace-and-Equality, [all persons] will be independent and free: clothing that is unusual will not be harmful to the public weal, and in everything people may do as they will. Men and women may dress in any way, even in the old style [if they wish]. However, in public meetings, when formal dress [is worn], men and women will all adopt the same style, and may not [wear] different colours, in order to revert to complete unity. There being no distinctions of form or colour, there will of course be no difference in their manner of behaviour. This being so, women will not be regarded as different [than men] when, as teachers, superiors, officials, or rulers (sic, chün, although there will of course be no princes in that Era), they hold office and perform their duties.

Item: All marriages of men and women will be by the personal choice of the parties. Their affections and will [in this matter] being mutual, they will then form an alliance. [This alliance] will be called an 'intimate relations contract.' We will not have the old terms of husband and wife. For, since men and women will be entirely equal and independent, their love contracts will be like treaties of peace between two states: there will be no distinctions of [either party being] unimportant or important, or superior or inferior. Should there be the slightest [distinction of] superior and inferior, then [the relationship of the contracting parties] would be that of half lord and [half] vassal, and we could not call it an alliance. Since [such] a flouting of the Heaven-conferred principles of human rights, equality, and independence would gradually lead to the practice of esteeming men and repressing women, the [public] government should forbid it. [The marriage alliance] should only be like the joining together of two friends, nothing more.

Item: Alliances of men and women should have a time-limit, and may not be life contracts. For all whom we call humans necessarily have natures which are unlike. Metal is hard, water is soft; yin and yang promote differing [conditions]; charity (jen) and avarice are each to be found [among human beings]; sweetness and bitterness differ in goodness [to the taste]; wisdom and stupidity are differing degrees; progressive and reactionary are differing characteristics. Thus, those who are in love never have exactly identical principles [in their natures] (or, never have exactly identical ideas or ideals), and it is easy [for them] to come [to consider each other as] perverse and peculiar.[8] Therefore, no matter who they are, people can merely vow to be united, [but find it] very difficult to hold to [their union] for long. If they are compelled to it, there will inevitably be quarrelling between them. They may see each other but not speak; or they may live apart to the end of their lives; or they may hate each other and get divorced; or they may secretly scheme to poison [each other]. Innumerable are those in the world, past and present, who, because of being compelled to be united to the end of their days, have eaten bitterness, or lost their lives. If they desire to end their relationship, then this would damage their reputation and be [thought] immoral, unfeeling, and ?unpleasant.[9] If [in consequence] they do not desire to end it, then they sit, [the wife] regarding this wild husband, [the husband regarding] this cruel wife as perverse and unreasonable. It is difficult for them to be content for a single breath, being forced to put up with [this situation] all their lives.[10] Therefore, even for those with the natural endowments of worthies and sages, there is absolutely no principle through which they can for a long period be mutually happy while mutually united.

Furthermore, human affections [are such that upon] seeing [someone] different, one thinks of changing. Familiarity breeds boredom. Only novelty is desired; only beauty is loved. Supposing an alliance was made formerly, [whereby] one obtained a beautiful person [as one's spouse]; but then one sees someone whose ability and learning are still higher, whose appearance is still more beautiful, whose temperament is still more congenial, whose wealth is still richer: then love will assuredly be born, and one will assuredly think of changing one's relationships. And after that, there will again be [new persons] one will see [who will excite the desire for novelty and change]. The years and months are not the same; those we love are still more unlike.[11] Hence we necessarily follow our feelings, abandon the old, and scheme for the new.

(Another point is made next, showing that it is a violation of the principles of individual freedom and equality to tie partners together permanently, regardless of the changing circumstances of life, as was done when women were subject to their husbands and shared the husband's status.)

Again, the old practice of the Age of Disorder [was based upon the fact that] the idea of husband-and-wife was solely for the purpose of transmitting posterity. This being the private duty of the individual man, it was therefore unavoidable that unions should be constrained to exist for life. The husband and wife being permanently fastened together, then the father and sons were [always] related to each other. [But] now, when the Age attains to Complete Equality, men and women will be equal, and each will have their own independence. People having been nurtured by the government may not be private individuals of one surname, but will be 'Heaven's people'[12] of the world. The matter of men and women [will concern] only the satisfaction of the human feelings, and not the regulation of the transmission of the line from father to son.

And how can we take the constrained union for life, and thereby [create] suffering and difficulties for human nature? Thus, to compel union is also immoral. If there actually are [couples whose] unions are eternally happy, naturally they will be permitted to renew their contracts repeatedly and cleave to each other till the end of their lives. But [all unions] must be because of the human feelings, and in accordance with [the principle of] freedom.

Therefore we cannot but fix a time-limit to the contracts, to enable [the parties] easily to honour them. Then, if they have new loves, it will not be hard to wait for a little while. The term of the contract must not be too short, and so human propagation will not become [too] promiscuous. Thus we can bring about that many desires will yet not poison the body. When two persons love each other forever, they may of course [remain united] all their lives. Should they form new relationships, they will be permitted to change their arrangements; their former love being renewed, they may also renew their [former] alliance. In everything there will be freedom; thus we will accord with human nature and harmonize with natural principles.

(The idea of divorce was sanctioned in China by Confucius and Han Fei Tzu.[13] Divorce is widely practised in the West, and provided for in Chinese law. Nevertheless, throughout the world, marriages are contracted for life, and persons who become divorced are slandered and ridiculed for it. Hence, most people do not go through with this solution to their unhappy relationship, but instead patch things up and suffer in patience. In the Era of Complete Equality we will not infringe upon the rights of independence, or cause suffering to people through forcing them to remain together even when incompatible. By our short-term contract system, we will do away with the idea that separation is cause either for condemnation or ridicule. We will also do away with the great problem of sexual immorality which has plagued the world through the ages, and which no preventive measures can control. The more we try to prevent lust, the more it arises. In One World we will make it easy for everyone to satisfy his desires, so how can there be any problem of sexual immorality? We will neither force people to marry nor to stay married, when they do not wish to do so; nor will we prevent those who wish to, from doing so.)

Item: The length of the marriage period may not exceed one year, and at the shortest it must be one full month. Those who are happy [in their marriage] may renew the contract.

Item: The office of marriage agent is established. Whenever a man and woman join in marriage they will go to the marriage agent of the locality in which they live, receive the stamped certificate, and make out the papers. They will vow to love each other during the period [of the contract].

Item: Women who have not gone to school and completed their education, who have not been able to receive their diplomas of graduation, cannot be independent. Those who must look to their husbands for support [can]not utilize this right [of independence]. For there are now still many old customs, and hasty changes would certainly entail many disadvantages. If it happened that a woman had received the husband's support all of her life, and [then she] suddenly abandoned him, it would be unjust ingratitude. If it happened that the man doubted the woman and abandoned her, there would likewise be discontent in the matter of bearing children. Now that which enables women to be independent is scholarship and knowledge. [But even if a woman] is fully prepared in the qualifications of a public citizen, then it is still human nature that she should temporarily be dependent on her husband and receive his support. Now, if we bring about that women seek to gain the rights of independence, to increase their [sphere of] responsibilities, and to incline towards studies, then human abilities will increase daily. How could this help but be admirable!

What has been discussed above is only a plan for future progress. If at present, when the education of women is incomplete, and their personal qualifications are immature, we were recklessly to introduce regulations for the independence of women, so that they would be free to indulge their feelings of revolt against their husbands, or their lustful passions, this would be the road to great disorder. 'Linens for summer; furs for winter': to everything its appointed time. Until we have arrived at that time, we must not mistakenly adduce comparisons. The author does not want to corrupt the moral customs; he does not wish to be guilty of that.

REFERENCES

[1] 抑揚 literally, suppress and raise.

[2] This quotation actually occurs in *Mencius*, I, B, 5.5, immediately following a quotation from the *Shih Ching*. In this conversation of Mencius with King Hsuan of Ch'i, he is pointing out that it will be easy for the king to carry out good government as well as satisfy his own private desires; all he has to do is to afford his subjects the same gratifications. Thus, the poem in the *Shih* tells us that a former king loved beauty, and according to Mencius he so ruled that there were no dissatisfied wives and no unmarried men.

[3] *I Ching*, Appendix III, Section 2, Chapter II, p. 15 (according to the arrangement in Legge's translation [see his *Yi King*, as cited above in Part II, p. 129, n. 1]). The quotation comes from a passage describing the successful reigns of the legendary emperors Shen Nung, Huang Ti, Yao, and Shun. The Wilhelm-Baynes rendering (vol. 1, p. 356; see same note) applies the words of the text to those emperors themselves, while Legge applies them in a general sense. I have translated somewhat differently than either of these. The reader will see the connection between this alteration of the Changes and the evolutionary changes of the Three Eras explained above in Book One, Chapter III.

[4] Correcting 耶 to 也. This is surely not a question.

[5] Taking 溺 as equivalent to 弱.

[6] 尊親 This term includes 'direct honoured relatives' (parents, grand-parents, great-grandparents, etc.), and 'collateral honoured relatives' (uncles on the father's side, mother's uterine brothers and sisters, and others).

[7] Correcting 皆 to 不, which seems to make better sense.

⁸ Taking 暌 to be 睽

⁹ 失懽 I would assume that the second character is a misprint; but one could not determine which of several possible compounds was intended.

¹⁰ Taking 古 to be 身 .

¹¹ Reversing the positions of the characters to read 尤 殊.

¹² On 'Heaven's people', see above, Book One, Chapter II, pp. 35–6, n. 28.

¹³ Han Fei Tzu (d. 233 B.C.) was a great philosopher of the Legalist—one might almost say Machiavellian—school.

PART VI

ABOLISHING FAMILY BOUNDARIES AND BECOMING 'HEAVEN'S PEOPLE'

[Introduction]

The Natural Principle of Love Between Parents and Children

(USING the examples of birds, fish, and beasts, it is demonstrated that love of the parents for their offspring is fundamental to all life. This love is not due to any recompense or expectation of recompense from the offspring; nor is it compelled by either public opinion or law. No, it is spontaneous.) This is the Heaven-[conferred] (or Natural-) nature, the root of *jen*. [All creatures] love [that to which] they have given birth; [all creatures] love their [own] kind. That whereby the ten thousand creatures multiply their kind, and do not become annihilated, depends upon this nature. Should the species of creatures lack this constitution of love, then human beings would not [continue] to be born, and the ten thousand species would become extinct for ever. Therefore, the ever-continuing production of life, and the principle of love for [one's own] kind, are the 'ancestors' of human beings. Now, if the love of birds and beasts for their children and for their mothers is like this, how much more so among humans!

The Original [Relationship] of Father and Children

(In the beginnings of mankind, before there was the institution of husband and wife, a woman required the help and protection of a man in order to raise her children. From this necessity, through long experience the institution of parentage became custom, and then law, of which the final product is the three-year mourning still observed for the father.) Analysing it from this [background], it is not essential to ask whether or not the father is the begetter of

169

the children; all of them having been born of the wife whom he
loves, he therefore extends his love to include them, and extends his
support to support them. This actually has been universally understood and universally practised from the first people of remote
antiquity up to the present. It is really the thing upon which the
relationship (literally, the Way) of father and children is based.

The First People of Remote Antiquity had Mothers but not Fathers

(Since mating was indiscriminate in remote antiquity, no man
knew his father. There were no family names; or if there were, then
they were derived from the mother's side.)

After the Fixing of [the Institution of] Husband and Wife, the Family System and Clan System came into Existence

(The establishment of a permanent relationship between a man
and a woman came about naturally in the course of time, both
through the desire of certain couples to remain together, and because
of the advantages of this permanent union. The institution was
'sanctified' by sages who saw in it a safeguard against the quarrels
of men over women in that warlike age. Once this institution was
established, the family came into existence, because the children knew
their father, and were all children of the same father, and close to
each other both because of the blood tie and because of their same
environment. The clan came into being upon the marriages of the
brothers and their begetting children, who likewise married and had
children. But all the clan existed only because of the one pair of
parents in the first generation; without the institution of husband
and wife there would not exist the family or the clan.)

On the Difference in the Power of Loving between Humans and Animals, and the Difference in their Strength and Weakness

(While the family relationships are inherent in the scheme of
things, both for humans and for animals, the difference lies in the
fact that humans have a greater power to love, and can fix their
love more permanently and extend it more broadly than can the
animals. In this power lies the strength of humans compared to
animals, as the former can form groups through their power of
love, while the latter are essentially individuals through their

relative weakness of love.) Therefore, those whose groups are larger, and whose propagation is most abundant: their knowledge and experience is greatest. Those whose power of extending their love is not very broad, whose consolidation [into groups] does not [extend] very far, and whose propagation is not very abundant: their knowledge and experience is not great.

On [the Fact that] All Nations have the Social Relationships, but None have a Clan System as Well Developed as China's; therefore, [the Chinese] are the Most Numerous

(While there are no nations which do not have the social relationships in varying degrees, China has extended them the most. Thus, the honouring of ancestors, and the various charitable and social institutions carried on by Chinese clans even in foreign lands, are unmatched by other peoples. This is the reason the Chinese now form a third of the world's population; it is due to the extended family and clan system enacted by Confucius for the Age of Disorder, which is very conducive to propagation and to consolidation into groups of like kinds. This is a great accomplishment of Confucius. The Westerner's home is where he happens to be; the Chinese always retains his ancestral home, even though he be away from it. Thus, the Chinese system is the ultimate development of the family.)

On [the Fact that], because of the Clan System, the Evils of Division and Estrangement Come into Existence

However, if there is that which is especially dear [to us], then there is that which is not dear. If there is that which we love, then there is that which we do not love. The Chinese, having the clan group, therefore hold dear those of the same surname, and [feel] estranged from those of different surnames. Those of the same surname care for each other, [while] those of different surnames do not succour [each other]. Because of this, those of two [different] surnames fight [with each other]; those of two [different] surnames are enemies. Having been habituated [to this way of thinking] uniformly [since] olden [times], [the Chinese] do not know they have a nation, but only know they have a surname (i.e. family, in the broad sense of those of the same surname) . . . Within a nation, if the various surnames are divided, then it is like ten thousand nations. Thus, [China] has persons who are wealthy and Good as well; they give offerings to the ancestors, contribute to public fields, succour the poor, found schools: [But in these acts], likewise, they only protect their clansmen, and other clans cannot benefit [from them], much less their fellow-countrymen. Besides this, we sometimes consider [people] as dear [to us on the basis of] a division by locality, by district, or by province. Those of the same locality, the same district, or the same province, we hold dear; those of different localities, different districts, or different provinces, are estranged from us.

Therefore, all outside of one's own clan are rejected, the individual district [stands] alone, and the individual province [stands] still more alone. When it comes to subscribing large sums of money for the schools, hospitals, poor-houses, or homes for orphans and aged of the whole country, it is unheard of. Therefore, the spread of this corrupt practice [has led to] dividing the single nation into numberless nations, and from the whole we have made tiny pieces. Therefore the hands and feet of our four hundred million people cannot help each other, and it has come to pass that the largest nation in the world is the weakest. This is a thing that has not existed among the ten thousand [other] nations of the world. Investigating the cause, we find that it is due to the spread of the corrupt practice of piling up the divisions between clans and localities.

On the Advantages and Disadvantages of China and the West having, and not having, the Clan System

(The Chinese system, with its maintaining of memory and respect for the ancestors, is very beautiful. Nations which do not do this forget their roots. Nevertheless, despite the fact that the other nations do not carry on this beautiful system, Europe and America are not only civilized and strong, but actually surpass China. They spend huge sums of money on public institutions for the benefit of the whole nation, and not just the individual clan. If we weigh the respective advantages of either system we must choose in favour of the one which gives the greatest advantages; although the Chinese system is good, the Western system is better, all things considered.)

On the Family being a Good Means for Mutual Protection among Mankind

(The family is the basic institution for all human beings throughout the world. Upon the family we depend for protection, support, and spiritual solace from the cradle to the grave. The best of friends may abandon us in a crisis—and may even turn against us—but the family sticks together through thick and thin, and does so even though its members sometimes may wish otherwise.)

On the Suffering of being without Parents

(The state of an orphan is indeed pitiable. Even though, in a civilized country, he may be cared for by an orphanage and not be abandoned to die in a ditch, yet his chances in life are very poor. He or she will have no one on whom to rely for anything, may become a slave, and will have no chance at an education. Good men who pity orphans have no remedy for this problem.)

On the Toil of the Parents in Raising Children

(A description of the endless toils and sacrifices of parents for their children; only because of their tireless devotion can the young grow up to adulthood. It is upon this fact that the ideal of filiality is based.)

On [the Fact that], having the Way of Father and Son, Mankind then Flourishes

(Despite the devoted toil of the parents, there are many children who do not live to grow up; many who do are not filial; for one reason or another, the ideal of the filial Way between parents and children is often not carried out. Nevertheless, the natural love between the parents and children being the very basis for the survival of mankind, the ideal of the filial Way is the ultimate Way for the flourishing of the human species.)

On Filiality as [that which] should be Emphasized in Requiting the Virtue [of the Parents]

(No grace, no virtue, can compare with those of parents, to whom we owe the very fact of our existence. Now, the smallest debt of money, or even of a meal, must be repaid. One is punished by law or by public opinion if one does not pay such debts. The principle of requital is a universal, unchangeable principle. Since our greatest obligation is to our parents, our greatest responsibility is to repay this debt. Confucius emphasized filiality, considering this to be simply the requital of that debt. Those who are unfilial are thus punishable, [for the same reason as any other debtor, only more so, the debt being greater].)

On the Ingratitude of the Children of Europeans and Americans

(The Western nations are termed civilized; and yet this is the way their family system works: despite the fact that the toil of raising children is no different from that in China, yet when the children grow up they separate completely from their parents, and devote themselves to their wives and their own children; the relationship of parents and grown children becomes like that of friends only. If the children become rich or attain high position, they do not include the parents in their activities, but only their wives. And so the parents are not requited for their pains in raising their children, but are abandoned by them. Old parents, those who are sick or widowed, have no one to take care of them or console them. Westerners prefer to have daughters rather than sons, as I have been told by an English-woman, because the sons will grow up and leave their parents, while daughters who are not married will stay at home and help to care for their parents.

(When the American President McKinley died, he left almost his entire fortune to his wife, and only a thousand dollars to his mother —a thing unheard of in China. We can see that even when a man becomes president, he lives only with his wife, and even though his parents may be poor, he only supports his wife. Even in countries which may have a law that, when a person's parents are very poor, a third of his earnings should go to support them, and if not, then the state can deduct this amount, this is rarely carried out.

(The Westerners do not carry on the remembering and honouring of ancestors, the sacrifices, the family temples, the tending of graves, and so forth. A European to whom I spoke of the Chinese way of the father and son greatly admired it. An American woman with whom I was discussing social relations said it was necessary to gain wealth, but not to have children, as children were no advantage, but only more trouble. Two English governors of Singapore with whom I was acquainted had not married. Nowadays Frenchwomen do not wish to bear children; the population of France is declining. This is because the dangers and difficulties of bearing and raising children are great, while the rewards are so negligible in the Western system.)

On the Cause of Westerners Neglecting their Parents being that they hold their Wives [More] Important

(If we seek the reason why in the West, whose government is near to the Age of Increasing Peace-and-Equality, there is this un-filial system, we see that it is because of the West's basic ideas of freedom. All men have the right to self-determination and to seek the satisfaction of their own desires. This makes the enduring relationship that of the husband and wife who have married of their own free will; wives cannot be subordinated to mothers-in-law, nor can sons be subjected to fathers. The abandonment of the parents and following of the desires of husband and wife is a grievous fault.)

On the West not being as Good as China in Filial Requiting; and on Christianity not being as Good as Confucianism

(It is the human way to calculate the rewards or losses when we undertake any action. And, even though the love of father and son is a natural thing, yet with all the toil and trouble of raising children, the parent is not without some thought of eventual reward. We contrast the conditions of the old and sick who have or do not have children and grandchildren; we see the benefits brought to the man who has wealthy descendants in contrast to the man without children; we see the strength of the man with many descendants as contrasted with the childless; we note that the man with descendants will be properly interred, and his sacrifices will continue, whereas the childless are cut off without sacrifices for ever. Confucius established the importance of filial requiting of the parents; since these rewards come from having children, people gladly undertake the toil of raising them. This is the only reason why China's population is the largest in the world.

(In the West, the responsibility for raising children is based on the law, or, in the lack of such a law, the people must be like the

Frenchwomen and consider the bearing and raising of children as undesirable. To do it without any expectation of recompense is against human nature. Therefore, many Westerners leave their fortunes to public institutions when they die, rather than to their children to whom they are not close and on whom they have already spent so much. This is also human nature.

(Suppose we say that people are children of God, or of the state, and not the parents' private property, as in Christianity or in ancient Sparta; then we minimize the importance of the parents. But since it is the parents who do raise the children, the natural principle of requital still holds.) 'I take China; I follow Confucius.'

On the Filiality of the Chinese being an Empty Ideal, and there being Few who have the Strength to carry it out

'However, when China talks about filiality, it is also only [using] a name.' (The Chinese, having bodies and souls, are just like the Westerners in seeking to satisfy their human desires. Those who can resist the call of their own desires and care for their parents instead are but few. The difficulties of earning a living for one's own wife and children are too great for most Chinese to be able to support their parents in addition. [The author gives figures next for the amount of money people in various kinds of occupations in China are able to earn.] Such incomes are not even enough to support a couple, as in the West, and hardly enough to support an individual, as in the case of a bonze. Westerners can take pleasure in having a family because they have enough to support their families; whereas in China, even a man with a job makes too little—and there are great numbers without jobs. I have seen many cases in my own native place where for one reason and another there are people who are not receiving support from the family system—almost seven or eight out of ten. In all of China, alas! how few can, with their utmost exertions, recompense their parents.)

On the [Relative] Difficulty and Easiness of [Parental] Compassion, and of Filiality, being due to Opinions

(I have noticed that among parents, no matter how ignorant, crude, uncultivated, or even cruel they may be, there are none who are not able to love their children. And yet among children, no matter how good their education and moral training, there are few who are filial, and countless numbers who are refractory. Why is this?)

Well, then, is the reason because it is in human nature to accord with virtue in [the case of parental] compassion, but to defy virtue in [the case of] filiality? Looking at the human body, [we see that] to bow the head is very easy, and to raise the head is very hard. [But] how can we also say that looking down (i.e. bowing the head) and caring for [children] is easy, but that looking up (i.e. raising the head) and serving [the parents] is hard? In case that were so, then to be filial would be to defy virtue (i.e. natural morality), and not to accord with virtue, [since it would be natural for parents to be compassionate, but unnatural for children to be filial]. If we seek out (literally, test) the most fundamental natural principle [involved], [then we see that] it is the parents who have bestowed favour on me; were I without parents, I could not have been born. [My] sons and daughters are ones upon whom I have bestowed favour, not ones who have favoured me. It is human nature to requite favours, but it is hard first to bestow them. It should be [the case that] men would always find it easy to be filial and hard to be [parentally] compassionate. Why is it that men [actually] find it hard to serve their parents but easy to nurture their children? This is inexplicable.

[In] trying to find the reasons [for this paradoxical situation], [we note that] a person's children having been born, they have then come [into the world] as a part of his own body and, loving his own body, he [therefore] loves them. This is the beginning of love. [Again], it is human nature to like to play with creatures that can move, and which have little knowledge. Hence many people keep pet cats and dogs, and go as far as to sleep with them. How much more is it so with a human being! When babies laugh and cry, move about and play, they are naturally interesting. As compared with cats and dogs, being also of the same form [as the parents], they are more lovable. Nowadays there is a child-rental society in America. Babies from the ages of several months to several years can be rented by the day for two or three dollars, and then the childless can play [with them]. If [people] will put out several dollars daily to play

with them, how much more [will they do] for the children born to
them! This is entirely for their own pleasure, and absolutely without
thought of recompense. How much more joy will there be in
nurturing [children] who are one's kith and kin, and flesh of one's
flesh, and from whom one may also hope for future requital.
There is little requital in Europe and America; therefore the desire
for children is likewise not ardent. There is much requital in China;
therefore the desire for children is much more ardent. This is the
difference between them.

Even though in principle the parents should be requited, when
[children] have as yet not become adults, they do not know it. But
because they respect their elders, they serve them respectfully. However, when they have parted from [the parents], gone away to study,
and themselves become different, then very many of their opinions
will become dissimilar. Now there is nothing in the world so great
as opinions. Coerced by opinions of the east and yet agreeing with
opinions of the west,[1] [the children] are placed in a dilemma,
and so it is difficult for them to accord with both. If they do not
accord [with the parents], then they are refractory. If they do
accord with them, then they suffer extremely. Despite the favour
of having been given birth [by the parents], those who disagree
completely [with them] and who can never accord [with them],
for this reason do not live on good terms with them. In teaching and disciplining their children, [the parents] can merely use
opinions. If [the children] repeatedly disobey, and they then angrily
scold and beat them, [this] will assuredly cause [the children]
violently to disaccord with them. This is one thing.

Again, while to support [only] the persons of [their] parents is
still easy, if the father and mother have several children, they must
then love them all. If they love them all, then it will take more than
they have, and yet it will not be enough to meet the need. Hence,
in this supporting of several persons,[2] if the son's strength is deficient,
his will-power is weak, or he is in difficult [circumstances], [then]
in his supporting of one child after another, there certainly will
be no share to give to anyone else (i.e. to the parents).[3] This is a
second thing.

Again, there are still more who support [only] their mother. The
mother is a single person with few desires. But the father may have

secondary wives or concubines, and may have still other desires, and then it is difficult to meet them.

(In the West, the son has to support his wife, but not his parents. Hence, parents prefer girls to boys, since the girl may stay with them and help them, if she does not marry. The mother who is supported by a married daughter must get along with the son-in-law, or else there will be trouble, and they will be unable to live together . . .) Of the sufferings of man, there are none like those of begetting a rebellious son. To cut him off is unbearable; to put up with him is impossible . . . Comparing the two, the reason filiality is difficult and [parental] compassion is easy, is due entirely and solely to opinions. [If parents and children] are unable to hold the same opinions, then they are unable to live together; those who can hold the same opinions can thus easily live together, and that's all there is to it. For the 'living' is the living of their opinions, and not the living of their bodies . . .

On the Sufferings of Members of a Family who are constrained to Live Together

(In this section the author details the discord, the quarrelling, and the evils which are the inevitable consequences of forcing several human beings to live together, what with all their prejudices, special affections, dislikes, frailties, and cross-purposes. This situation is worst in China, because of its large-family system, despite all the preaching about the exemplary cases of large families. The more people that are in a family, the more troubles are bound to arise. This is truly one of the basic causes of suffering.)

On [the Fact that] the [Very] Advantages of having the Family then Cause the Disadvantages of having the Family

(The sages established the family system as the best way to meet the needs of human nature; because of the difficulties of people living together, they also continually admonished, threatened, punished, and rewarded them, to try to eliminate these difficulties. But all has been without avail. The difficulties—detailed in the previous section—make it impossible that this system can ever lead to Complete Peace-and-Equality, or to the perfection of human nature. The family is too exclusive: parents try to give the best only to their own children. Since there are very few wealthy and high-class families in comparison to the poor and low-class families, and each gives only to its own as best it can, it follows that there can never be any universal equality, and that there will always be only a few in a nation who are strong, intelligent, good, and brave, and vast numbers who are weak, stupid, vicious, and cowardly. Further-more, the necessity to marry a wife from another family dissipates the strain of the few who are superior, as it is hard to find a wife who will bring equally superior qualities to transmit to the children. This condition is aggravated in China, where children are so often begotten of concubines, who are of poor quality as human beings, both physically and culturally. Thus the propagation of the unfit is so widespread that it is impossible to bring about universal equality.)

On [the Fact that] if there are Families, then there is Selfishness, which Injures [Human] Nature and Injures the Species

(In this section the author elucidates the thesis that, given the family as the social unit, the result is inevitably a narrowing and concentrating of the individual's efforts upon the support and better-ment of his own family. Since it is very difficult for one individual to support many, this leads inevitably to the development of those qualities of deceit, cunning, and violence which are essential to succeed in this struggle. And only one family in ten thousand can secure the wherewithal to give their children the physical, mental, and moral qualities that they would like to give. From this we have the extreme disparity between the fortunate few and the unfortunate multitudes. In the West, which talks a great deal about individual liberty, it is likewise impossible to reach the conditions of complete equality, because there too each looks after his own. Even though there are public institutions, the opportunities they give to those without parental support are meagre. Thus we have the spectacle of the hungry, the poor, and the friendless. In the West, moreover, the importance of money, as regards power, position, and friend-ship, is even greater than in China. This leads to the use of any and all means, no matter how evil, to get money. This vicious system is perpetuated and handed on to successive generations; thereby the hope of perfecting human nature and attaining One World is rendered vain.)

*On [the Fact that] the Injuries [due to] having the Family Form the
Great Obstacle [in the Way] of Complete Equality*

Now I am going to list the injuries of having the family, as
follows:

Item: Customs are not the same. Teachings are not identical.
If the family itself is unrefined, then its posterity is mostly bad,
and human nature cannot be perfected.

Item: The nurturing of children is not identical. There being
many who are diseased, their posterity will then mostly be weak,
and the human body cannot be made hale.

Item: When begetting children, [the parents] cannot always find
a good place [to live]; hence [the children's] temperament will be
bigoted and narrow, and [humanity] will be unable to advance to
broad and lofty intelligence.[4]

Item: If from birth to adulthood they are not able to have twenty
years of equal education in school, then men's characters will not
be equalized or perfected.

Item: If people do not have effective medicines and physical
examinations daily during their lifetime, then their bodies will be
susceptible to diseases.

Item: If all people from birth to adulthood are not compelled to
attend school, then they [develop] into uncultured and half-tutored
persons. Because men are constituted variously, they must be
smelted and carved. If we begin at birth to smelt and carve, then
it is easy; if we smelt and carve them after they have grown up, then
it is hard. Therefore, not to have the family, but to leave it entirely
to the schools to educate people, is [the system of] the Age of
Complete Peace-and-Equality; to have schools and [also] to have
the family to educate people is [the system of] the Age of Increasing
Peace-and-Equality; to have people educated entirely by the family
is [the system of] the Age of Disorder.

Item: [If children] go to school, but do not leave the family and
live completely within the school, then education will be hetero-
geneous and unequal. For, if people do the teaching themselves,
and if the family itself is a school, then confusion and narrow-
ness are already extreme, and we cannot have breadth, lofty
intelligence, and purity.

Item: Because of having a family, [a man] will necessarily be partial towards his wife and children, and the world cannot be made public.

Item: Because of having a family, [a man's] dependants are numerous; and so the schemes devised in his mind are necessarily selfish, his experience is necessarily narrow, and deceit, fraud, and greed will necessarily be born.

Item: Having selfish, deceitful, fraudulent, and greedy natures, which are mutually fanned (i.e. incited) and mutually spread, the human race is necessarily evil, and [human] nature has no way to become good.

Item: If people all hold selfishly to their own families, then there cannot be much public expenditure for the extensive support of physicians whereby to promote the people's health. But if there are many who are diseased, the human race will not be perfected.

Item: If people hold selfishly to their own families, then private property cannot be used as public property, and there is nothing whereby to publicly support the people of the whole world; but there are numerous poor and suffering people.

Item: If people all hold selfishly to their own families, then there cannot be much of a levy for public expenditures to provide public benefits: to put into operation the rearing of infants, the caring for children, the support of the aged, and the succouring of the poor.

Item: If people all hold selfishly to their own families, then there cannot be much public expenditure for keeping up roads and bridges, [developing control over] mountains and rivers, and [constructing] dwellings for the sake of giving humanity happiness in their dwelling places.

Therefore the family is an institution essential to mutual support among men during the Age of Disorder; but it is the most obstructive and divisive great injury to [mankind's progress towards] the Age of Complete Peace-and-Equality.

CHAPTER I

Introduction

On [the Fact that] if We Wish to Attain One World of Complete Peace-and-Equality, We Must Abolish the Family

N ow, we desire that men's natures shall all become perfect, that men's characters shall all become equal, that men's bodies shall all be nurtured. [That state in which] men's characters are all developed, men's bodies are all hale, men's dispositions are all pacific and tolerant (? literally, broad), and customs and morals are all beautiful, is what is called Complete Peace-and-Equality. But there is no means whereby to bring about this Way [and yet] to eschew abolishing the family. Thus the family is a necessity of the Ages of Disorder and Increasing Peace-and-Equality, but is the most detrimental thing to [attaining] to the Age of Complete Peace-and-Equality. To have the family and yet to wish to reach Complete Peace-and-Equality is to be afloat on a blocked-up stream, in a sealed-off harbour, and yet to wish to reach the open waterway. To wish to attain Complete Peace-and-Equality and yet to have the family is like carrying earth to dredge a stream, or adding wood to put out a fire: the more done, the more the hindrance. Thus, if we wish to attain the beauty of complete equality, independence, and the perfection of [human] nature, it can [be done] only by abolishing the state, only by abolishing the family.

On [the Fact that] to Leave the Family is to be Ungrateful, and would [Lead to] Annihilation of the [Human] Species; [hence] It Cannot [be Done]

(The 'Brahmins' seek for this complete equality, independence and perfection of human nature through leaving the family and abandoning the world. However, this practice violates the principle of requiting the favours done us, since the parents are given no return for their having given birth and nurture to such a person.) I genuinely respect, but differ with, the subtlety and profundity of Buddhist principles. And as to the turning of the back on the parents and fleeing, the not repaying the debt of the early [years], but instead planning [only] to take and use [for oneself]: [as to these ideas], I shall always consider them to be impossible. Moreover, civilization in the world is actually dependent upon mankind for its extension. Should mankind decrease, then intelligence would likewise diminish, and [the world] would revert to savagery. Still further, by prohibiting intercourse between men and women, the human species would be cut off. If we [followed] this path, then of the one-and-a-half billion human beings on this earth, in not more than fifty years the human form would be completely extinct. After a hundred years . . . the whole earth would have [on it] only shrubs and forests, [with] only birds, beasts, and insects throughout its length and breadth. This is not only a thing that we cannot [allow] to happen, but is also certainly a non-existent principle . . . [Considering in this manner what it involves], this may be one Way, [but] it is not [the Way] that the bulk of mankind will universally consent to.

On the Good Method of Abolishing the Family and Making the World Public

Now [supposing] we desire to abolish the family and attain to Complete Peace-and-Equality, and yet also cannot bear to cut [ourselves] off from parents and spouse, for the preserving of our humaneness; then by what Way can we achieve this? K'ang Yu-wei says there is a Way to get there. Gaining it will be gradual; [we must proceed] in orderly sequence to perfect it. [This Way] can bring about that men will have the happiness of having abolished the family without suffering leaving the family.

K'ang Yu-wei says man is not [a being] that can be produced by man. Men are all [beings] to which Heaven has given birth. Therefore all men are directly subject to Heaven. But independent governments are [institutions] which are established jointly by men. The publicly established government should publicly educate them and publicly succour them.[5]

The Nature of Public Nurture

(Public nurture will be carried on through the following institutions):
The first is called the human roots institution. All women after

becoming pregnant will enter it. Because it is the institution which from the root beginnings of human beings gives education in the womb, I wish to call it the human roots institution. It will not be necessary for the husbands to care for [their pregnant wives].

The second is called the public infant-rearing institution. After a woman has given birth, the infant will be transferred to the infant-rearing institution to be cared for. It will not be necessary for the mother to take care of it.

The third is called the public nursery. All babies after the age of three years will be transferred to this institution to be cared for. It will not be necessary for the parents to take care of them.

The Nature of Public Education

(Public education will be carried on by the following institutions):

The fourth is called the public primary school. All children after the age of six years will enter this institution to be educated.

The fifth is called the public elementary school. All children from the age of ten years to the age of fourteen years will be in this institution to be educated.

The sixth is called the public middle school. All persons from the age of fifteen years to the age of seventeen years will be in this institution to be educated.

The seventh is called the public college. All persons from the age of eighteen years to the age of twenty years will be in this institution to be educated.

The Nature of Public Succour

(Public succour will be carried on by the following institutions):

The eighth is called the public hospital. All persons who are ill will enter [this institution].

The ninth is called the public institution for the aged. All persons after the age of sixty who are not able to support themselves will enter [this institution].

The tenth is called the public institution for the poor. All persons who are poor and who have no one on whom to depend will enter [this institution].

The eleventh is called the public sanatorium. All persons with incapacitating ailments will enter [this institution].

The twelfth is called the public crematorium. All persons who have died will enter [this institution].

Now the way of life is not otherwise than to be born, to be nurtured, to be educated, to be supported, and [to encounter] old age, sickness, suffering, and death. These matters will all belong within the public [domain]: for, from begetting to burying, all will be managed by the [public] government, and will not be provided for by the individual's parents or children. The parents will not have the toil of nurturing and caring for the children, or the expense of educating them. Moreover, the children will be cut off from the father and mother and will not see them very often, for being removed to distant places. Yet again, [because of] moving about, they will not be acquainted with each other. This is not *to leave* the family, but to be naturally *without* the family. Having neither given favours nor received favours, there will naturally be no ingratitude. To carry this out will be very easy; its result will be great contentment.

It may be said that for the parents to be with their children is [inherent in our] Heaven[-conferred] nature; and that to give them up is contrary to natural principles. And yet nowadays in France, America, and Australia there are many illegitimate children. In Japan every year there are likewise eight hundred thousand of them (*sic*). [This] is what was described by K'ung Jung[6] as children merely being due to the sexual desires of the parents. After men and women are free, there will necessarily be many illegitimate children. And then, taking all the people in the world and reckoning it, [since] the poor, who cannot raise and educate their children, are numerous, [while] the wealthy, who can raise and educate their children, are few, we will settle [the matter] on the basis of the majority. Because it is clear[7] that those who will desire to have public nurture will be more numerous, therefore it is certain that the world will become public. After that we can attain One World of Complete Peace-and-Equality.

The Human Roots Institution

THE human roots institution: the roots of human beings are all in the womb. [Here] are the beginnings of man's life and the sources of its ten thousand transformations. Those who through the ages have talked of *ch'ih* (ruling, governing, regulating), have spoken of clarifying the government's punishments, and also of revising its laws. [But to take] untutored people and multiply the meshes of the law so as to deal with their offences: this is to deal with beasts by the snare, to deal with fish by the net.[8] This is truly the *ch'ih* of the Age of Disorder. [Its result is] what Confucius described as 'the people avoiding without shame'.[9] Its distance from the Age of Peace-and-Equality in which [human] nature has become perfected cannot be reckoned. Those who have advanced, and who talk of education, understand that to *ch'ih* humanity the customs and the human mind (or/and heart) are primary. And so they are unceasing in teaching, in polishing them by *jen*, in imbuing them with a sense of moral responsibility (*i*), in demonstrating [the Way] to them by sincerity (*hsin*), in putting them in order (*ch'i*) by the rules of correct social behaviour (*li*), in exhorting them to goodness and admonishing them against evil, in giving honour to *chieh* (moderation, restraint, purity, chastity) and esteeming shame (*ch'ih*).[10]

(Now, while the traditional method of education has as its aim the perfecting of conduct and custom, it is not successful, because it is in the first place a book-learning which can affect only a few, and in the second place it is applied too late. There are too many influences from the home and from society which have already formed the child's character.) Whenever matter has become hard and firm, it is difficult to twist or bend it. Therefore, [in trying] to educate [people] only after they have become adult, when their dispositions have become well developed, it is difficult to change them . . .

Moreover, if we educate them [only] after birth, their disposition has already been formed, their sight and hearing have already commenced, their experiencing has already begun. Now the brain is the best thing in the world for accumulating. Once having been impressed by an external thing, [the brain] retains it permanently. In whatever circumstances—good or bad—it grows and develops. Chia I said:

> 'If one studies with an upright man and holds to it (i.e. to what one has studied), one cannot be un-upright. It is just as, if one is born and grows up in Ch'i, one cannot but [talk with] the language of Ch'i. If one studies with an un-upright man and holds to it, one cannot but be un-upright. It is just as, if one is born and grows up in Ch'u, one cannot but [talk with] the language of Ch'u.'[11]

When now one is born into the evil and corrupt Age of Disorder, when men devour each other, [these conditions] are communicated to the child through sight and hearing, and he is habituated[12] to them as customary. To plant this bad seed, and yet to hope for excellence in the fruit: how can [such a result] be obtained? To hope to attain the Age of Complete Peace-and-Equality and the perfection of [human] nature by this [means] is then like 'wishing to go northwards by turning the shafts southwards'. Such a day will never come.

The man of antiquity: Confucius! Profoundly, deeply he thought, because he understood this [problem]. Therefore he went back to the root, traced the source, and propounded the principle of education in the womb, of educating [children] before their body and disposition (literally, matter) were yet fully formed. Were it brought about that everyone was [educated] like this, that the whole world was [educated] like this, then before [the child] had taken his first breath, at the very beginning of the soul['s existence], he would not already be dyed in evil and corruption. The spring being pure, the stream would naturally not be foul. It must be this way before we can attain the perfection of [human] nature, before we can attain Complete Peace-and-Equality. Unfortunately, not having attained One World, it is not possible that everyone will suddenly carry out [this method].

(There follows here a description of the pre-natal and post-natal education and ceremonial observances of ancient times, as set forth in the *Li Chi*. If such practices were followed, the character of the prince was bound to be refined.)

Now the human roots institution will be for the special purpose of making correct the roots of human beings, and of making sound the beginnings of human lives.

(There follows here a discussion of the influence of topography and climate upon human physique and intelligence. Since such influences are very important, the first consideration in our pre-natal education must be to establish the human roots institutions in places where the climate and topography are favourable. This means we must move people from the unsuitable areas of the earth to the suitable, so that there will be no more propagation of the poorer types.[13] Though this will be difficult and will take time to accomplish, it is essential. Hence, the human roots institutions will be located in surroundings most conducive to the healthy development of the foetus: they will avoid dampness, cliffs, deep valleys, etc., and will find seashores, island plains, pleasant countrysides by the banks of rivers, and the like.

(The remainder of this chapter details the organization and functioning of the human roots institution. We may summarize the main points as follows:

(1. The personnel will be selected from among the kindest and most intelligent graduate nurses.

(2. Women will enter this institution earlier in their pregnancy as civilization advances. Ultimately, they will stay there for the entire time of pregnancy.

(3. As for women in this institution having intercourse with one man, or several, and how often, it will be up to the doctors to decide. It will be prohibited by law, if there is danger of harming the unborn child, because, while in One World people are to be afforded all possible pleasure, yet the children are given to the public by women, and the protection of the children is a public concern. Women's bearing children will be their official duty, and they will be honoured and respected by the public government for this responsibility. But, it being a public duty, they must be careful to discharge it well, avoiding emotional extremes which will be harmful to the unborn child. This applies to sexual intercourse also. And yet terminating intercourse for ten months is a very difficult thing, and will cause much unhappiness. The attempt must be made to moderate desire, to satisfy it some other way, and to maintain

emotional stability by having only one man during the months in which intercourse is permitted. Of course, the latter will not hold if the particular man is not himself healthy and happy. The whole problem is unavoidably difficult.

(4. Because of the central importance of motherhood, and in consideration of its suffering and lack of pleasure, it will be especially honoured in One World. In that Age, there will be no other honours than the three titles of teacher, senior, and mother. But since the former two do not involve suffering, while motherhood does, this latter will be especially honoured, ranking below the great teachers and great seniors, but above the ordinary teachers and seniors. There will be gradations within this title also, with each child born bringing a new medal. Along with the honours for bearing children will go the strict prohibition against abortion. In this way there will be pleasure in having children, and the population will flourish.

(5. The physicians will all be women.

(6. Pregnant women will receive frequent periodical physical examinations; doctors who permit their patients to develop any ailments will be punished according to law.

(7. Diet and medicines will be prescribed by the physicians.

(8. The living quarters of the pregnant women will be suitable to their condition: pleasant, clean, healthful, with due regard to weather factors and aesthetic factors. This will all be determined by the physicians.

(9. The physicians will likewise determine the proper clothing. All harmful practices, such as foot-binding or the Western-style corseting, as well as dancing and carousing in general, will be prohibited to the pregnant women.

(10. Women who have stopped their usual occupations and entered this institution will occupy their time by receiving instruction in, and studying the principles of, love and morality, health and hygiene, child-birth, and infant-care.

(11. The mothers being responsible for the propagation of the species, and for the excellence or lack of it among the species, it will be most important to see to it that they are protected during their pregnancies from harmful influences which would adversely affect the unborn children. An eminent woman physician will be elected to be the 'tutor' for each group of pregnant women, to supervise in

this matter. [There follows additional elaboration on the previously discussed theory that the foetus is effected for good or ill by outside influences. The point is emphasized that the temperament and character of the future person will be determined by these pre-natal influences, including especially the actions and characters of the parents, and most especially the mother. Thus nothing is more fundamental to the improvement of the species than this pre-natal education.]

(12. The women in these institutions will wear tinkling girdle-ornaments which will help them to regulate their actions by the reminder of their sounds, which will be rhythmical and pleasing only when there are no discordant movements resulting from discordant emotions.

(13. The books and pictures inside the institution will be only of a kind calculated to stimulate ideas of love and beauty and goodness in the mother, for the sake of the unborn child.

(14. The supervising tutors will have power to keep out persons whose behaviour or speech is not suitable to the environment of the unborn children.

(15. Music will play an important part in these institutions, for nothing is so potent in affecting our natures. The music will be of the most peaceful and correct sort.

(16. We can see, by observing the example of France, how it will be when women have greater freedom and education: they will not willingly endure the sufferings and handicaps of bearing and caring for children. If this is the case in France today, how much more will it be the case in the era of One World, when there will be complete equality of women with men! Yet if women do not continue to bear children, of course the world will soon revert to the grasses and trees, the beasts and birds, and human civilization will be annihilated. In such a case the complete happiness of all people which is the goal of One World would end by producing the same disaster as would be caused by the universal adoption of the extreme asceticism of the 'Brahmins'.)

But we know that man's Way lies entirely in gaining the Mean. Always, in ideas, we cannot go to extremes. The north and south poles are the farthest apart and the most opposite; and yet in their being seas of ice they are then the same—which exemplifies this principle. Therefore, we clearly understand that the usages of the Ages of Disorder and Increasing Peace-and-Equality are defective, but that this could not be helped. Thus, the ancient custom of repressing women, and their inequality [with men], certainly is a vestige of the custom of the strong oppressing the weak. Holding children dear, and nurturing them with esteem, certainly is due to the fact that we love those to whom we have given birth. But the usages of the Age of Disorder in the various countries all come from these [causes]. [And] even though [such] ideas are not just, and are not [productive of] happiness, yet they are actually the cause which has enabled mankind to become numerous, to triumph over the birds and beasts, and to become established on the earth (literally, heaven and earth). And they are likewise the cause which has enabled civilization to arise, to triumph over savagery, and to form great nations: [This] is, then, the path along which progress must pass, and there is no help for it.

If men eat birds and beasts, then they are extremely non-*jen*. The ancient teachings of India prohibit killing, and the Indians are the most compassionate [of peoples]. They do not [even] tread on insects and ants. But the number of Indians who are eaten every year by fierce beasts is, as a result, ten thousand and some. Moreover, man's intelligence depends a great deal upon eating meat to supply its essence. Thus he is able daily to invent new institutions, and thereby to improve civilization. Hence, the cruelty of eating beasts, and the *jen* of benefiting people, are mutually opposing yet mutually dependent.[14] Roads do not go [only] one way; bodies do not have [only] one surface.

Thus, how difficult it is to establish laws!. We prop up the east, and then the west falls down. We establish laws, and then corruptions arise. And so things just born now [start] to die, [things] just flourishing now [start] to decline. After all there is no total principle. Whenever the sages have established regulations, they have always done so in accordance with the conditions [of the times], and only by way of repairing what was defective.

Now when we consider that all people are given birth by Heaven, and are all alike in body and intelligence, then it is extremely unjust and extremely unequal to honour men and repress women. (Yet there is this problem that when we have equalized men and women the result is bound to be that women will not desire to bear and care for children, and that population will therefore decline, and civilization will be endangered. This is the gravest problem of One World. For that reason, abortion will be the most serious crime, even more serious than killing a person who has already been born. The heaviest punishment for abortion will be life imprisonment at hard labour, and the guilty person will be dishonoured as 'non-*jen*'. The lightest punishment will be imprisonment for the number of months of pregnancy at the time of the abortion, and complete social ostracism thereafter. It may be that if the sufferings of child-birth are made slight, while the sufferings of imprisonment and inequality are great, abortions can be prevented. [The same deterrents will be applied to physicians and medicine shops.]

(17. The physicians will receive honours for their achievements in constantly finding new ways to alleviate the sufferings of childbirth.

(18. There will be special delivery rooms with music and pleasant conditions; the best physicians will deliver the babies. There will be specially trained nurses to care for the infants. Except when nursing the baby, the mother will be free to listen to music, to read, and to look at pictures. The mother will be given proper foods and drinks to nourish her in her special condition. There will be music and poetry played and sung, suitable to harmonizing body and soul.

(19. The census officer will visit these institutions once a week to record the new births, which will be reported to the degree government. If the father is known, he may be notified.

(20. Whereas in ancient times children were named at first from the name of the mother [knowing their mothers but not their fathers], and later from the name of the father, in the Age of Increasing Equality it will be suitable for the children to be given the names of both parents. But when we come to One World, children will be publicly reared, and there will thus be no reason for carrying on 'family names'. If we have family names then we have relatives; and if we have relatives then we have selfishness, which is the greatest obstruction to our principle of making the world public. Thus, instead of family names, each child will be named according to the 'stems and branches' system[15] as follows: such-and-such a degree, such-and-such an institution, such-and-such a room, and such-and-such a day in which the child was born.

(21. Careful supervision will be exercised by the physicians over care of the newborn infant and the nursing mother. The physicians will prescribe the time after which a mother may resume normal activities, as well as the duration of the nursing period.)

22. All mothers, during the period they are in this institution and nursing their babies, naturally must not have sexual intercourse with men. But, fearing that it may be difficult for human nature to refuse to permit them to be with men and sleep with them for several tens of days or for several months, prior to the time when they may be permitted to sleep with [real men], it may be that they will have pleasure only by substituting a mechanical man. It will always be according to the study and decision of the physicians as to the proper number of days . . .

(23. Mothers will regain complete independence as soon as they leave this institution. They will be given tokens of honour upon their departure; if they live a long way off they will be taken by car. All who see them will pay them respect for having borne a child.

(24. The nurses of these institutions will be selected by the physicians from among the healthiest, most intelligent, and highest-charactered women. They will be judged according to the reports of the mothers for whom they care: if the reports are good, they will receive decorations; if the reports are unfavourable, they will be disgraced, and will be barred from ever holding a high position. All women must serve in these institutions, or in the infant-rearing institutions, or in the public hospitals or institutions for the aged, before they can be eligible to hold a high office of any kind.)

CHAPTER III

Infant-Rearing Institutions

A NOTE attached to this title states that this is the same as the compassionating children institution, designed to take care of those from the ages of three to five. If this institution is not set up, then the infant-rearing institution will take care of them during these ages also.

(The main provisions of this institution are as follows:

(1. Babies will be placed there as soon as they have been weaned, and the mothers have left the human roots institution.

(2. The nurses will all be women, who are selected by the physicians for their character and health, and who have the desire to do this work.

(3. These women will be held in the highest esteem because of the great importance of their work for mankind, and because their job is so arduous and yet without any recompense in the sense that a natural mother might be recompensed, since these children will grow up and will not even know them.

(4. The physical surroundings of these institutions will be the same as those of the human roots institutions; their physical plants will be perfectly suitable to the nature of children, with flowers, trees, ponds, toys, pictures, etc., and nothing evil or jarring will be permitted there.

(5. The supervisors will be physicians chosen from among those of highest ability and character. There will be frequent physical examinations, and the physicians will order the food and clothing and in general regulate everything for the babies. Up until the age of two each baby will have one nurse assigned especially to it; after that, perhaps two or three will be assigned.

(6. The population office will give names to the babies after they have entered this institution.[16]

(7. Educational toys will be provided to acquaint the children with the world and its civilization, according as they become older and their understanding develops.

(8. Since the children's minds will easily be influenced by any surroundings, care will be taken to keep these institutions away from such bad environments as theatres, factories, crematoriums, etc.[17]

(9. To avoid the bad influence of climatic factors, these institutions will not be established outside of the 50th degree north, and the 20th degree south latitude.

(10. Nurses in these institutions who have performed their duties meritoriously will be given decorations of the first degree; their labours and responsibilities are even heavier than those of the actual mothers.)

CHAPTER IV

Elementary Schools

(THERE is a discrepancy between the outline of the educational system as set forth at the end of Chapter I above, and the following. Here, the public primary school has been omitted; this was to have taken children from six through nine. The elementary school as here described will take them from six through ten, or perhaps five through nine, as human knowledge and ability improve.

(The main provisions regarding the elementary schools are as follows:

(1. All the teachers will be women, since women are more patient, refined, and compassionate than men. These teachers will be selected for their high qualities of character and their loving nature; it is most important that the children at this age be subjected to good influences, since the impressions they receive at this age are lasting and will mould their characters for life.

(2. Education at this age will in general emphasize the body more than the mind. The foundations of lifelong good health are laid at this time. Children will play a lot and work little. They must be guided and supervised carefully, however, as they are easily led astray; the teachers in these schools are really mothers as well as tutors. One teacher will not have to handle more than a few children.

(3. As in the case of the other institutions, these schools will be located in places suitable as to physical surroundings, and away from bad influences.

(4. The schools will be completely equipped with all suitable educational toys, playgrounds, etc. Singing will be important.

(5. The curriculum will be decided according to the needs of life at the time. Since there will be a universal language, this will save much time and energy for other things. There will be more time for play and enjoyment during this era, with the better organization of education. The only restriction will be that this play and enjoyment must not be improper or harmful to the development of character.

(6. These schools will not be established in the areas of unfavourable climate beyond the 60th degree north or within ten degrees of the equator.)

CHAPTER V

Middle Schools

(IN continuing with the system according to the foregoing, there is a continuance of the discrepancy with the original outline at the end of Chapter I. There it was said that the middle school would take students from fifteen to seventeen. Here the ages are to be from eleven to fifteen.

(The main provisions regarding the middle schools are as follows:

(1. The curriculum will be adjusted to the nature and intelligence of the students, and will comprise the higher level of common studies. Improved education will make these students of this age the equals of students of fifteen years and older in former times.

(2. These students will gradually develop freedom and independence of will; emphasis will be placed on physical education, music, and the rules of correct social behaviour and conduct.

(3. Both men and women will teach in these schools, as the students are now maturing. Increasing liberty is given to the students; but at the same time emphasis is laid upon morality, correct behaviour, and academic studies. The latter will still not be overstressed, however.

(4. The teachers must be persons of outstanding character, learning, and diligence, as the characters and abilities of their students in later life will depend upon the soundness of their training at this stage. The head of the school must likewise be a superior person.

(5. Equipment of these schools will include all things suitable for study, recreation, enjoyment, and learning about the work of the world.

(6. These schools will be located away from bad social and physical environments.

(7. These schools will be improved in this era to the point where their highest class will be almost superior to the college classes of the present day.)

Item: Each middle school will be able to hold ten thousand persons, or several tens of thousands. [In] the dining-hall, and in rising, retiring, going out and coming in, all will be [regulated] in an orderly manner. The division of classes and the arranging in order will be strict, as in an army. The great teacher will be like a general, the department heads will be like unit commanders, and the ordinary teachers will be like sub-unit commanders. Sitting, working, advancing and retiring, lecturing, studying, resting, playing—all will have their set times. The clothing will be uniform; when we look at them, [the students] will appear like soldiers. The more people there are, the greater the seeing and emulating. The greater the group gathered together, the deeper the incitement. Morality [thus] will easily be made uniform. Mores [thus] will easily be made identical. What is wrong will never enter into the group. Being considered shameful, there will then be little [of it].

CHAPTER VI

Colleges

(**A**GAIN there is the discrepancy with the original outline at the end of Chapter I above; there it was stated that college age would be from eighteen to twenty; here it is given as sixteen to twenty, following on the middle school plan as given directly above.

(The main provisions regarding the colleges are as follows:

(1. In One World all persons will go to college.

(2. Having completed the common studies in the middle school, the five college years will be spent in specialization. These studies will include business, agriculture, and the trades, as well as the more academic subjects. Students will pursue whatever course of study they desire, and for which they are by nature suited.

(3. With the advancement of civilization in this age there will come about an increasing division of knowledge into special fields; every person will be a specialist of some kind. The superior persons will be able to study more than one thing; but even the least talented will be able to master some one thing sufficiently to support himself.

All persons, even those without much natural ability, will naturally be stimulated to learn because of their environment: for twenty years they will live communally, spurred on by the opportunities available to them and the encouragement of all their fellows engaged in the same learning process. They will know that they cannot do without learning because they must support themselves after leaving the college, or else go to the public institution for the poor and lose their status. This universal education will enable every person to develop whatever abilities he has; which is the opportunity that so many are denied nowadays, resulting in their stupidity and lack of usefulness, their suffering, and oftentimes their turning to crime.

(4. The studies of the college will be practical, applied, and experimental; in studying agriculture, for example, the student will go out into the fields and study it. This education will not be concentrated on an empty literary learning.

(5. The various branches of the colleges will be located in whatever places are most suitable to the subjects to be studied in each branch; the objective is practicality and usefulness.

(6. Teachers will be men and women of the greatest knowledge and experience. Knowledge is to be emphasized most importantly in the colleges, but physical education and moral education will also not be slighted.

(7. Like the middle schools, the colleges will be run on a regimented pattern, with uniforms, regulations for all activities, and authority by the teachers—like an army. The various educational institutions of One World will each be like a small state, with the students as the citizens, and the teachers as the ministers and high officers.

(8. Graduates will receive diplomas; those who fail to graduate will not receive diplomas—the government will not support them, but they will also seek employment.

(9. Especially able students will receive the opportunity to go on for further studies with governmental support.

(10. Persons who cannot find other employment after leaving school will have to take menial jobs; if they cannot get such jobs, they will have to enter the public institution for the poor, where they will perform hard labour and will not be considered equal to other people.)

CHAPTER VII

Institutions for the Poor

THE main provisions regarding these institutions are as follows:

(1. All persons without employment, who cannot otherwise maintain themselves, may enter; they must work at hard labour; if they do not know some kind of work, they will be taught.

(2. They will sell the products of their work and use the money for their maintenance; the institution will supplement whenever this is insufficient. Industry will be encouraged, and laziness will be punished.

(3. Inmates will have times for rest and recreation, and may go out of the institution, but only at certain times.

(4. There will be teachers and physicians attached.

(5. Inmates will wear adequate but poor clothing; their living quarters will be clean but poor; the institutions will be only meagrely provided with such amenities as gardens, libraries, and recreation facilities.

(6. Those who enter this institution more than once will be considered unequal to ordinary citizens; they will be shamed by wearing special clothing and their names will be defamed. Only students just graduated from the colleges will not be so shamed, providing they leave and find employment within one year. Inmates who work well and commit few faults may be recommended by the officials in charge for outside employment, and may have their names restored to honour.

(7. The main problem will be to keep people from being lazy, since during this era no one will have to be afraid of having no way to live; therefore the institutions must stress the punishing of laziness, and exhortations to work.

(8. Persons who enter these institutions four times will be punished by extra-hard labour; those who enter five times will be put in prison for seven days in order to shame them and warn them to reform.

(9. Officials of these institutions will be publicly elected on the basis of their good character and educational ability.)

CHAPTER VIII

Hospitals

THE main provisions regarding these institutions are as follows:

(1. Although we will have these hospitals to take care of the sick, yet, since every person throughout the world will be visited and checked by a physician once each day, there will be universal prevention of disease.

(2. Medical care and medicines will be government-provided, free of charge.

(3. The facilities of the hospitals will include pleasant surroundings, music, plays, books, etc.—all the things calculated to foster pleasure of body and mind for the patients.

(4. The physicians will be awarded decorations by the government for their accomplishments in devising new methods of treatment, and for excellence in taking care of patients. Physicians who by making mistakes are responsible for the death of a patient will be severely punished: they will be deprived of their right to practise, disgraced, and possibly imprisoned for a time.

(5. The nurses may be men or women; they will be given awards for each year of service, or deprived of their positions and disgraced, according to the reports of their patients. All physicians must first serve as nurses in these hospitals for one year before they can become great physicians or superintendents.

(6. Those with physical handicaps will all enter this institution for treatment, and there will be no distinctions made in the way they are treated and the way ordinary patients are treated [i.e. they will be given just as good treatment]. The permanently handicapped will be placed in special institutions, and given education through college, with special training in some art. If they are able to go out and support themselves after the age of twenty, well and good; if they cannot, they will be supported by this institution, with half of whatever they can earn from their work being given to them. However at this time there should not be many such people.

(7. The insane will be placed on special islands. They will not be allowed to procreate their kind. They will be taught agriculture and

other work, and half of whatever they can earn will be given to them. However, there will not be such people in this age, since they will not be allowed to have children.

(8. Persons with malformed bodies, harelips, etc., will not be permitted to marry and propagate their kind. They may receive official permission to have sexual intercourse [presumably with contraceptive control] if they have such desire; however, at this time, there will be 'mechanical persons' to substitute for real persons for sexual relief.

(9. The medical authorities will control epidemic diseases by suitable measure; they may even move sections of the population to other areas. Such removals would be paid for by the government.

(10. The hospitals will be located in pleasant and healthful spots.

(11. At this time there will be huge numbers of physicians, as each physician will be responsible only for a few hundred persons. Medical control will be supreme over the world, regulating food, drink, clothing, architecture, sanitation, and so on. The public institutions will all be under medical supervision. Every person will be given a medical check-up once each day. The physicians may enter into any dwelling to check on sanitary conditions.)

For in the Age of One World there will be no military forces. Its government will be for the purpose of expanding men's knowledge, perfecting men's moral virtue, preserving men's bodies, prolonging men's lives, and making men's lives happy. And that which expands men's knowledge and perfects men's moral virtue is ultimately to be found in preserving men's bodies and making men's lives happy, and nowhere else. Therefore the preserving of men's bodies and the making happy of men's lives is the most weighty [responsibility] of government. And so, in the Age of One World, physicians will be the most numerous, medical capabilities will be the most highly developed, medical responsibilities will be the heaviest, medical [personnel] will be selected from the finest [talents], and medical authority will be the greatest. For in the Age of Disorder force is respected; and so militarists are the rulers and military authority is the most important.[18] In the Middle Age (i.e. the Age of Increasing Peace-and-Equality) letters are respected; and so scholars are the rulers and the authority of philosophy[19] is the most important.

In the Age of [Complete] Peace-and-Equality *jen* is respected; and so physicians are the rulers and medical authority is the most important. The people of all the world, from life to death, entrust their lives [to the physicians]. How could there be [a responsibility] more important than this! Therefore we may call the Age of One World the Medical World.

(But there is a danger here, because of the tremendous number of physicians and their great authority. It might happen that some kind of a medical religion would be started up, with a doctor as the religious leader; and it might be that medical political parties would be started up, with doctors as political leaders. This would result in conflicts and a reversion to the Age of Disorder. Hence there must be a ban on these two kinds of activities, or One World will be destroyed.[20] The prevention of abortion, in order to ensure the flourishing of the human race, and the prevention of the formation of parties among the physicians, are the two things which must be done if One World is long to endure.)

CHAPTER IX

Institutions for the Aged

(THE main provisions regarding these institutions are as follows:

(1. Anyone over sixty may enter; since the public citizens labour for the public government for several decades, it is fitting that they should be recompensed by the government.

(2. The greatest freedom and happiness will be accorded these old people. Even should someone among them commit some grave crime, he will be punished only by comparatively minor social ostracism and disgrace.

(3. The attendants in these institutions will be both men and women. They will be decorated if the testimony of the old people is that they have been *jen*; they will be disgraced, and will never be allowed to hold high position, if the old people hate them. All men must serve in this institution and in the hospital before they can go on to become rulers,[21] teachers, or officers-in-charge. Similarly, all women must serve in this institution, and the infant-rearing

institution, before they can hold a high position. In the Age of One World, old people being without their own children, these attendants must take the place of their children, and serve them with love and respect.

(4. The number of attendants each old person will have will be determined by his age.

(5. The facilities of these institutions, including gardens and ponds, entertainments, books, furniture, and instruments, all will be calculated to make the old people as happy as possible.

(6. Of all the institutions, the institution for the aged is the only one in which there will be distinction of grade among the inmates. Those who enter will be classified according to what they have achieved during their lives, into six grades: the upper two being those who have held the most responsible positions and accomplished important works; the middle two being those who have lived good lives and have been decorated for excellent service; the lower two being those who have not done anything meritorious or who have been disgraced for their misdeeds. The reason for thus grading the old people is to serve as an example for everyone, so that they may retire in the greatest possible honour and pleasure.

(7. To give point to this differentiation, the treatment to which the old people are entitled will also be different according to their grade. For example, the upper two grades will live in spacious houses with every possible convenience and beauty; the middle two will live in six-room houses [bedroom, guest-room, living-room, study, bathroom, and extra room], while the lower two, deserving nothing from the public government as they have never contributed anything to the public welfare, will only get consideration because of their age, and will live in two-room apartments [bedroom and living-room] of a poor sort, and share a public bath.

(8. The physical location of these institutions will be in suitably healthful and pleasant spots.

(9. Quarters will be assigned to those entering, in the order in which they enter; if they wish to move in with someone else for companionship, or if they wish to travel to some other spot, they may do so.

(10. It will be permissible for inmates to have a companion living with them, even though that person has not yet reached the age of

eligibility to enter this institution. However, such persons will not get free board and room.

(11. Each inmate will receive a daily physical check-up. Those with serious illnesses will be transferred to the hospital.

(12. The old people will have horses and carriages for going out. Use of these will also be differentiated by grade. Or perhaps by that time electric vehicles will have replaced horses and carriages.

(13. The public government will pay railroad fare for the old people as follows: the low grades, third class for a distance within one hundred miles of the institution; the middle grades, second class for a distance within one thousand miles; the upper grades, anywhere in the world, first class.

(14. For the spiritual nourishment of the inmates, there will be daily lectures in the auditorium on the Way (*Tao*) and other suitable topics. Inmates may also have bonzes live with them, and there will be special temples within the institution.

(15. Upon the death of an inmate his body will be wrapped in silk, and his coffin will be escorted to the institution for those who have enjoyed their allotted span, attended by police-soldiers, and with all suitable evidences of the grade and attainments of the deceased.)

CHAPTER X

The Institution for
Those Who Have Enjoyed Their Allotted Span

(THIS is the same institution that was called the public crematorium in the original outline at the end of Chapter I. Its main provisions are as follows:

(1. All persons will be sent here after their death.

(2. There will be lying in state, assembling of mourners, dressing of the corpse, procession from the mourning hall to the crematorium, and all appropriate public manifestations of grief and respect, according to the grade and achievements of the deceased. However, there will not be any continuance of such mourning after the body is cremated. Such mourning is bad for the health and happiness of

the living; it will not be necessary or appropriate in the Age of One World, when there will not be private families.

(3. The matter of wearing mourning apparel will be up to the personal feelings of those concerned. It will usually happen in this era that the mourner's teacher or nurse will be more dear to him than his parents, since the latter will likely not have had much to do with him since his birth. But in any case it will be a personal matter.

(4. Being in mourning will be indicated by a piece of black cloth worn on head, shoulder, waist, or arm, to indicate degree of feeling. The mourner will abstain from listening to music for a couple of months. Prostration will not be appropriate, unless the individual really feels deeply enough to wish to perform this act.

(5. Schoolchildren who die will be given only three [for college], two [for middle school], or one [for elementary school] day of lying dressed, before cremation. They will be attended by their respective teachers, nurses, and fellow-students. Those dying in the institution for the poor will be given three days; those in prison, one day.

(6. Persons of unusual accomplishments and great virtues may be signally honoured by embalming, if there is a method of doing this. They will be buried, and a tombstone erected, with a portrait. It will be the responsibility of this institution to have the golden tablets with the portrait and accomplishments of such outstanding persons engraved, upon resolution of the public parliament. Such persons will be designated as *hsien* ['worthies'] or as *sheng* ['sages'], according to the degree of their *jen* and knowledge. Those outstanding for the former will be honoured with square plaques; those outstanding for the latter will be honoured by round plaques; those outstanding for both will be honoured by both kinds. The size of the plaque will also indicate the degree of attainment. The raising of the tombstone and plaque will be attended by gathering of the people from near and far—even from all over the world, in the case of a very great person—and will be accompanied by music and incense and scattering of flowers, by bowing and appropriate manifestations of respect. The accomplishments of the deceased will thus be preserved. 'With this, the concerns of mortal man are ended.'

(7. Cremation of the dead is the best custom, because it is the

quickest method of disposing of the decay. There is no good purpose in preserving the carcass, which is of no more value than the nails and hair and excretions of the living person. It is not that from which the living spirit comes, nor knowledge, nor soul. There is a natural aversion to cremation, because the living hate to see the body of a loved one destroyed before their eyes; so in this era cremation will be done by electrical machines, completely and cleanly. As 'man's life comes from non-being to being, it also [goes] from being to non-being'. Hence this returning of the body to Heaven, instead of burying it in earth, is more beautiful. The whole purpose of One World is to make human existence happy. It is much more compatible to that purpose to do away completely with the burden of the dead upon the living. This is better: to create a happy world here, everywhere on this earth, than to find happiness by the Buddhist method of escaping from the troubles of this earth.

(8. This institution will keep careful records of the deeds and of the personal property of the deceased. Half of the property and effects, aside from what is willed by the deceased, will go to the public. The accomplishments and virtues of the deceased will be forwarded to the historians office for transmission to posterity.)

REFERENCES

[1] This would seem to be used here in a figurative sense, rather than as referring to Occident and Orient.

[2] 美 is used to set off the phrase.

[3] The foregoing paragraph contains difficulties which make me hesitate to affirm the correctness of the rendering here given, but it seems to carry along the author's train of argument consistently enough.

[4] This has reference to the supposed influence of the environment upon the foetus, affecting the physical, mental, and spiritual constitution of the individual for life.

[5] The point of this otherwise seemingly irrelevant observation is to be found in its derivation from an opinion of Mencius: in a passage in which he is discussing the function of Heaven in giving the empire to a ruler, he states that the difference in character, ability, and length of rule among certain early emperors 'was all from Heaven, and what could not be

produced by man. That which is done without man's doing it is from Heaven . . .' (Legge's translation [see citation in Book One, Chapter II, n. 28], p. 798.) Such things are ordained by Heaven, but governments are instituted by men, and it is the responsibility of men to perfect them.

⁶ 孔融 flourished A.D. 153–208.

⁷ Transposing the positions of 願 and 明 .

⁸ Compare *Mencius*: 'The way of the people is this.—If they have a certain livelihood, they will have a fixed heart. If they have not a certain livelihood, they have not a fixed heart. And if they have not a fixed heart, there is nothing which they will not do in the way of self-abandonment, of moral deflection, of depravity, and of wild license. When they have thus been involved in crime, to follow them up and punish them:— this is to entrap the people' (Legge's translation, III, A, 3.3, p. 611). Almost the identical words are found in I, A, 7.20 (p. 463). The 'untutored people' recalls the famous passage in VI, B, 8.2 (p. 917): 'To employ an uninstructed people [in war] may be said to be destroying the people.' The use of snare and net refers, of course, to the use of unfair methods—we recall that the Master (Confucius) 'fished with a line but not with a net; when fowling he did not shoot at perching birds' (*Lun Yü*, VII, 26).

⁹ *Lun Yü*, II, 3: 'The Master said, "Lead them with laws and keep them in order by punishments, and the people will avoid [the laws and punishments] without shame. Lead them with moral example (德) and keep them in order by the rules of correct social behaviour, and they will have [a sense of] shame and will become [good]."'

¹⁰ A veritable code of the Confucian gentleman. The virtues catalogued are difficult to translate for the very reason that they are the most common, hence the most meaning-filled, of concepts in the Chinese Great Tradition.

¹¹ Chia I (201–169 B.C.), *New Writings*: 'Guarding and Instructing' (新書、保傅篇).

¹² 習 , the same word translated as 'studies' in the passage quoted above from Chia I.

¹³ Compare above, Part IV, pp. 145–6.

¹⁴ For an elaboration of this subject, see below, Part IX, throughout.

¹⁵ i.e. the traditional system comprising two sets of characters, one set of ten, and one set of twelve, which are combined in sequence and thus give sixty different combinations. This system is used for dating and for other purposes and the two sets are used for the same purposes as we use

A, B, C, or I, II, III, etc. (For example, the Parts of the *Ta T'ung Shu* are numbered by the ten 'stems'.)

[16] See above, Chapter II, p. 193.

[17] We are reminded of the mother of Mencius, who changed their residence three times to avoid the bad influences of environment upon her young son.

[18] Changing 尚 to 重, since it thus conforms to the wording of the following two sentences, and avoids repetition of 'respected' in the same sentence.

[19] 哲 Philosophy here equals 'wisdom', in the broad sense. 哲學 is taken as the technical term for philosophy in the narrower sense when Western philosophy becomes influential in China, a little later on.

[20] See below, Part VIII, Chapter XV: 'The Second Prohibition . . .'

[21] 君 It must be presumed that the author has used this word here and in the passage quoted directly above in a special sense, as meaning officers who have been elected to serve in the public government in some most authoritative capacity.

PART VII

ABOLISHING LIVELIHOOD BOUNDARIES AND MAKING OCCUPATIONS PUBLIC

(After noting the 'new world' which is in the making because of all the technological advances of the present day, the author makes the following statement):

However, the new techniques, although marvellous, are merely a superficial aspect of the world. As for the livelihood of the people —the poverty and suffering of the individual, and the deficiencies in our regard for the public welfare—they cannot in the slightest rectify the situation.

CHAPTER I

If One World is Not Carried Out in Agriculture, then Production Cannot be Equalized, and there will be Starving People

Now to speak of it with regard to the farmers. In China people may buy and sell land, hence they each obtain a small piece of land. It is difficult to use machinery to farm [this small piece], not to mention that agricultural schools have not been opened, [so that the farmers] do not know how to improve [their methods]. And the landlords ordinarily do not farm themselves; most of [the farmers] are tenants. The leasing [of the land] is already expensive; [then if] the wet and dry [periods] are unseasonable, [the farmer] will labour the entire year with calloused hands and feet, his entire family working together, [and still] not have enough to support them. They will eat yams and cook gruel, and still will not satisfy their hunger. In extremities they will sell their children to pay the rent. Cadaverous, in tattered clothing, their sufferings are such that one cannot bear to describe them.

Even if agricultural schools were everywhere to be established, if the [best] species [of crops] were to be thoroughly known, if fertilizers were to be perfected, and machinery were to be widely employed as in Europe and America, still, the fields being too small, it will for ever be difficult to bring about equalization. There may be many large fields neglected and uncultivated, but it is in vain that [the farmer] uses his ingenuity on the small fields. And there may perhaps not even be fields to till, [with the result that we have] famine and beggary and vagrancy and [dying in] the ditches. This is not only so in China; aside from the newly opened-up [territory of] America, where it is possible to have large fields, nearly every country is unable to avoid [these conditions]. But in the old countries of Asia, where there is little [new] land, and there are many people, [the situation] is still more acute.

Confucius was already concerned about this in ancient times, and so devised the well-field system.[1] But later, men did not concern themselves over [the causes and prevention] of famine, and this 'checker-board' arrangement could not actually be carried out in countries that were not just being developed. The saying of Confucius, 'With equality, no poverty',[2] is the highest ideal. Later scholars daily talked about equalizing the fields, and devised the method of limiting the fields of each person. Wang Màng[3] did not follow this path, but recklessly abandoned[4] it; and so brought on disorder. The Englishman, Mr. *Fu*,[5] in his theory of livelihood, wanted to support [groups of] a thousand persons by means of large 'well-fields' of ten [square] *li*. His idea was very *jen*, but also impractical.

For if we permit people to buy and sell private [real] property, if they all have private real property, then there will not be a levelling of wealth, and there will never be any way [to bring about] equality. It is like Holland's governing of Java: there are local owners who receive their land from the state, and [receive] revenues from the people [who work this land]; hence the taxation is heavy. It is like the [system of] feudal lords and emperor.

Because this is not the Way of Complete Peace-and-Equality, then even though there be good men who desire to bring about that the people of the whole world shall be supported without the calamities of cold and hunger, without the unhappiness of inequality, it cannot actually be accomplished. Therefore, by present practices—even though we bring about that machines are daily improved, that people add more and more to their abilities and knowledge, that the governmental laws are made ever more detailed—yet if we do not carry out the methods of One World, we will never enable human beings to become contented and happy.

For enabling the farmers to obtain equality in subsistence, we may perhaps advocate the methods of communism.[6] But if we have the family, if we have the state, selfishness is then extreme. If we have the family, then the individual has wife and children dependent upon him; if we have the state, then the marshalling of troops and the levying of taxes daily increases. With such a polity, to hope to carry out communism[6] is like 'wishing to go southwards by turning the shafts northwards'. Not to mention that it could not be carried out during the French Revolution, even America up to the present has likewise been completely unable to carry it out.

CHAPTER II

If One World is Not Carried Out in Industry, then Struggles between Labour and Capital[7] will Develop into[8] National Disorders

WITH regard to the struggles between labour and capital: in recent years they have increased, because of machines being used to make things, and completely taking over from the artisan. What formerly could be made by the enterprise of a single man's hands and feet is now all taken over by the machines of the large factory, and the artisan has no way to make a living. But those who have the ability to set up the machines of the large factory must necessarily be big capitalists to be able to do it. Hence nowadays the large factory, the large railway, or shipbuilding shop, the large emporium, and including the large farm—all are run by big capitalists. One factory, one [? market]-place [employs] a thousand or ten thousand labourers who depend upon it for their living. While the capitalist in his turn can be strict or lenient, easy or hard on the livelihood of the labourer, and control him or oppress him. Whereby the rich become richer and the poor become poorer.

Machines, during these [past] hundred years, have been merely in the budding stage; and yet the cleavage between poor and rich is [as great] as this. After several more decades we shall see the autumn-time [*sic*] of the machine's development and growth, the time when the tree-trunk divides into branches and puts out leaves. The time is near when the capitalists' factories and emporiums will be ever larger, ever more extensive, when banks will be found every-where in the land, when railways will span the world, when com-mercial vessels will cross [the seas between] the five continents, when telegraph wires will enwrap the earth. The utilization of workmen [in these enterprises] will reach to a hundred thousand, to a million, and will not stop [even there]. [Such an enterprise] will be like a small state; its wealthy owners will be like the state's princes; its hundred managers will be like the gentry and great officers; its workers will be like the common people. The disparity between poor and rich will be like the distance between sky and abyss. We will assuredly fear that what was anciently a struggle over territory —in which nobles and plebeians were spoken of as constituting the state—will [then] be changed into a struggle over factories and emporiums—in which poor and rich will be spoken of as constituting the state. Then the wars of the old states will cease, but the wars of the new 'states' will occur just the same. The calamities which this would bequeath to mankind—how can we calculate them!

Now, in the struggles of human affairs, 'those who are unequal will cry out',[9] which is a natural circumstance. Therefore in recent years there has been a springing up of struggles by labour unions to coerce the capitalists, in Europe and America. At present [such phenomena] are merely the germinating of the root, and the formation of labour unions will certainly increase in the future. One fears lest [this development] foment the disasters of 'blood and iron'.[10] This struggle would not be between strong and weak states, but between poor and rich groups. A hundred years hence it will certainly be this [problem] to which the whole world will be giving its attention. Therefore nowadays socialism is flourishing, communism is thriving. And in the future [this problem] will be the greatest subject of controversy. But if we have not yet done away with the selfishness [caused by] having the family, the idea of private property will still be active; [in which case] it will be practically impossible to seek to tranquillize this unusually great struggle and to relieve [the situation].

CHAPTER III

If One World is Not Carried Out in Commerce, then Men will Develop Artful Natures, and will Waste Things through Surplus of Goods

WITH regard to the future of commerce: its struggles will be still more fierce. At the same time that high abilities emerge, pressing into service [the cleverest] mental calculations [for the] piercing of gold and the carving of stone, cleverness in deceit is also born, because of contention for profits. Hence spurious goods are manufactured, which injure [the innocent] public. In the case of medicines, foods, boats, and vehicles, the harm done is still greater. Even if [the goods] are not actually spurious, yet [the merchant] demands excessively high prices for goods of poor quality. They are satisfied to cheat people; trustworthiness is non-existent; all shame is lost.

And in the struggles between [firms engaged in] the same business, they subvert and crush each other. If A prospers, then B is envious of him; if C is weak, then D rejoices in it. In their struggling over profits (or, in their struggling for the advantage), they 'kick those in front and fear those behind'. Even the best of friends have no pity on each other. Or they make pitfalls and traps, and a hundred cunning frauds are devised. This being central in their planning, and the only thing to which they devote [themselves] to the limit of their strength, nothing is left over whereby to serve the people. The daily ruination of character, the daily frustration of natural functionings accumulates [among] men, and becomes habitual. With this, to hope to attain to the age when [human] nature will be perfected—how can it be done!

Nowadays the theory of natural selection is being proclaimed, and the idea of competition is being regarded as most rational. Hence, state and state, they marshal their troops and look at each other, considering the swallowing up [of another state] as a matter of course. Man and man, they cunningly deceive and entrap each other, considering cheating and abuse to be the accomplishment of their plans. The hundred affairs, the ten thousand businesses are all founded upon competition. It is thought that talent and knowledge progress through competition, that implements and techniques are refined through competition, and that survival of the fittest is a law of nature. And in making a living in commerce still more is competition considered the great principle. How can it be, that only [by] depraving men's mental processes and overthrowing men's persons, [men] learn how to fulfil the Way of Heaven, and to assist nature!

Now the [same degree of] strength or weakness not being common [to all,] wisdom or stupidity not existing [in the same] extremes [in all,] when two merchants fight, there must be a loser. [He will be] 'reduced to mud and earth'.[11] His capital exhausted, the rich one changes and becomes poor. Then his whole family cries out without avail. Their livelihood having been lost, grief and misery are born; their bodies being without nourishment, sicknesses multiply; the family being without support, deaths follow upon each other. I have seen numerous [cases of this kind]. And then there are poor men who have suddenly become rich through commerce; but since [it is only] one man out of ten or a hundred or a thousand or ten thousand [who succeeds in this,] the inequality is very great. Now [if a man] is richer than ten, they are subordinate to him; if he is richer than a hundred, they serve him; if he is richer than a thousand, they are slaves to him. Among the rich there is pride; among the poor there is obsequiousness. At the extreme of pride, [the proud one] gives orders with contemptuous [gestures] of chin and fingers; at the extreme of obsequiousness, [the obsequious one] becomes depraved, licking the sores [of the rich man]—for there are no [limits] to which [pride and obsequiousness] will not extend. Therefore pride and obsequiousness are not that whereby to cultivate human nature and perfect human character. But if we follow the way of competition, and have the boundary of poor and rich, then we will necessarily bring about this [pride and obsequiousness].

Those who discuss [these matters] nowadays hate the calm of

unity, and exalt the hubbub of competition. They think that with competition there is progress; without strife there is retrogression. This is for a fact suitable to the Age of Disorder; but it is most pernicious to the Way of One World of Complete Peace-and-Equality. Now with deceit and corruption confusing [men's] thinking processes like this, the ruination [of human nature] is complete; with misery and exhaustion, sickness and death like this, with pride and obsequiousness confusing men's characters like this, the calamity is most severe. This is in direct opposition to our desire to lead men to peace and happiness.

Hence those who advocate the theory of competition understand nature but do not understand man. There is no way to correct them, their stupidity is so enormous. Alas! This is truly a theory of the Age of Disorder! However, if we do not free the way of man from the selfishness of having the family and private enterprise, and yet we desire to do away with competition, how can it be done? Therefore, [so long as we have the family and private enterprise,] we cannot but consider competition a good method. If we have the selfishness of the family, and private enterprise, then certainly individuals will manage their enterprises themselves. There is actually no help for this in the Age of Disorder. Now let us take enterprises as managed by individuals and enterprises as managed by the public, and compare them.

CHAPTER IV

Comparison between Independent Agriculture and Public Agriculture

(THE point made in this section is that the individual farmer cannot predict the market for his produce; hence without public, planned agriculture, there is an incalculable waste of time, labour, and produce.)

CHAPTER V

Comparison between Independent Commerce and Public Commerce

(IF business is run by independent individuals, there is no way for them to calculate the supply and demand. Thus we have the problems of over-supply, under-supply, and over-stocking, and the consequent rising and falling of prices. The cleverest business men may become rich, but the majority will be ruined. The prospect of failing in business also leads to the merchant trying to pass off spurious or spoiled goods on the public, which works great harm to everyone. Even with government regulation, should the merchants not be prevented from accumulating an over-supply and hence dumping it on the market, there is a great waste of raw materials.

(In the One World era, when the whole earth is opened up, the population will be enormous, and the quantity of goods which will be needed will be tremendous. But while the population will be unlimited, the amount the earth can produce is limited. Now we can calculate all the various goods which are needed by the consumers; to turn out an excess of this requirement is not only beyond the capacity of the earth [to continue] to produce, but is also a great loss to the people. But unless we base our economic system on One World we will not be able to regulate commerce.)

CHAPTER VI

Comparison between Independent Industry and Public Industry

(GIVEN independent industries, we likewise have the problems arising from over-production of one item and under-production of another, and of the rising and falling of prices brought about by this and the difficulty of disposing of out-dated products. There is also the matter of disparity of wages, which are higher or lower according to whether there are many or few competing for the capitalist's factory jobs. These things of course bring about inequality and lowering of the moral character, in the struggle for livelihood. The total loss of goods and energy and natural resources consequent upon this competition, with its enormous quantities of goods produced only to be 'rejected', is incalculable. This can be done away with only by abolishing private industry.)

CHAPTER VII

Public Agriculture

(I N One World all agriculture, industry, and commerce will revert to the public. All lands will be public. There will be no private enterprise, and no acquisition or selling of lands. The public government will establish a ministry of agriculture; the degree governments will establish boards of agriculture; each [area] of several tens of *li* will establish its agricultural office. Students of agriculture will study under the supervision of this office, and when they have completed their studies it will assign them lands to farm. The amount of land, as well as the amount of production, will be regulated according to the needs of the times. Yearly reports will be made to the public government concerning production, and these reports, transmitted to the ministries of industry and commerce, will enable calculations to be made regarding supply and demand for the world's population. The agricultural organs will also report on natural disasters, climate, topography, suitability of the various lands for cultivation, etc., so that comparative statistics can be worked out for planning purposes. Based upon these reports, each area in the world will be assigned the most suitable and necessary type and amount of agricultural production. [Here follows a detailed breakdown of what is most suitable to be produced in various places.] The planning will extend to every detail, such as the amount and type of fertilizers, the farm animals, the machinery, and the number of farmers to be used in each case. There will be an ever greater specialization and refinement. Through the reports going up to the ministry of commerce, advance planning will be done, which will provide for proper amounts of produce to be stored up in each respective area of the world as provision against natural disasters. The farmers will purchase their implements and fertilizer from their local commercial stores.

(Under each agricultural office every few *li*, there will be a farm. Each farm will have the following officials: director, inspector, assistant inspector, manager, supervisor of storage, secretary-treasurer, clerks and apprentices. The size of the farm and the fields within it will be determined by the conditions, including the machinery, degree of cultivation, and the stage of man's knowledge at the particular time.

(Under each agricultural board there will be a geological research office which will conduct continuing studies of climate, soil, topography, suitability of various fertilizers and crops, etc., and over the years its reports will determine the progress of the degree territory. There will also be agricultural associations which will work towards such progress. Each agricultural school will have a research bureau. Graduates may become heads of farms; those who have not graduated may be farm workers, but not heads, unless they demonstrate special knowledge and creativeness—in which case they may also be given diplomas.

(The organization of the agricultural boards will be similar to that of the farm [see directly above]. They will establish sub-sections as suitable to the situation, with research bureaux to study problems of each type of product, and make public reports. These bureaux will be staffed by graduates of the proper colleges. Below the boards will be the offices, in charge of supervising and assisting the farms in their respective areas.

(Working hours, as well as the whole organization and operation of the work of the farms, will be regulated; as the world progresses and machinery becomes more refined, the hours can be shortened.) However, working hours, sitting, rising, advancing, and retiring will be almost like [the execution of] military orders.[12] The amount of talent and experience of each farmer, fisherman, and miner will be appraised, and from that his worth as a worker will be determined. [The workers] will be divided into ten grades. Those who are still superior may then be picked out and moved into the various sections of the agricultural bureaux. But the two top [officials] must be graduates [in agriculture or] engineering. [They] can be officials of the public government and the agricultural boards of the branch governments of the various continents. Those farmers, fishermen, shepherds, miners, and foresters of the lowest grade will receive salaries sufficient for their food and clothing. [They] may rise from this grade.

(Each farm will have the same kinds of facilities as the various public institutions described previously—libraries, music-halls, gardens, etc., along with living quarters, dining-halls, and stores, each as nice as a present-day wealthy home. On their days off there will be lectures and entertainments for pleasure and education. The public quarters will be furnished free; food and clothing will come out of the individual's salary. One-tenth of the salary will usually be kept back for savings. The individual may choose not to work when he wishes; however, those who are too lazy and take off too much time will be cast out and their names dishonoured. The officials, even though holding superior positions with higher salaries, will live just like everyone else to show complete equality.

(Everyone in these agrarian occupations will have the opportunity to get to the top, since there will be schooling and service afterwards which will allow talent to be developed and experience to accrue. Free from the concerns of family, free from the caprices of nature [science having overcome natural calamities], with opportunities for personal development, with transportation readily available to every place, with civilization—its new machines and its high culture—available to everyone, work will be easy and pleasant for all, and pleasures will be such as emperors could not have in past times. Along with all this, when there is planning and carrying out of plans on a world-wide scale, the evils of under- and over-production will be avoided. The benefits of this One World over the present system are so great that we cannot even describe them.)

CHAPTER VIII

Public Industry

I N One World all industry will be publicly controlled. Under the public government's ministry of industry there will be established the various degree government boards; under these there will be the public factories. It will be determined what industries are best suited to each locality, and production will be regulated accordingly. Officials of the factories will correspond to those of the farms [see above, Chapter VII]. Graduates with appropriate degrees will be eligible to hold these offices, as well as higher government posts. They will hold their positions for life, being qualified specialists, and will be placed according to the excellence of their work into one of the ten grades.

(Each board and each factory will have a professional society, to which the industrial personnel will belong. The purpose of these societies will be to disseminate knowledge of new discoveries.

(During this era factories will be unimaginably large. They will be like whole states, with their officials like the rulers and officials of states, and their offices like rulers' courts. They will be provided with the same kinds of facilities for living and enjoying life as the farms [see above, Chapter VII].)

Now the barbarous ages esteemed simplicity,[13] the Age of Complete Peace-and-Equality will esteem refinement.[14] Esteeming simplicity, [we] therefore value agriculture; [given] sufficient food, this is enough. Esteeming refinement, [we] therefore value industry. [Whatever] is wonderfully rare, extraordinarily beautiful, startling as demons and spirits, new every day without end, then [these things] are what human nature likes. Therefore, in the Era of Complete Peace-and-Equality, nothing will be more esteemed. What is most esteemed will be only industry. In the Era of Complete Peace-and-Equality, nothing will be honoured more highly. What will be honoured highly will be only the new things made by industry. In the Era of Complete Peace-and-Equality, there will be no suffering. Those who work will only enjoy it. Therefore, to make work enjoyable, art, painting, sculpture, and music will be the basis (literally, the root), and 'shrinking' the earth[15] and flying through the air will enable men to benefit themselves. Daily, new wondrous implements which are efficacious[16] and clever [will appear]. That which the government will encourage, and that to which the people will be inclined, will be entirely in [the devising of] new articles. (Those who invent new things will be awarded honours like present-day scholarly degrees, as well as large monetary prizes; this will be the way to fame and fortune in that era.)

Therefore, in the barbarous ages, industry was the humblest [occupation], the [occupation employing] the fewest; and industry was shabbily treated. In the Age of Complete Peace-and-Equality, industry will be the noblest [occupation], those who are workers will be most numerous, and industry will also be the most generously treated. After having left school all official business, agriculture, commerce, postal administration,[17] electric power and highway [construction] of the entire country will be nothing other than industry. Only medicine can be treated equally with industry. By this time, hard labour and bitter toil will be transferred to machines, used like trained animals, and men will merely control these machines. Therefore the use of one man can replace the labour of a hundred men of past times. Because [those who] work will all be educated, they will all be literate. In the Age of Complete Peace-and-Equality, the population will be increasing daily, and new machines [will appear] daily, sufficient to substitute for human labour. (This tremendous development in machines will bring about a great shortening of the working day, so that in that age workers will put in only three or four, or even less, hours per day. The time gained will be used for the education and recreation of the workers; so short will be the working day that there will be no lazy workers. Free from the cares of family, ancestral sacrifices, and marriage, with no worries about unemployment, and plenty of free time, plus the advantages of all the cultural and recreational facilities of the factories, in this age the workers will be completely happy. The individual will be able to develop himself according to his abilities; world-wide planning and control will eliminate problems of over- and under-production. Mankind will progress, becoming stronger and morally better and happier. How much better this will be than things are at present cannot even be calculated.)

CHAPTER IX

Public Commerce

I N One World all commerce will revert to the control of the ministry of commerce of the public government. The function of this ministry will thus be the distribution of all agricultural and industrial products according to the needs of the population in the various parts of the world. Each degree government will have its board, and every few *li*, as necessary, there will be offices and commercial stores. These will be administered by officials corresponding to those of the farms and factories [see above two chapters]. The boards and offices will carry on the compilation of relevant statistics concerning production and population and consumer needs; in the light of this information, distribution will be effected to the stores.

(Each city will have just one store, as big as a present-day town in some cases. The quantity and variety of goods displayed will be like a present-day exhibition fair. Goods will be sold for a fixed price. Goods may be ordered by telephone and will be sent to the buyer's home. Daily necessities may be ordered in advance and will be delivered to customers' doors as required. The size of these stores, like that of the factories, will be comparable to a small state, its officials comparable to the officials of a state, and its workers comparable to the people of a state. Of the three—farms, factories, and stores—however, the latter will be the smallest, employing the fewest persons. The 'commercial atmosphere' will be absent, since these stores will be entirely run by the government for the public. Prices will be determined according to the conditions of the times, but they will be much lower than present-day prices.)

Now the untimely fluctuations in [the prices of] goods from which people suffer are caused by the untimely production, manufacture, and distribution of [goods in] the various localities, and the private obstruction of goods [for the purpose of] cornering the market. Moreover, what is made by private industry and sold by private commerce is always [limited to] one [particular] factory or store. Small ones [employ] tens of persons, large ones employ thousands; but all have many administrative personnel [just] sitting [around] and eating. And then [there is] the expense of distribution: one distribution uses up to hundreds of persons, and the expenses of the administrative personnel and distributors is entirely a consumption of profit and not a making of profit. In one Chinese store the consumers of profit are almost half [of the total personnel]; in the various European countries, [they are] also a third or a fourth. If we take a city as a whole and figure it, then [we could] provide one emporium for one city, and [this would be] merely the same as providing ten thousand emporiums. Then we would save nine thousand nine hundred and ninety-nine. If we take the world and figure it, those who sit in stores and consume the profit are probably more than nine hundred million out of a billion. If commerce be put under public [control], then the distribution of goods will become a single [process]. Using electric and steam vehicles and boats, entirely by machines, [goods] will be distributed directly to the stores. There will not be the consumption of profits by countless distributors. All the various jobs will be done together in a single store; all the kinds of goods will be displayed [there]. There will be few employees. Where formerly each of the ten thousand stores of a single city employed ten persons, making one hundred thousand persons [altogether], now there will be [only] one store employing one thousand persons, who can handle all of it. Or if not [that few], then [at most] ten and several thousand persons will not be unable to handle it. This will enable a saving of a hundred- and several tens-fold. If we completely eliminate [this] hundred- and several tens-fold of profit-consuming persons, the price of things can [thereby] be reduced a hundred- and several tens-fold. The prices of things being cheap, buying will naturally be easy. All the goods of the whole earth being collected [in a single store], every day will be like an exhibition. Familiarity [with the latest products of all the world] will naturally be extended [among all the people], and there will not be the misfortune of people living in out-of-the-way places finding it difficult to buy [things]. Likewise, there will not be the misfortune of prices soaring a hundred and several tens-fold in out-of-the-way places [because of] the difficulty of distribution. Countries (*sic*) will provide for their people only by means of public commerce, estimating their needs, and fulfilling the public needs. Hereby the wages spent by the innumerable people of the whole earth will simply go [back] to the public. By no means will there be the taxing of individuals among the public. The evil of heavy exactions, which has existed from of old in every country, will be swept away, and the men of the Age of Complete Peace-and-Equality will not know the suffering [caused by] squeeze and extortion.[18] They will receive their wages and use [them] only for the pleasures of singing and dancing, travelling about and sightseeing. As for pleasure and profit, what could compare [with this]?

(The same provisions for living conditions will be made for the commercial workers in their stores, as for the agricultural and industrial workers [see above two chapters]. They will be educated in commercial schools—located right in the stores—and will have the same opportunities for advancement according to ability.)

CHAPTER X

General Remarks [on the Proposition that, if it is] Desired to Carry out One World in Agriculture, Industry, and Commerce, then [this must] begin by Clarifying the Human Rights of Men and Women

SUPPOSING we are anxious to obtain that the officials under whom [control of] agriculture, industry, and commerce will belong will not be corrupt, [and by their] usurpations and filchings [work] the worst harm; this anxiety is of the Age of Disorder. In the Age of Complete Peace-and-Equality, men will be without private families, without private homes, without private estate, without private stores. Being without families they will be very happy; their natures will be excellent and [their] educations thorough. [Therefore] it is certain that they will not have minds bent upon peculation, [so] peculation will just naturally not occur. [Even] should [an official] have the desire to peculate, yet there being no other private stores, though he should misappropriate and steal things, where would he sell them? If by any chance [such a case occurred and] were disclosed, then [the guilty one] would be outcast until the end of his life. Moreover, at this time people's money will all be kept in banks; the amount they earn will be equal to their labour-value and the rewards [they have been given for] their inventions. Everyone will be able to know [this amount]. Should [an official] in charge of commerce, [for example], suddenly acquire a lot of money, the traces of peculation would be obvious. Now [as for such] shameful things: if there are no family cares or poverty which compel [to them] unavoidably, who would be willing to do them, and cause [himself] to be ostracized for life? The people of the Age of Complete Peace-and-Equality will be without family cares, without poverty; a smooth road will be unending before them, and public opinion will press them from behind; morality will already be excellent, and the cultivation of education will improve it. [This situation will be] what Confucius described by saying, 'Even though you rewarded them, they would not steal.'[19] So why should we worry [about the danger of peculation]?

All the agricultural, commercial, and industrial enterprises: [considering] the immensity of the earth, how are they to be turned over to the public? If we wished to raise a public loan to undertake this [task], it would be completely impossible. Certainly the most difficult [matter to accomplish] in wishing quickly to attain One World is to abolish national states. [But] if we were to abolish private enterprise, this matter would be very easy. Then we will begin by abolishing the family. Thus our wish quickly to abolish national boundaries will also begin with the abolishing of the family.

Do we wish to abolish the family? Merely bring about that the principle of the Heaven-conferred human rights is clearly understood. Men and women are all equal and independent. [In] marriage we will not again use the terms 'husband' and 'wife', we will only permit the signing of a contract of union for [a number of] months and years, and that is all. Carry these [measures] out for sixty years, and then the peoples of all the world will no [longer have] families. There will [no longer] be private husbands and wives, fathers and sons. There will be no one to whom to bequeath property; money and personal possessions may all be given to others, [but] as for fields, factories, and merchandise, [these] will all be returned to the public. Then we can attain to One World.

The people of the earth being without families, it will then be very easy to abolish national states and attain to One World. In this time, the most difficult to abolish will be the boundary of race. [Even so, this] should only require [a few] months and years.

(Here follows another assertion of women's essential similarity to men, and their right of independence.)[20] Therefore, do the people of the whole world wish to abolish the cares of the boundary of family? It lies in making clear the equality of men and women; it begins in each having the right of independence. This is a right which Heaven has bestowed on Man. Do the people of the whole world wish to abolish the evils of private property? It lies in making clear the equality of men and women; it begins with the independence of each. This is a right which Heaven has bestowed on Man. Do the people of the whole world wish to abolish the fighting between national states? It lies in making clear the equality of men and women; it begins with the independence of each. This is a right which Heaven has bestowed on Man. Do the people of the whole world wish to abolish the struggles [caused by] the boundary of race? It lies in making clear [the equality of][21] men and women; it begins with the independence of each. This is a right which Heaven has bestowed on Man. Do the people of the whole world wish to arrive at the Age of One World, the bounds of Complete Peace-and-Equality? It lies in making clear the equality of men and women; it begins with the independence of each. This is a right which Heaven has bestowed on Man. Do the people of the whole world wish to attain to the Era of Utmost Happiness, the way of immortality? It lies in making clear the equality of men and women; it begins with the independence of each. This is a right which Heaven has bestowed on Man. Do the people of the whole world wish to refine the soul and nourish the spirit, to be without coming into being, without extinction, without increase, without diminution? It lies in making clear the equality of men and women; it begins with the independence of each. This is a right which Heaven has bestowed on Man. Do they wish [to enable] their spirit-substance to ramble, to roam all the heavens, inexhaustibly, illimitably, immeasurably, infinitely? It lies in making clear the equality of men and women; it begins with the independence of each. This is a right which Heaven has bestowed on each. I have singled out a method to obtain One World of Complete Peace-and-Equality, of utmost happiness, of immortality, without coming into being, without extinction, roaming through all the heavens, immeasurably, infinitely; and I yearn to save my fellow-men of all the world, eternally to save them from their sufferings. [This method] is but the right which Heaven has bestowed on Man: [the right to] equality and independence![22] If my Way is carried out early, [this] happiness [will be attained] early; if it is carried out late, [this] happiness [will be attained] late. If it is not carried out, then there will [continue to be] suffering without happiness. Alas! The sufferings of the world's people—is it better to be content with them, and not to seek for happiness?

REFERENCES

[1] See above, Part III, pp. 138–9, n. 2.

[2] *Lun Yü*, XVI, 1.10.

[3] 王莽 One of the most famous characters in Chinese history, he usurped the throne from A.D. 9 to A.D. 22. During his reign sweeping reforms were undertaken in the social and economic institutions of the empire; among which was the nationalization of the land.

[4] Text reads, 'recklessly carried it out' (or, 'walked it', if my rendering were to be followed through). Which is not disturbing in the Chinese, but needs modification when put into English.

[5] 傅氏 This is apparently a reference to Francois M. C. Fourier (1772–1837)—who was, of course, French, not English—and his system of *phalanges*: these were units consisting of 1,620 persons who would form communistic groups called *phalanstères*, dividing the work among them according to the talents and inclinations of the individuals composing the group. (This idea was a moving cause in the various communistic experiments in America, such as Brook Farm, Massachusetts, and Red Bank, New Jersey.)

[6] 工產之法(說). Compare below, Chapter II, p. 213, which in the Chinese text is expressed by the term 均產之說. For discussion of what our author means by 'communism', as found in the *Ta T'ung Shu*, see above, Book One, Chapter III.

[7] 工黨業主.

[8] 別成.

[9] 不平則鳴. A stock phrase.

[10] i.e. militarism and war (from Bismarck's policies).

[11] (or, 'beaten to the ground') i.e. being utterly defeated (一敗塗地 a stock phrase).

[12] Compare above, Part VI, Chapter V, no. 7, and Chapter VI, no. 7.

[13] 質   Following the rendering of Fung and Bodde, *History of Chinese Philosophy*, vol. II, p. 61.

[14] 文 Following Fung and Bodde (same reference).

[15] Through progress in transportation and communication, one presumes.

[16] 靈 飛 A rather insipid translation for the Chinese, which is made up of the words for 'spiritual power' and 'flying'.

[17] Omitting punctuation after 郵 .

[18] The Chinese is much more expressive: 'levies which flay, and pursuing-and-beating-on [for payment]'.

[19] *Lun Yü*, XII, 18.

[20] See above, Part V, throughout.

[21] Supplying these words which have been inadvertently omitted from the text.

[22] Text repeats this sentence, whether for emphasis or as typographical error is uncertain.

PART VIII

ABOLISHING ADMINISTRATIVE BOUNDARIES AND GOVERNING WITH COMPLETE PEACE-AND-EQUALITY

CHAPTER I

Dividing the Earth into a Hundred Degrees

THE entire earth will be divided into 100 degrees [each] of latitude and longitude, with 50 degrees north of the equator, 50 degrees south of the equator, and 100 degrees east and west: altogether, 10,000 degrees. The degrees near to the north and south poles will be smaller; the other degrees will each [measure] close to, and a little less than, 400 Chinese *li*, corresponding approximately to 100 English miles.[1] Taking all (literally, the four) the continents, with the sea and land [areas], and reckoning it in round figures:[2] Asia from east to west can be [put at] 7,000 English miles, and from north to south can be [put at] 5,300 English miles. Figuring in the island [areas] as well, the [total] surface area can be [put at] 700 billion square *li*, corresponding to 17 million square English miles.[3] Every 10,000 square *li* being 1 degree, altogether we obtain 1,700 degree areas.[4] Europe's length from east to west can be [put at] 3,400 English miles; its width from south to north can be [put at] 2,400 English miles; being altogether 21 billion square *li*, corresponding to 3,700,000 square English miles (*sic*). Altogether we obtain 370 degree areas. North America's length from south to north is 4,500 English miles; its width from east to west is 3,000 English miles. Figuring in the island [areas] as well, the total surface area is 8,600 square *li*, corresponding to 8,600,000 English miles.[5] Altogether we obtain 860 degree areas. South America's surface area is altogether 6,500,000 square English miles, corresponding approximately to 30 billion square *li* (*sic*). Altogether we obtain 650 degree areas. Africa and [its adjacent] islands [comprise] a surface area of 1,548,000,000 square English miles, making a total of 5,480,000,000 square *li*.[6] Altogether we obtain 1,550,000,000 degree areas (*sic!*). Australia and [its] various [adjacent] islands [comprises an area of] 92,800,000 square English miles, a total of 9,280,000,000 square *li* (*sic*). Altogether we obtain 423 degree [areas]. The grand total of the earth's land [area] is 5,238 degrees.

(The present use of 360 degrees in celestial and terrestrial measurement, being only an inexact and unhandy system carried down from the astronomical crudities of antiquity, will be replaced by the system of 100 degrees, which will greatly facilitate calculation.)[7]

CHAPTER II

The Whole Earth will be Opened Up

(IN One World, transportation, communication, and settlement of population will open up the whole earth, so that there will no longer be any isolated or backward areas. Only those regions—the torrid and frigid zones—climatically unsuited to the human constitution will remain undeveloped.)

CHAPTER III

Local Governments will take Degrees as Boundaries

(IN One World there will be no need to attach importance to geographical factors in deciding boundaries—there being no states or military strong-points—and the only boundaries will be the degrees. Markers will be set up to indicate these boundaries, and within each degree area the functions of government will be carried on [i.e. the public institutions and the establishments for public agriculture, commerce, and industry].

(The establishment of governments has in the past been a matter of geography, which determined the size of the area governed, whether a locality of ten *li* or a modern state or continent.) But this is entirely unsuitable to One World. For if we were to take one locality as a single government, then [people] of great talent [within it] would still be too few, and its material resources would be insufficient; [hence] it would be difficult to bring about prosperity. And as for the public government controlling them, [since they] would number in the hundreds, or thousands, or tens of thousands, we would fear they would be too numerous and difficult to superintend. And as for the election of persons to the public parliament, [since they] would number in the hundreds, thousands, or tens of thousands, we would fear they would be too numerous and it would be difficult to carry on [the elections]. The posting of names and distinguishing of appellations would be utterly confused, so that there would be no way to handle [the problem]. Therefore, [taking localities as the subordinate unit of government] cannot be done. Should we take individual continents, or the present-day individual states as [the subordinate unit of government], then below them we would have to set up many area sub-units of government. But [these] would be separated and far removed from the public government. It would gradually come about that gradations and inequalities would again emerge.

In the Age of One World, the [peoples] of the whole earth will all be self-governing, and the whole earth will be entirely [under one] great administration, publicly elected by all the people. The telephone, extending everywhere, will bring all places into communication. [Since] everyone will be in direct touch [with everyone else], why should we undertake to set up these many sub-governments [by] dividing up continents or dividing up the [present-day] states? Only [the units formed by] the individual degrees of territory, which will connect with the public government of the globe above, and will unite the people [within them] below, are suitable by size and fitting by number. Therefore, we can establish [these degree-areas] as the [unit of] local self-government.

(The network of communication and transportation in this era will make an area of that size no bigger than a city of today, so far as convenience of administration is concerned. Yet such an area will have a sufficient population to ensure the development of human and material resources. The total number of local degree governments will be three thousand and some; hence there will be three thousand and some members of parliament. Although this may seem a rather large number, yet it will not be impractical to elect them, since each degree area will publicly elect its own representatives, and the administrative officers of the public government will likewise be elected by their own degree areas. Not only will the tremendously increased speed of transportation and communication make it easy for such large units as the public government and the degree governments to carry on their functions, but the substitution of degree governments for the present forms will also help to abolish the boundaries between men.)

CHAPTER IV

The Governmental Structure of the Universal, One-World Government

(THE public government will have the following twenty ministries:

(1. Ministry of the People [the senior ministry, in charge of the various public institutions].

(2. Ministry of Agriculture.

(3. Ministry of Pasture.

(4. Ministry of Fishery.

(5. Ministry of Mines.

(6. Ministry of Industry.

(7. Ministry of Commerce.

(8. Ministry of Finance [most powerful of the ministries, controlling all banks and fiscal affairs].

(9. Ministry of Development [in charge of public works and opening up of inaccessible or unused regions].

(10. Ministry of Waters [in charge of rivers and waterways, including the oceans].

(11. Ministry of Railroads.

(12. Ministry of the Post.

(13. Ministry of Electrical Communications.

(14. Ministry of Ships.

(15. Ministry of Air [in charge of 'flying machines' and 'flying boats'].[8]

(16. Ministry of Health.

(17. Ministry of Letters. [Also in charge of meteorological observations.]

(18. Ministry of Encouraging Knowledge.[9]

(19. Ministry of Teaching the Way. [Charged with promotion of, and control over, ethical, religious, and soul-purifying teachings.]

(20. Ministry of Utmost Happiness. [Charged with promotion of the arts, museums, zoos, etc.]

(There will be the following four *yüan* in the public government:

(1. Conference *Yüan* [meetings of appropriate ministries to confer on particular topics which may arise in connection with the government and its business].

(2. Upper House of Parliament [composed of one representative elected from each degree area. This body 'will deliberate on the world laws and official regulations, and will also control the important legal judgments, the exhortations of the government (to the people), and the criticism (i.e. ? censorship) of literature and art'].

(3. Lower House of Parliament [merely a recording and communicating office, without representatives].

(4. Public Information *Yüan* [collects and disseminates information from and to the degree governments and the public government. Staffed by persons publicly elected from each of the degree areas].

(There will be boards [under the various ministries], with the following officials: director, branch director, sub-director, manager, or executive secretary, treasurer, secretary, and clerks and servants. Directors and sub-directors will be elected from among the directors and sub-directors of the degree governments, and must be persons of the highest wisdom and *jen*.)

Regarding political parties: Only with competition can there be progress. Without competition there is no advancement. But competition depraves the workings of human nature. Nowadays, [wherever] constitutional government has been established, the political leaders all compete [by means of their] political parties throughout the country. All is darkness and confusion[10] [as they] go clamouring about the roads, calling for party followers. They plan secretly and attack each other, sometimes going so far as to use military force to stab [each other]. Before the elections, when the multitudes of people are gathered in a crowd, milling about irresolutely, [the politicians] spread out quantities of food and drink so as to coax the people [to vote for them]. It is thus improbable that the selection will be fair. [Or] even if it is fair, there will still be a big fight. [Such things] deprave the workings of men's minds, attacking the roots and the seed. This absolutely cannot be tolerated.

In the Age of One World there will be no national struggles, no secret schemes. In great undertakings it will not[11] be necessary to put the power into [the hands of] political leaders or to set up autocratic leaders. The laws and regulations of the ten thousand and some hundreds of administrative [? organs] will all [be determined] through universal public discussion. Other affairs will be carried on solely by the various small degree governments. All matters will be decided by public vote. Even though the public governments were by name a presidency, in actuality [the president] would be without power. He would merely sit and receive the formulated [decisions] of the various degrees, and would preside over the accounting, the regulation of details, the encouragement [? of excellence in wisdom and *jen*], and that is all. Therefore it is not necessary that we have a person to carry out the functions of president. The various ministers cannot be appointed by a single person (i.e. a president), [but] will all be elected by the various boards of the various degrees.

On election day the questioning and answering (i.e. the process of voting) will be done by telephone, and [officials] will be given office (literally, used) according to the majority [vote]. There will be no competing or clamouring; there will decidedly be no mutual attacking or assassinating. Thus there will be no injury to the workings of men's minds. [When the people of that age] look [back] at the political strife of today, they will consider it as the behaviour of savages, and ridiculous. (Moreover, one will decline twice and thrice before accepting office, fostering the spirit of modesty. One who did not so decline would be thought shameless, and be damned by public opinion. High office in this era will be more of an honour than a real responsibility, as actual decisions on affairs will be in the hands of the public.

(In the conduct of parliamentary business, a certain dignity and decorum is called for which is so lacking in present-day representatives that they are utterly barbaric and shameful. This will not be so in the One World era, as the standards of virtue and education will then be so high that members of parliament will be persons of lofty morality and character.

(There will be three levels of government: the local, the degree, and the public government. There will be no distinctions between the people of the world, except for the special honours bestowed on those outstanding for knowledge and *jen*.)

CHAPTER V

The Governmental Structure of the Degree Governments

(FOLLOWING in general the pattern of the public government, the degree governments will have the following boards:
    (1. Board of the People.
    (2. Board of Agriculture [includes fishery, forestry, pasture, and any other special kind of agricultural production of the particular area].
    (3. Board of Mining.
    (4. Board of Industry.
    (5. Board of Commerce.
    (6. Board of Finance.
    (7. Board of Development.
    (8. Board of Waters.
    (9. Board of Communications [roads, ships, railroads].
    (10. Board of Medicine.
    (11. Board of Letters [the educational institutions, libraries, and meteorological bureaux].
    (12. Board of [Teaching] the Way.
    (13. Board of [Encouraging] Knowledge.
    (14. Board of [Utmost] Happiness.

(Likewise following the pattern of the public government, there will be the following four *yüan* in the degree governments:
    (1. Conference *Yüan*.
    (2. Upper House of Parliament [composed of the most

distinguished elders of the degree, their number to be determined in accordance with the population, but generally speaking, several hundred. Heads of the boards will be members also].

(3. Lower House of Parliament [merely a recording and communicating organ].

(4. Public Information *Yüan* [an official from the Public Government will be delegated to act jointly with the elected officials of the degree. They will investigate and report on conditions within the degree, upwards to the public government, and downwards to the people of the degree].

(The absence of legal organs and foreign affairs organs is explained by the fact that there will be no punishments or litigation, no armed forces, no international intercourse [there being no sovereign states]. Officials are merely 'public servants'.

(There will be five grades of officials in the various boards, who will be elected from the local self-government districts, and who will serve for life. These officials will be elected by the officials of the local district and the officials of the board concerned [rather than directly by the people].)

CHAPTER VI

Public Communications

(THE entire earth will be served by complete networks of communications, all of which will be under the public government, and manned by graduates of special schools.)

CHAPTER VII

Public Development

(THE opening up of isolated and undeveloped territory will be 'the greatest task' of the One World era. The public institutions will be placed on high mountains to take advantage of the healthful mountain air. Places of natural beauty, such as crags, peaks, torrents, and the like, will be made into public parks, and equipped with suspended bridges, hanging glass rooms for taking in the view, etc.) [In the Age of] Disorder, people lived mostly in caves in the mountains; [in the Age of] Increasing Peace-and-Equality, people live mostly in buildings on the plains; in the Age of Complete Peace-and-Equality, and of Utmost Happiness, people will again live in the mountains, completing the cycle and returning to the beginnings.

(Ships in this age will be unimaginably huge, equipped with everything conducive to the happiness of travellers. People may live on them and enjoy the pleasures of the sea for days and months. Water will be brought to the deserts; great canals and bridges will be constructed. With all the resources of the public government brought to bear, the whole earth will be made habitable and productive within less than several hundreds of years. The machinery which will be developed will enable all these great works to be carried out without even much labour.)

CHAPTER VIII

Local Self-Government

(THE cities of this era will mostly be located on mountain tops, seashores, and islands, with many also along the upper courses of rivers. The population of the world will dwell in the quarters provided by whichever ministry their work falls under—agriculture, industry, [one of the ministries concerned with] transportation, development—or in one of the public institutions; there will be almost no private homes. Hence people will be gathered together in these great institutions and will not be scattered about in small villages. The transportation and communication facilities of this age will make it easy to get out to the fields while living at a distance from them; and so these fields likewise may be very large. Wherever there are farms, then the other establishments, such as stores, post offices, railroad stations, etc., will naturally follow. Hence the farm, with its attached establishments, will be the equivalent of today's village, and will constitute the unit of local government. The director of the farm will be the head of the local government, and the directors of the subsidiary establishments will be his assistants.

Local questions will be publicly discussed and voted upon. Matters requiring to be brought to the attention of higher governmental agencies will be presented by the farm director in his capacity of representative of those signing a petition on the matter. Meetings of the local government will take place monthly and reports of the proceedings will be transmitted upwards to the agricultural office.

(Similarly, the equivalent of today's towns and cities will be the factory of that era; and the director of the factory will be the head of the local government. Procedures will be identical with those for the farm as described above.

(In every case there will be, in addition to the ten public institutions, banks, parks, zoos, museums, botanical gardens, music-halls, art galleries, halls in which the Way will be expounded, great stores, postal and telegraphic offices, airfields, ship docks, and railroad stations. In the factories there will be departments of roads, police, sanitation, teaching the Way, courts,[12] and weather forecasting. Where suitable, there will be departments of waterways or of developing the mountains.

(Personnel for all these agencies will be elected by the council, which will meet every few months. All persons will have the right to speak at these meetings, and all decisions will be made by majority vote. Officers will be elected from among those of the populace who have been decorated for their *jen* and knowledge. There will also be a public information office.

(There is a brief chart at the end of this chapter, illustrating the above-described local government system. Included under the control of local governments are the ten public institutions.)

CHAPTER IX

Public Banks

(THERE will be a completely centralized banking system, with branch banks established in the various governmental levels, institutions, farms, factories, etc. There will be no private banks. People will save money in these banks, and may be paid from their savings when they are not working. The banks will all make yearly and monthly statements of receipts and expenditures to the public government.

(The money of this age will be of two kinds, gold and silver; with paper currency representing the metals. It is also possible that silver may not be used, but only gold. Denominations [of currency] will be 10's, 100's, and 1,000's. Banks of this time will actually be 'gold stores' rather than 'silver stores'.[13] All paper notes will be issued solely by the public banks.) '[Paper currency] will be issued by the public printery inexhaustibly, affording the people an abundance, and [enabling them] to have much happiness.'

(There will be the same kinds of officials staffing the banks as in the previously discussed organizations. The superior grades will be filled by wealthy persons from commercial or other occupations. For in this age to have accumulated wealth will mean that a person has contributed towards the advancement of civilization through new ideas or inventions, or through great manifestation of *jen*.)[14] Because, in the Age of One World, of those whose power will be greatest, none will be equal to the banks; therefore it cannot but be that we take [their functioning and effective operation] as highly important.

In the Age of Complete Peace-and-Equality, all agriculture, industry, and commerce will proceed from the public government. There will be absolutely no competing. The root of [human] nature will be completely tranquil. Now, things progress through competition, and without competition there is laxness and decadence, as in the Age of China's First Reign (i.e. the First System, or Hsia dynasty). Than decadence, nothing could be more injurious to the world. [In such conditions] men would revert to stupidity. Men having become stupid, then their activities would all be destructive, and grave calamities would ensue. Before long One World would have reverted to the Age of Disorder. This we cannot but guard against.

[However], should we lead men to compete, we would also fear that [this] would implant [the spirit of strife] in the root of [human] nature, and that the disaster of fighting[15] would arise. The two are related ills.

Moreover, in the Age of Complete Peace-and-Equality, agriculture, industry, commerce, education, railroads, postal service, electric lines, steamships, and flying boats all proceed from the public. Men all work, and all have only their work-wages. There being no poor or wealthy, then it will be difficult for new imple-ments[16] to be widely sold, and new machines will cease [to be produced]. Moreover, it is certain that these [various things] could not then be [continually] improved, and that decay would ensue. When in all things there is decay, and men have reverted to stupidity, One World can likewise not endure for long. Then [the world] would again revert to [the Age of] Disorder.

Now, the Way of Heaven (i.e. nature) is not peaceful. Not being peaceful, it is then disorderly. The Way of Man (i.e. human life) is affected by the afflictions of [this] disorder, and so [men] decide to co-operate and seek with all their might for peace. But when they have won through to the time of peace, then the afflictions of peace also arise. [We must] 'complete the partial and restore the deteriorated';[17] we cannot but worry about [this danger] and deeply [ponder a means] to guard against it. This is our gravest anxiety for [the Age of] Complete Peace-and-Equality. In thinking of means of guarding against [this] deterioration, and of finding a middle way between [these] two ills, there are then two paths [to accomplish this]. (For which, we turn to the following two chapters.)

CHAPTER X

Striving for Excellence

RECKONING by the progress of mankind as a whole: In the Age of One World . . . everything will proceed from the public [government]; if there is no competition, how can there be improvement, how can there be progress? Assuredly, if we sit [idly] by and permit this deterioration, the damage [thereby wrought] will also be severe. This [being the case], we cannot but spur them on.[18]

(The degree governments will be responsible for seeing to the management and improvement of the various public institutions, and will also have charge of the planning, operation, and improve-ment of the transportation and communication facilities within their area—or this latter may be handled by the public government if it

242 THE ONE-WORLD PHILOSOPHY OF K'ANG YU-WEI

is more feasible. The degree governments will be autonomous in their control of the farms, factories, and stores. Thus the benefits and losses from these enterprises will be received by the people of the degree concerned as a result of their own decisions and actions. A rise of prices would be the result of the decision of the people themselves, and not of the oppression of the public government; the benefits would accrue to the public, with but slight loss to the individual. Hence everyone would agree happily to such a thing. The public government will publish lists of those who have distinguished themselves in the advancement of the public weal. There will be inter-degree expositions at which the people of the various degrees will strive to outdo each other. From this kind of competition will come both individual benefit and public honour. We will not fear stagnation and retrogression.)

CHAPTER XI

Encouraging Knowledge

RECKONING by the progress of the individual: In the time of One World everyone will perform work, there will not be high and low, and wages—although there will be slight disparities—cannot be very disparate. And so human knowedge [might] fail to develop, and implements, plans, theories, and ideas [might] be unable daily to come forth, new and different. Then there would be obstruction and loss, and more than that, there would be a decline [of civilization].

(Therefore, in order that knowledge may continue to advance, we will encourage four types of contributions:

(1. New books—on any subject, scientific, artistic, literary. There will be three grades:

(a) Books on new principles; those who establish new principles will be considered sagelike and wise.

(b) Books on new methods; those who establish new methods will be considered clever and ingenious.

(c) Books on new benefits; those who establish new benefits will be considered intelligent and sagacious.

(2. New inventions—material objects. There will be established grades according to the amount of individual or public benefit resulting therefrom.

(3. New theories—by which is meant the usual type of scholarly activity. The theories will be graded according to their importance.

(4. New techniques—including not only techniques used in manufacturing, but also in government, education, the arts, and music.

(There will be in the public government a *yüan*, in the continents sub-*yüan*, and in the degree governments offices,[19] for the granting of patents and the awarding of subsidies to assist those who are engaged in advancing knowledge. Rewards for contributions to the advancement of knowledge will be of two kinds: rewards of 'name' [honourable titles] and rewards of 'substance' [money].

(As for the former kind of reward, such honourable titles will be awarded in a scale corresponding to the number of new inventions and discoveries of the recipient: for one, 'person of knowledge'; a new award to be given for each additional contribution until after ten contributions the title of 'person of much knowledge'; the title of 'person of great knowledge' for outstanding contributions; and after ten times receiving this award, the new title of 'person of highest knowledge'. Those still more eminent will be titled 'wise person'; those of surpassing eminence will be called 'sage'. However, there will be no regulations established for earning these latter two titles; they will be given by unanimous decision of the public parliament to rare individuals chosen from among the 'persons of highest knowledge'. The title of 'person of knowledge' will correspond to the present-day *hsiu-ts'ai*; 'person of much knowledge' will correspond to our *chü-jen*; there will be a title of 'scholar' which will correspond to our *chin-shih*; 'person of great knowledge' will correspond to our *han-lin*; there will be a title of 'doctor of learning' which will correspond to our *ting-chia*, [the highest three in the Palace Examination given to *han-lin*]; 'person of highest knowledge' will correspond to our *chuang-yüan* [the highest in the Palace Examination]. Those called 'wise person 'and 'sage' will be very few and far between; this will ordinarily be a posthumous title.

(Although there will exist the above-described grades of title, relatively few persons will attain the higher titles. However monetary rewards will be given out much more liberally, on a scale divided into hundreds of grades. Even the lowest reward will be substantial enough to enable such persons to continue to contribute new things.

(All the grades of honour will be publicly manifested by the wearing of badges.[20] After death the memory of exceptional persons will be kept alive by means of statues and plaques.[21]

(Conferring of the title of 'person of knowledge' will be done by all the 'scholars' and 'doctors' of the degree area concerned acting in committee together with designated officials of the various public enterprises and the schools, as well as other appropriate consultees. The continental sub-*yüan* will confer the title of 'person of great knowledge' by selection of the 'doctors' and other suitable persons acting in committee. Scholarly degrees will not be given by the degree governments themselves. Authority to confer the titles of 'doctor' and above will rest with the ministry[22] of encouraging knowledge of the public government, composed of the most distinguished scholars of the world; the continental sub-*yüan* will not have this authority. All awards will be made only on the basis of ability, and without any fixed limit as to number.

(During this time the thoughts and wills of people will be directed to finding new things and new ways): For the Age of Complete Peace-and-Equality will be without competition. Its striving must be in making the new! Its struggling must be in encouraging knowledge! The more the struggling for knowledge, the more it will develop. The more the striving for the new, the more it will arise. Thus man's life on earth will daily be advanced, and we will not fear retrogression.

CHAPTER XII

Encouraging Jen

(THERE being no royalty, nobility, or classes in One World, the only two things to which people will aspire for honour's sake are knowledge and *jen*. There will be no point in accumulating a lot of money, since people will not have such expenses as supporting a family, providing for sacrifices, laying up against sickness, etc. They will not need money for a large home, as they will live together in couples [the children of course being in the public institutions]. Art treasures will belong to the public. Aside from use in travelling, therefore, people will not need much money. A 'climate of goodness' will encourage the general tendency of men's natures towards goodness. Within the public government there will be established a [?] ministry of encouraging *jen*:[23] there will be sub-*yüan* in the continents, and offices in each degree.[24] Titles of honour will be given to persons distinguishing themselves for *jen*, similarly to the system of awards for knowledge. In ascending degrees of merit, there will be the following titles: 'person of *jen*', 'person of superior *jen*', 'person of great *jen*', 'person of utmost *jen*', 'great person', and 'divine person'. The latter two titles will rarely be conferred.

(The awarding of these titles will be made to those persons who have distinguished themselves for their services in the public institutions, or for other acts contributing to the public weal, such as giving books to libraries, donating to public institutions, establishing parks, repairing bridges, putting through roads. Since the 'social security' coverage under the One World system will be so complete, there will not exist the opportunity for many of the philanthropic deeds typical of today. However, such a great undertaking as cutting through a mountain or digging a canal would be worthy of high honour. Monetary awards will accompany the titles for *jen*, as in the case of titles for knowledge.

(And those persons who are distinguished both for knowledge and *jen* will receive fitting titles, ranging from 'excellent person' to 'godlike person'—for one who was accounted a 'divine person' as well as a 'sage'.

(In conducting public business, in public gatherings and at banquets, there will be an order of precedence based on the grade of title of knowledge or *jen*.) For in the Age of Complete Peace-and-Equality they will honour virtue and not nobility [of blood]. Thereby men will be caused to exert [themselves] in *tao* and *te* (the highest ideals of human morality), and to make excellent their behaviour. Thereby men will be caused to become compassionate and propitious (*sic*), and complete in public morality. Thereby men will be caused to increase in intelligence and to receive universal benefits.

(However, the honouring of sages and great men will also have its limits. Should there be a return to the unification of people's beliefs under a religious leader, then there would result a return to the stupidities of the past. Those sages and religious leaders of ancient times who contributed to the universal principles of One World will be honoured according to the extent of their contributions to these ideas. As for other influential persons in history, some will be honoured, others not. Those who worked only for their own state, such as Chu-ko Liang,[25] would not be honoured. Men of war, such as Bismarck, would be regarded as bandits. However, men like Napoleon, who fostered the people's rights, would be honoured accordingly. And aside from the religious leaders, thinkers like Lao Tzu, Chu Hsi, Wang Yang-ming,[26] etc., would be honoured for their important influence on later generations, as would [for example] Martin Luther, Manu of India, or Columbus.)

CHAPTER XIII

Schools

(THE increase of knowledge being a main objective of the Age of One World, great emphasis will be laid on schools. There will be universal education until the age of twenty. Language and culture being unified, there being no worry about livelihood, and all necessary books and equipment being provided, the progress of education will be great. We cannot specify the contents of the curriculum, as that will be determined according to the needs of the time.)

[However], as to its general principles, aside from moral, intellectual, and physical education, practical education will be most important; therefore the curriculum of the colleges will specialize in this [practical education]. When we come to ancient history, it is a review of antiquity for those preparing themselves in broad scholarship, and that is all. Its usefulness is very slight, [for at that time the civilization of the Age of Disorder] will seem like contemporary men's view of the wild *Yao* and *Man* savages: examined for evidences of advancement [in civilization], we may be but a laughing-stock. As for the obscurities of logic and empty [? speculations] on the soul, scholars may pursue them on their own [initiative], and scholarly societies may be founded to investigate them; [but] they are not what will concern the public schools, and so they will not be taught in the public schools.

(Schools will all be equal, and we will not have the present situation in which the good schools are all concentrated in the cities, and the countryside has but inferior schools. Things will be equal everywhere, except for the climatically unsuitable regions in which public institutions will not be established at all. There will be a ministry in the public government, and boards in the degree governments, to supervise education. Changes in the schools will be decided upon by vote, following upon joint discussions by the schools of the degree area concerned.)

CHAPTER XIV

Punishments Discarded

CONFUCIUS said, 'It is essential that there be no litigation.'[27] In the Age of Complete Peace-and-Equality, good order will extend to the point where punishments are discarded. Then there will be perfect order. How tragic is the Age of Disorder! In human existence dispositions are evil and natures are stupid. [People] provoke punishment and fall into the meshes [of the law]. [There are] the slicing off of flesh, the severing of [the head from] the body, the exacting of retributions from the relatives. As for the injury and shame, the depraving of customs, and the steeping of the Heaven[-conferred] nature [in evil], this is still worse.

Now there are always reasons for men originally sinning to the point of incurring punishment. If during a man's life he has a body and has a family, then he cannot help but be in straits. It is natural. Being poor, he cannot bear it. Since he cannot bear it, then [he commits such] deeds as robbery, swindling, bribery, fraud, counterfeiting, smuggling, blackmail, [unlawful] levying of taxes, usurpation, extortion, absconding, gambling—to the extreme [crime] of murder. We do not try to save him from the original cause of poverty, but treat him with severe punishments. [But] if clothing and food are inadequate, who can have considerations of shame, or fear of the law?

Men are born because there are the life-planting organs, and we cannot do without the desire for sexual intercourse. It is natural. Because it is natural, it necessarily cannot be prevented. Since it necessarily cannot be prevented, then there will necessarily be deeds inspired by lust, ranging from passionate desire, rape, taking [a woman] by force, and adultery, to incest, disordering the blood-line, murder, and ruining the family. Even though there be tens or hundreds of thousands of Brahmins, Buddhas, and Christs who want to save them and wish to extinguish their desires, it will certainly be impossible to bring about the extinguishing of the desire for sexual union among mankind throughout the world. [And even] supposing it were possible to extinguish it by causing them to follow their teachings, then the human species throughout the world would, in only a few decades, become completely extinct. Then the earth would again become a world of grasses and trees, birds and beasts. But supposing it were possible to bring about that for an age (literally, for ever) it would be a world of grasses and trees, birds and beasts; yet, before long, the animal species would progress and evolve into humans. Abilities and knowledge would again develop, and there would likewise be competition. Such a futile reversion of the world to a jungle, after the infinitely long ages of sufferings whereby it has been able to become civilized, would be the greatest of calamities. The harm of this would exceed the harm caused by universal sexual immorality by no less than as many times as there are sands of the Ganges. For this reason it is fortunate that men do not completely follow the teachings of all the religious leaders. Should they completely follow them, then the human species would be annihilated, and the worse calamity would have befallen.

We do not approve of the source whence springs the seeking to gratify the desires, but vainly treat [men] with severe laws. [But] if not given [gratification of] the sexual desires, who can have considerations of shame, or fear of the law?

If we have rulers and superiors, then we shall have [political] struggles, and overthrowing of the state by military force. If we have fathers and sons, elder and younger brothers, and the clan, then we shall have relatives, and lawsuits will arise out of the need (literally, hope) to support them, the compulsion to do the right thing by them, and the wrangling over [property] shares. If we have husbands and wives, then [we shall have] contentions over sex, contentions due to lust; and with the prohibitions [placed on] lechery, the grievances and hatreds [so engendered] will lead to cases so serious as to warrant the punishment of death. If we have hereditary nobility, then there will arise cases of intriguing for position, toadying, fraud, reliance on force, arrogance, and exaction. If we have private property, then there will be much litigation over fields and houses, over industry, over articles of commerce. If we have burial of the dead, then we will have litigation over the cemetery. If we have customs barriers, then the crimes of evasion and smuggling will result. If we have military forces, then military laws are even more severe, and men are cut down like weeds. If we have class divisions, then will arise the oppressive laws of the superior [class], and their violation and opposition by the lower [classes].

All this aside; to disregard man's passions, to depart from man's nature, to go counter to man's desires, is to [hold to] visionary hopes without [possibility of] attainment; it is to weight [men] down with responsibilities [they] cannot bear.

Things being like this, [then we have] set up a snare and dug a pit, and [thereby] caused that men should be punished, and have incited them to litigation. [For under these conditions, punishments and litigations] are things which cannot be avoided in the course of life. If we do not know how to remedy this, but daily amplify the laws like the hairs of the ox, daily discuss the lightening of the punishments like a compassionate mother, daily talk of *tao* and *te* (morality) like all the religious leaders, [then] we shall never be able to save [humanity] . . .

This being the case, what is to be done? The medicine [to cure] the present age has not yet been provided. [But] I have thought of a prescription to save it. The healing in the future of this immeasurably great illness must lie in the application of this [prescription].

Confucius said, 'The Way is not far removed from men. If the way a man pursues is far removed from men, it cannot be considered as the Way.'[28] Chuang Tzu (369?–286? B.C.) criticized Mo Tzu (c. 479–c. 381 B.C.), saying, 'To have a mind to set themselves apart from this world, human beings are not able. To set oneself apart from the world is to go far astray from the Kingly [Way].'[29] The teachings of Mo Tzu cannot be carried out, for the reason that they cannot be tolerated by human beings. Now do not the Ways [taught by] all the religious leaders likewise set [men] apart from the world, [so that] human beings cannot tolerate [them]? It is only the Way of One World [which can be tolerated by human beings, and can save the world] . . .

Man is endowed with Heaven[-conferred] rights. Each [human being] is independent. [Hereby], women are already not [creatures] whom men can compel to be their own [property]. They mate together, and have intercourse, only because each is gratifying [his or her] Heaven[-conferred] nature. With regard to the forms of male and female, it may be compared to the mechanism of a lock. The 'finger' is inserted into the 'mouth', and 'saliva' flows into the place. What has this to do with the law, that strict prohibitions should be established to deal with it? Constructing a strong wall just when notified of an artillery attack, or setting up a high dyke just as the water inundates, certainly cannot prevent [disaster]; we had just as well level them. Therefore [this] is not as good as being completely without walls and dykes.

Moreover, when a man has a concubine,[30] it is considered morally right; [but] when a woman has a paramour it is considered wicked. Thus [we see that] severe punishments and stern laws have been especially devised by men only [to serve their] selfishness. In the time of One World, when human rights have all been established, how could we have [such punishments and laws]!

(Therefore, in One World, absolute freedom will prevail with regard to sexual relations, so far as adults are concerned. Minors—those under twenty—who will still be in the educational institutions will not be allowed freedom; however, control over minors will be in the hands of their teachers, and will not be a matter for the law. Offences will be punished by the force of opinion, and by dishonouring of the person's name. Adults who force minors into sexual relations should be severely punished; however, that sort of thing is caused by the repressions which prevail in the Age of Disorder, and when people are free to satisfy their sexual desire in a natural way, there will be no need to satisfy it in a criminal way. Should this latter nevertheless occur, the matter will be referred to the public parliament for decision as to the punishment.)

For laws are established for the purpose of preventing the doing of evil. If there still remain those with evil desires like this in the Age of Complete Peace-and-Equality, they would certainly be men without self-respect, who would not fear the law [in any case]. Hence there is no need to toil [over the writing of] books on laws and punishments. With other cases it will be the same. For in antiquity, when laws had not been established, affairs were regulated by discussion. In the Middle Age there are laws to prevent evil [deeds]. In [the Age of] Complete Peace-and-Equality there will be no laws—a return to the ways of antiquity: because men will not be evil, it will be unnecessary to guard against [evil deeds]. Sexual relations with women being easy [for men to obtain], there certainly will be no [sex] crimes. But 'a beautiful man breaks down [? the indifference] of age',[31] and there certainly will also be [men] who enjoy sexual relations with men. Even Socrates had this [inclination]. Although [homosexuality] does not conform with *yin* and *yang*, and may be harmful to the body, yet [normal] sexual [relations] are also not without harmful [effects]. The passions having been permitted their freedom, if [homosexual] union is not accomplished by coercion, then there is no reason to prohibit it.

Now in universal principles originally there is no 'good' or 'evil'. [Our concepts of] right and wrong are all according to what the sages have constituted. The Buddhist Law proscribes fornication; hence, that Confucius had a wife was a transgression against [this] proscription, and he should be cast down into hell. Confucius said that to be without posterity is the gravest unfiliality; hence, the two religious leaders, Buddha and Christ, likewise transgressed against the proscription [laid down by Confucius]. The Lotus [School][32] produced Shinran,[33] and [he and] Martin Luther publicly founded new teachings (or, religions) within the bounds of Buddhism and Christianity, and carried on fornication; but the world likewise did not [consider] them to be wrongdoers—in fact, there were many who followed them ... Thus we know that [what constitutes] 'good' and 'evil' is difficult to determine, and 'right' and 'wrong' [take their meaning] from the times. However, 'right' and 'wrong', 'good' and 'evil', all [take their meaning] from human life; universal principles likewise are determined from the [circumstances of] the times. As I figure it, whatever is injurious to man is wrong; whatever is not injurious to man is right.

The old prohibition against homosexuality [was based on] the fear that [the husband] would like that and dislike this (i.e. he would like relations with men and dislike relations with women); it was a precaution against injury to [continuance of the family's] posterity, and the decline of the human species. Therefore it was prohibited. In the Age of Complete Peace-and-Equality, men and women will be equal, everyone will be independent, everyone will be free. There will be no differences of dress. In the holding of positions [men and women] will be entirely alike. There will be no return to the distinctions between men and women. [So] if we are talking about sexual relations, then the intercourse of a woman with a man, or of a man with a man, will be the same thing. At this time people will be completely content; we [need] not fear that mankind will not be numerous, or be overly anxious [about continuation of the species]. Those who take delight in intercourse [with each other], regardless of whether it be a man and a woman, or two men, will always go to the official [in charge of these matters][34] and make their contract, so as to avoid other disputes.

However, intercourse of men with beasts greatly disorders the intelligent species; because it leads to decadence [of the human species], it cannot but be strictly prohibited. In remote antiquity, intercourse with beasts was most frequent. Man's own origin is likewise from the intercourse of intelligent beasts. [From thence] he evolved into [his present form]. (Among certain peoples, as for example in India and among the Jews,[35] the practice of copulation with animals is still not entirely abandoned. The author cites several stories about the offspring of such unions—one from a report in a Canadian newspaper. Such great offences against the species should be strictly forbidden.) However, investigating their cause, [we find that] all of [these abnormal acts] result from [the fact that] the laws of the Middle Age against [normal] intercourse are too strict; while the great surges of human desire cannot be restrained. (There being no such restrictions in One World, there will likewise be no abnormal outlets needed for the desires. Should there be cases of perversion, then the punishment will be public shame and degradation from the status of equality with other persons.)

In One World[36] there will be no states, therefore there will be no severe military laws. There will be no rulers, and so there will be no cases of opposing the superior and creating rebellion. There will be no husbands and wives, and so there will be no fighting over sexual desire, no provisions against sexual immorality, no repressive regulations or bearing of grievances, no resentment or hatred, no divorces, no miseries of punishment and killing. There will be no family relationships, and so there will be no need to support [one's family members], no compulsion to do the right thing [by them], no wrangling over [property shares]. There will be no nobility, and so there will be no depending upon intimidation or coercion, no oppression, no grabbing, no intriguing for position, no toadying.[37] There will be no private property, so there will be no litigation over fields and houses, over industry and commerce, or over production. There will be no burial of the dead, and so there will be no litigation over the cemetery. There will be no customs barriers, and so there will be no crimes of evasion and smuggling. There will be no class divisions, and so there will be no mistreatment or oppressive laws [on the part of the superior class], and their violation and opposition [by the inferior classes].

Aside from this, then, what crimes will still exist, what punishments will still exist? I think that in the time of One World, while there may be faults (or, mistakes), there cannot be sins (or, crimes). What will these faults be? In a job or in official position, there may be negligence or mistakes, or discourtesy or gossip. Through the influence of twenty years' schooling, conduct and customs will be excellent, human nature will have become perfected, and [men's] energies will also be abundant; with this, even faults and mistakes should just about be eliminated. [Even] if we say they will necessarily exist, yet they will not be [serious enough] to be dealt with by laws and litigation. Therefore, in the Age of One World, there will be the hundred (i.e. all kinds of) officials, but two [kinds] of officials—military and punishment—there will not be. [Cases of] faults and mistakes [within] the various jobs and official positions, [cases of] discourtesy and gossip which are contrary to correct social behaviour, will all be referred to the officers [of the offender's] own [organization]. [Such cases] will be [dealt with] by precept and example, or at most by adding on a fine. Now even superior men have arguments,[38] and it may be that in the Age of Complete Peace-and-Equality we shall not be able to be without [them]. In that event we will publicly invite men to judge and settle the rights and wrongs (literally, the crooked and straight) [of the argument]. It will not be necessary to establish officials to adjust [such arguments].

Therefore, in the Age of Complete Peace-and-Equality, there will be no litigation; in the Age of One World punishments will be discarded. For everyone will act like a scholar and a gentleman[39] without being controlled. Therefore, in the Age of Complete Peace-and-Equality, punishments will not be established; there will exist only the rules and regulations of the various official positions and jobs. Though there be negligence of duty and breaking of the regulations, they will not involve punishments under criminal law. Aside from the regulations of the official positions [and jobs], there will be established a law of only four provisions. (For which, see the following chapter.)

CHAPTER XV

Four Prohibitions

The first prohibition: [against] laziness

IN the Age of Complete Peace-and-Equality, [there will be] parks and music, and men and women will enjoy themselves together, drinking and eating, singing and dancing. [But if] people are too given over to pleasure, then they will not do work. Besides which, there will be the institution for the poor to take them in. Should everyone become [lazy] like this, then everything would go to ruin, machinery would gather rust, and civilization would fail completely. [Thus, One World] would go into decline. Therefore, in its ability to bring about a reversion of the Age of One World to the Age of Disorder, there is nothing more damaging than laziness. Hence it should be strictly prohibited.

Those who are lazy in their work will be fined according to the number of days [involved]. Should [their laziness] exceed a month, then they will be disgraced. [Should it] continue still longer, then [the offender] will be deprived of eligibility to hold higher office. Those who enter the institution for the poor will be put to hard labour. If not exceedingly wealthy, and so certified by a bank, a person who does not work for a long time should always have a fine set for him. For the enterprises and the administration of One World are all the public responsibility of everyone. [Should] an individual not be responsible in his position, then one position will suffer loss.

[This is true] even of those who, wanting to purify their spiritual souls (*ching-hun*), [prefer] to dwell alone in the mountain fastnesses, clothed in grass, eating [the fruit of] trees, forsaking the world for ever. These are men who find their Way in abandoning the world, and fundamentally they cannot be judged by the laws of this world. But in the Age of One World a man's life will be nurtured by the public for twenty years.. How can he insincerely receive [their] nurture and yet flee from them? Even in the Buddhist Law, when one has already received the nurture of the parents, suddenly to abandon the family is really to be unfaithful to the principle of gratitude. How much more so now, [in the case of] the public government! 'Present a peach in return for a plum';⁴⁰ when in debt repay the money: such is the ultimate universal principle. One cannot flee away into the midst of heaven-and-earth. The public government having supported the people for twenty years, the people then should requite the public government for twenty years. Therefore, until the age of forty, [a person] will not be permitted 'to abandon the family' [to seek] purification. After that [age], [every person] is free [to do as he wishes].

The second prohibition: [against] idolizing an individual

In the Age of Complete Peace-and-Equality, everyone will be equal. There will be no concubines, no slaves, no monarchs, no military commanders, no religious leaders, no popes. It will be what Confucius described as 'seeing a flight of dragons without a leader'.[41] Should there be leaders and those who are idolized then gradually inequalities [will develop], gradually autocratic rule will become consolidated, gradually there will arise quarrelling and killing, and we shall revert to the Age of Disorder. Therefore, no matter how holy [a person may be], or in what occupation [he is engaged]—such as a political leader who is excessively respected by the great majority of the public—[idolization of individuals] must always be guarded against. Hence, in this time, those who covet to be emperors or rulers would be rebels against the principle of equality. All [such persons] would be [considered] seditious and wicked, and [their activities] the worst of crimes, so they would be cast into prison by decision of the public parliament. For if we were once to have an emperor or ruler, then [we should have] inequality, then would arise quarrelling and killing, and we should revert to the Age of Disorder. Whenever an individual has become idolized, [the result] must be the destruction of the happiness of [the Age of] universal, Complete Peace-and-Equality.

And so, that men of godlike intelligence surpassing all others should, as religious leaders, gather the multitudes [to follow them], will likewise be strictly prohibited. For even though the religious leader surround (literally, cover over) the multitudes with *jen* and wisdom, and do no harm to men, yet excessive idolization will, I fear, [lead to a recurrence of such] social principles [as those taught by] Moses and Muhammad. Should religious leaders become secular rulers, then we should again have autocracy, [the principles of] equality would perforce be disordered, and we would return to the Age of Disorder.

But in the Age of Complete Peace-and-Equality, human knowledge will have become profound, and it will be very difficult to covet to be a religious or secular ruler. There would hardly be such a thing; however, we cannot but guard against [the possibility of] it. We can reckon that in this time authority will be very much divided up [among men], and it will be extremely difficult to gather a great following. However, the power of the physicians will be the greatest, since men's persons will be mostly entrusted to their [care]. It might be that a man of unusual intelligence[42] surpassing all others, like Napoleon, [could], by his 'surpassing abilities and grand strategies',[43] and making use of the methods of medicine, teach [his own] Way and gather a multitude [of followers]. Thus, from being the medical leader of the globe, [a man might] become the great ruler of the globe; from being a great religious leader, [a man might] become the great emperor of the globe. In this [way] we should have Ch'in Shih Huang[44] all over again with the [consequent] curbing of [human] rights, the use of force, the burning of books, and the burying [alive] of scholars so as to make ignorant the people (literally, the black heads, meaning the Chinese people). Then, [from] the pole of Complete Peace-and-Equality we should return to [the opposite pole of] Disorder. Such a disaster defies description, and we cannot but establish rigorous laws to prevent its occurrence. Therefore all cases of idolization of an individual should be nipped in the bud, and not be permitted to reach maturity.

The third prohibition: [against] competition

In man's nature there is nothing but that [proceeds] from selfishness. Since there is only selfishness, therefore there is competition. This arises spontaneously, without any particular cause. It is already implanted [in us]. In the beginning, what the first men actually depended upon to win out in their struggles with the birds and beasts, and to preserve the human species and take over the earth, was this selfishness and competitiveness. At first, [men only had] themselves, and only knowing they had themselves they were partial [only] to their own selves. Whereupon they fought for what other selves possessed, and killed each other. Later on they had families, and then they were partial [only] to their own families. Whereupon they fought for what other families possessed, and killed each other. When they came to have clans and tribes, then they were partial only to their own clans and tribes. Whereupon they fought for what other clans and tribes possessed, and killed each other. When they came to have states, then they were partial only to their own states. Whereupon they fought for what other states possessed, and killed each other. Having [different] races, then they were partial only to their own races. Whereupon they fought for what other races possessed, and killed each other. The strong oppressed the weak; the bold cheated the timid; the artful deceived the ignorant; the majority harried the minority. This is all fantastic nonsense, and [to be described as] 'when knowing, to but half-comprehend'.[45]

For example, Darwin propounded the theory of evolution, considering that what is caused by nature (*t'ien*) is [therefore] right. [This] leads men to believe that competition is the great principle [of life]. Whereupon competition—which is the greatest evil to the public existing in the world, past or present—is carried on every day and month; and eminent men[46] all pay their respects to it without shame. With this, the earth becomes a jungle, and all is 'blood and iron'.[47] This great evil is worse than flooding waters.

Now natural evolution is a thing [which proceeds] without cognition. Human principles are things in which cognition is inherent. The way whereby we [can] unite men into a group, whereby we can completely pacify-and-equalize [them], is to take the basically loving nature [of individual men] and to extend it [to all men]. Thereby we shall 'fulfil the Way of Heaven, co-operate with Nature (literally, the Heaven-suited)',[48] 'abide in perfection',[49] and attain ultimately to One World. Then will the multitudes find their happiness and profit. Should we follow the example of natural evolution, then among all mankind throughout the world the strong will oppress the weak, mutually gobbling each other up, and wars will occur daily, like fighting among quail. But in the end, there will remain only the strongest individual, and then he will simply end up by being eaten by the birds and beasts.

Furthermore, [regarding] this principle: in former times, in the age when the different kinds [? of men] were separated from each other, and all the states coexisted, it was like being in an impossible situation without being able to prevent it: there was no help for it. [But] when we are in the Age of One World, then we shall have passed by the worst things, like children who bear the smallpox virus (i.e. who have had smallpox, and so are now immune to further attacks of it). Why should we return to the times of Chuang Tzu and Lao Tzu! In the Age of One World there will be no different kinds [of men], no different states; all will be of the same bodily type, [all] will be compatriots.⁵⁰ Competition is inevitable among differing kinds and differing states; [but] among [those of] the same bodily type and [those who are] compatriots it is very injurious. Why should we again sow this evil seed and scatter it throughout the world!

In the Age of Disorder, [each] man still fights for himself. In the Age of Increasing Peace-and-Equality, there are [still] limitations and boundaries among men: others do not have to do with me, and I do not have to do with others. Therefore, in the Age of One World [men] will regard others as [they regard] themselves, and there will be no barriers [between them]. '[They] will hate to have goods abandoned on the ground, [but] will not need to store them up for themselves. [They] will hate not to employ their strength, [but] will not need to employ it for themselves.'⁵¹ In this time, competition will be most hated, and [thus] there will be no competition. Their competition will lie solely in competing in *jen* and competing in knowledge. In these [two competitions] 'they will not yield to their teachers'.⁵²

However, change of colour⁵³ is a symbol of the flowing of blood in a great battle; flaring up of anger is the spirit (or, the same temper) of a cannon attack; clamour and hubbub are the echoes of the noise of battle [between] opposing ramparts. The people of the [Age of] Complete Peace-and-Equality will be joyful and not angry, happy and not sad. Although there may perhaps be [those of] a competitive [spirit in that age], we cannot but strictly prohibit it (i.e. competition). All those who have a quarrelsome⁵⁴ temper, a quarrelsome voice, quarrelsome language, quarrelsome actions, and quarrelsome ideas will therefore be held in great shame by public opinion. The newspapers will adduce [them] as warnings to others. Their names will be dishonoured, and it will be difficult [for them] to win election [to public office]. How about the use of military force? The people of the Age of Complete Peace-and-Equality certainly will be without this. If there should be anyone who talked about manufacturing armaments, then it would be contrary to the principles of Complete Peace-and-Equality, and [such proposals] would be [considered] seditious and wicked. The public parliament would deprive [such a person] of his equal standing [as a citizen of One World].

The fourth prohibition: [against] abortion

See the chapter on 'The Human Roots Institution' (above, Part VI, Chapter II).

REFERENCES

[1] Compare above, Part II, Chapter IV, 'Outline of the Public Government', item 7 (pp. 99–100).

[2] 截長補短之, literally, 'cutting off the long, adding to the short of them'.

[3] (*Sic.*) Although these figures are quite fantastic, the possibility that they are due to typographical error is ruled out when we note that equally puzzling results are obtained from the author's further calculations below.

[4] Literally, 'degree boundaries'. The author has in mind, obviously, the area bounded by degree lines on the four sides.

[5] (*Sic.*) The square *li* figure seems to contain a typographical error; however, it really doesn't matter, since the entire calculation is erroneous.

[6] Correcting 界 to 里.

[7] See above, Part II, Chapter IV, 'Outline of the Public Government', item 7.

[8] It will be interesting to recall some key dates in the history of human flight, and note our author's surprising apprehension of the future importance of this art—presuming that he wrote this material no later than around 1902: 1891—Lilienthal's glider; 1892—Langley's model aircraft; 1903—the first successful flight of a heavier-than-air craft, by the Wright brothers. (According to the Chao Feng-t'ien *Nien-p'u* (p. 218), K'ang Yu-wei himself made an ascent in a balloon while in France in 1905.)

[9] See below, Part VIII, Chapter XI.

[10] 大昏博夜 literally, 'great darkness and universal night'.

[11] 不 must be inserted before 須.

[12] Courts will settle disputes; however, there will be no prisons, and no punishments except for dishonouring the offender's name. Second offenders will be sent to the public institution for the poor, and put to hard labour. (See below, Part VIII, Chapter XIV; also Part VIII, Chapter XV, 'The First Prohibition', and Part VI, Chapter II, provisions against the gravest crime: abortion.)

[13] The present Chinese term for bank is literally 'silver store'.

[14] See below, Part VIII, Chapters XI and XII.

[15] The words rendered as 'compete', 'strife', and 'fighting' are all given in the Chinese by the same character 爭.

[16] 器 A word which is difficult to translate. It has had a long usage in Chinese philosophical thought, and perhaps should be simply given the all-inclusive English equivalent of 'things', meaning material objects.

[17] 補偏救敝. A stock phrase, rendered here in overly stilted terms.

[18] The Chinese is at least equally vivid: 'drum and dance them'.

[19] But this seems discrepant with what is said above, in Part VIII, Chapter III, where the continent is rejected as an unsuitable unit of administration. And for consistency with the governmental structure as given above in Part VIII, Chapter V, the degree organ should be called a board, rather than an office.

[20] See also above, Part IV, 'The Method of Mixed Marriages', where we are told that persons who enter into mixed marriages will wear badges entitling them 'race reformer'.

[21] See also above, Part VI, Chapter X.

[22] Correcting 院 to 部 (see above, Part VIII, Chapter IV).

[23] A ministry not included in the structure of the public government as outlined above in Part VIII, Chapter IV, but obviously parallel in importance and function to the ministry of encouraging knowledge; hence, the 院 of the text has been changed to 部.

[24] Compare above, n. 19.

[25] Chu-ko Liang (A.D. 181–234) was one of the most famous heroes in Chinese history. His wisdom, military genius, and fidelity was largely responsible for the success of Liu Pei in founding the Shu Han dynasty, one of the 'Three Kingdoms' of the third century.

[26] Lao Tzu's dates (if such a man really lived) are undetermined, and remain the subject of dispute among contemporary scholars; the traditional story makes him a somewhat older contemporary of Confucius, in the late sixth century B.C. Chu Hsi (A.D. 1130–1200) is the most famous philosopher of later times in China. Wang Yang-ming (A.D. 1472–1528) is the greatest philosopher of the Ming period, whose idealistic theories became very influential also in Japan.

[27] Slightly changed from *Lun Yü*, XII, 13 (which is also quoted in *Ta Hsüeh*, IV): 'The Master said, "In hearing litigation I am like anybody else. What is essential is that we bring about that there be no litigation!"'

[28] *Chung Yung*, XIII, I.

[29] Slightly modified from *Chuang Tzu*, XXXIII.

[30] 侍妾 literally, serving maid; here, obviously connoting a sexual relationship.

[31] According to *P'ei Wen Yün Fu*, the full quotation is: 'A beautiful man breaks down [? the indifference] of age; a beautiful woman breaks down [? the discretion] of the tongue.' 美男破老 美女破舌 Without knowing the context, it is impossible to be sure of the correct translation. The quotation occurs, according to *P'ei Wen Yün Fu*, in *Chou Writings* [*from*] *the Chi Tumulus* 汲冢周書, which I presume is the same work (or a part of the same work) *Tz'u Hai* and *Tz'u Yüan* refer to as *Writings* [*from*] *the Chi Tumulus* 汲冢書, a work said to be written in the ancient 'tadpole' characters, recovered from a former king's burial mound early in the fourth century A.D.

[32] Another name for the T'ien-t'ai (*Jap.* Tendai) School of Buddhism, deriving from the text on which the doctrine of the school is founded: the *Saddharma-Pundarika*, or *Lotus of the Good Law*.

[33] Shinran (A.D. 1173–1262) was the founder of the Shin sect in Japan.

[34] i.e. the marriage agent 媒氏 (see above, Part V, pp. 160–1 and 166).

[35] Our author states that up to the present time, before they are considered to become adults, Jewish girls first have intercourse with a ram.

[36] The following paragraph takes up the problems posed towards the beginning of the present chapter, and answers them (compare above, pp. 247–8).

[37] Taking 倭 to be 佞.

[38] Simplifying the text slightly at this phrase.

[39] Quite literal here— 有士君子之行.

[40] 投桃報李 A maxim. (Compare *Shih Ching*, Wei Feng 衛風: 'Mu Kua 木瓜'.)

[41] See above, Part II, pp. 131–2, n. 32.

[42] 異靈 (transposing the positions of 靈 and 異).

[43] 雄才大略 A stock phrase.

[44] The First Emperor, from the State of Ch'in, who completed the overthrow of the feudal polity and united China for the first time as a centralized monarchy (221 B.C.); but who has been detested throughout all ages for such tyrannical actions as those mentioned here.

[45] 一知半解 A stock phrase.

[46] 賢者 Usually rendered as 'worthies', which seems even less satisfactory than the present translation.

[47] i.e. warfare (from Bismarck's policies).

[48] Slightly changed from *I Ching, t'ai* 泰 hexagram: 財(裁)成天地之道、輔相天地之宜 (My translation differs considerably from both Legge and Wilhelm-Baynes [see their works cited above, Part II, p. 129, n. 1; on p. 281, and vol. 1, p. 50, respectively], both because of the context of the present text, and because of a divergence in interpretation.)

[49] 止於至善 From the famous opening proposition in *Ta Hsüeh*, the full statement of which reads: 'The Way of Great Learning lies in making abundantly clear [one's] moral virtue (德), in loving (I am here not following the Ch'eng-Chu alteration of 親 into 新) the people, and in abiding in perfection.'

[50] The Chinese term is 'of the same womb'.

[51] A quotation from the key passage in *Li Chi*, 'Li Yün'. (See above, Book One, Chapter II, for four English renderings of the passage. My translation differs somewhat from those versions.)

[52] See *Lun Yü*, XV, 35: 'The Master said, "when it comes to *jen*, do not yield to your teacher".'

[53] i.e. flushing or paling with emotion, such as anger or hatred.

[54] 'Quarrelsome' is the same character also rendered as 'competition' (爭).

PART IX

ABOLISHING BOUNDARIES OF KIND, AND LOVING ALL LIVING [THINGS]

FTER mankind have become equal, great *jen* will abound. However, the birth of the ten thousand creatures originates in the original ether;[1] man is merely one species of creatures within [this] original ether. In remote antiquity, at the beginnings of human beings, [men] knew only to cleave to their own kind and preserve them. If not of their kind, then they would kill them. Therefore love of [one's own] kind was considered to be the great principle. Those who were said throughout the world to be loving of [their own] kind were called *jen*; those who did not love [their own] kind were called not-*jen*. Should [a man] kill [a one] of a different kind, then, taking it [that thereby] injury was avoided and harm prevented, [the killer] was likewise called *jen*.

Now, what is called 'kind' is no more than a distinction of appearance and physique. [Those who] are the same as I in appearance and physique, [I] am then intimate with and love; [those who] are different than I in appearance and physique, [I] then hate and kill. For this reason, [in the case of] children, who are born from our semen,[2] and lice, who are born from our sweat,[3] we then love and cherish children, only fearing lest they should not grow up; [but] we kill and destroy lice, only fearing lest they should prolong their lives.[4] They are equally [creatures] which are born [from us], but our love and hate [for them] is quite dissimilar. How can this but be attributable to [the distinction of] kind? If there were born from the [mother's] womb a creature of a different kind, [such as] a snake or a dog, then we would certainly strike and kill it. And many even among children who are born with slight differences [from the normal kind of] ears, eyes, hands, or feet, are not nurtured [by the parents]. Hence [we see that] what men love is not their *children*, but what is of the *same kind* as themselves. Thus, in the instruction of adopted children, if they [turn out] to resemble us, then we love them. How great is the importance of love-of-kind!

264

Confucius took the ancestors as the root of the [human] kind. Therefore father, mother, sons, and daughters are the root of love-of-kind; elder and younger brothers and kinsmen are the extension of love-of-kind; husband and wife are the 'intercoursing' of love-of-kind—if there is intercourse with an animal, then [the human being] does not love that [animal]. Extending it from this, [then] love of friends [exists] because they are the same kind in sound of voice; love of prince and minister [exists] because they are [engaged in] the same kind of affairs; love of neighbours [exists] because they are the kind who reside in the same place. We love the people of our city, our country, or the world, more or less, according as they are of the kind who dwell nearer to or farther from [us]. We take the one kind of form (i.e. the human kind) as the limit [to our love], and on this basis we deal with them (i.e. our own human kind), civilize them, govern them. Hence he who kills a man dies; he who saves a man is rewarded; he who succours men is praised. [But] he who kills another [kind of] creature sins not; he who succours another [kind of] creature [gains] no merit.

(All the words and thoughts of all the saints and wise men have always been limited to this love of our own kind, and working to help our own kind. Thus), among the countless creatures produced by nature (literally, Heaven), we only are partial to one creature, love one creature, preserve one creature. Because we [only] are partial to one creature, love one creature, and preserve one creature, we are then not averse to slaying all [other] creatures, subduing all [other] creatures, injuring (literally, carving and hacking) all [other] creatures. With [this] daily serving of [only] the one creature—our own kind—so far as nature (or, Heaven) is concerned, so far as the virtue of love is concerned, what is gained is not more than one-myriadth; so far as universal principles are concerned, what is lost is more than a myriad. How terrible!

(The same applies to the beasts as well, since each loves only its own kind and preys on other kinds. We see that sages are not very different, therefore, from tigers. In fact, man's lack of compassion is far greater than that of the tiger, who cannot compare in destructiveness with man, due to the latter's crafty intelligence. Man is the most selfish and uncompassionate of all creatures.) Those who are termed bandits may kill men in the course of effecting the building up of their own family, and therefore the officials punish them. Those who are termed heroes may kill men in the course of effecting the building up of their own state, and [therefore] the sages reproach them. Then the sages may kill [other kinds of] creatures in the course of effecting the building up of their own kind, and [therefore] as Heaven sees it, they are equally culpable.

(However, the killing of other animals is a thing which humans cannot help. Had they not been able to destroy the animals that menaced them, they could not have survived. Therefore, if it is a question of choosing between killing animals or being exterminated, the human species is right in choosing the lesser of the two evils. And so, when One World is attained, all the earth will be completely inhabited by man, and the animals dangerous to man will be exterminated or represented only by a few specimens in zoos.[5] But how about the animals which are now customarily domesticated? When we consider that they are not far removed from man in intelligence, that they too have feelings of terror and pain, that they are not a threat to our survival or essential to our diet, then it is against natural principles and the greatest of uncompassion to kill them.

(Therefore, although the Hindus and Buddhists are the best of men because of their prohibitions against killing even insects, their Way cannot be carried out at present. The Way of Confucius is a progress in three stages: loving one's kin, loving all people, and finally loving all creatures. The stages correspond [of course] to the Three Ages. Though this Way is not as *good* (*jen*) as that of the Hindus and Buddhists, it is *practicable*. The final stage will be possible of attainment because, in the One World era, substitutes will be developed for animal meat. The people of that age will loathe animal meat, and thus will of their own accord abstain from killing animals. They will look upon their domestic animals as people of today look upon their servants: they will pity and love them and take care of them, while using them.

(But prior to the time when substitutes for animal meat are eaten exclusively, animals will be slaughtered by electrical machines so that they will not suffer. In this way, they may not be able to fill out their normal span of life; yet, since all must die some time, it is a 'having compassion in the midst of uncompassion'. Among the

various kinds of animals, those of superior intelligence and usefulness, or which give pleasure to man, will be widely domesticated
and protected. Thus, monkeys and parrots are the most superior,[6]
with oxen, horses, dogs, and cats next, and they will be extensively
domesticated, while animals like deer, which men love to raise, will
also roam freely through the parks and mountains and plains . . .)
The main rule to be followed in the treatment of the birds and
beasts is that those harmful to man will be exterminated, while
those which cannot harm man will be preserved.

Therefore, the refraining from killing of [animals] will start with
the kine, dogs, and horses, because they are intelligent and useful.
It will next [be extended to include] fowl, swine, geese, and ducks,
because they will *not* be useful [as food, in that age]. It will finally
be extended [to include] fish, because their intelligence is slight [and
yet they do have intelligence]. Thus, the [stage in which there is
still] eating of flesh and killing of living [creatures] is One World's
Age of Disorder; [the stage in which] electrical machines [are used]
to slaughter animals is One World's Age of Increasing Peace-and-
Equality; [the stage in which] killing is prohibited and the desire
[to kill and eat animals] is ended is One World's Age of Complete
Peace-and-Equality. [This] is a gradual progress.

But then, how about the Buddhist absolute proscription against
killing? It is likewise not right. Insects roam over the earth, and
there is no place without them. Should we insist upon absolute
proscription of killing, the insects will be able to attack man, and
[cause him] much sickness . . . Now we will draw up a law, that
all [creatures] which attack man may be killed; this being [a thing]
which cannot be helped. With regard to the insect species, in this
time there will surely be new drugs which can cause that insects
will of themselves not invade human habitation; in which case it
will likewise be unnecessary to kill them.

And yet, being humans, we have a body, have a form. We are
impeded by our form, and there are things which limit it. Even
though I desire to be *jen*, how can I perfect (literally, exhaust) my
jen? Even though I desire to be loving, how can I perfect my
lovingness? Among the forms of the ten thousand creatures, there
are large and small. Largeness is limited (literally, exhaustible), but
smallness is illimitable. The *chiao-ming*[7] nests on the eyelash[8] of the

mosquito, but the mosquito is not aware of it. Now the *chiao-ming* is the largest of [such] creatures. If we now place a drop of water in a cup, and look at it through the microscope, then we see ten thousand 'insects' wriggling and squirming. There are round ones, long ones, ones with 'wheels' and ones with horns, ones with wings (or, fins), and ones with feet—a thousand strange varieties, ten thousand different sorts, crawling and coiling. [In quantity and variety] they are inexhaustible. In the Age of One World, the power of the microscope will be one doesn't know how many times greater than that of [the instrument of] today. [Viewed through the instrument of today], an ant looks like an elephant. [Viewed through the instrument of] the future, the size of a microbe will be like that of the great, skyborne *p'eng*-bird.[9]

The air is full of microbes. Man being [comparatively] so huge, with a single yawn he kills countless numbers of microbes, with a single footstep or wave of the hand he kills countless numbers of ants [or other] insects. Well, then, I call myself good and *jen* (or, very *jen*), and yet, since my birth I have killed I don't know how many thousands of times more microbes than there are sands of the Ganges. Do you say they haven't the slightest consciousness? Yet when viewed through the microscope, they are then bigger than dragons or elephants. Thus [viewed], they are the greatest of living beings; thus [viewed], they are living creatures.

Buddha said to abstain from killing; and yet he daily killed countless living [beings]. Buddha told Ananda to fetch water in his bowl. Ananda said that water contains microbes, [and so] we ought not to take and drink it. Buddha said that what we cannot see, we may drink. Now Buddha referred to all living beings. But he should have [based his] discussion [on whether] a thing was animate or inanimate, not [on whether] it was visible or invisible. Should we effect that man would be invisible, then we could also kill men! At the same time, it is in fact impossible to carry out that we do not drink water. Therefore Buddha's reply was evasive. Or, even if we knew that Buddha did not drink water, yet he could not help but breathe air. When the air is exhaled and inhaled, then living [beings] are killed. Since I cannot retire outside of the atmosphere and not inhale them, then how can I be *jen* to living creatures and not kill them? *Jen! Jen!* We shall never be able to perfect [it]. Thus [it was that] Confucius [said]: '[The Gentleman] stays far away from the kitchen.'[10] Life! Life! Eternally there must be killing. Therefore Buddha limited [the proscription against killing to exclude] invisible [creatures]. Alas, alas! The production of life is inexhaustible; the Way is likewise inexhaustible (i.e. imperfectible). However, [given] this imperfectibility, [we should] bring [the Way] to [the highest possible] perfection and perfect it.[11]

Therefore, the Way is based on [doing what] can be done, and that is all. What cannot be done, even though we wish to do it, cannot but be thwarted. There is that which limits my *jen*. There is that which thwarts my love. Alas, alas! And even though the [kind of] *jen* [which will prevail in] One World, and the [kind of] love [which will then bring about] abstinence from killing were to be established in all the heavens; yet, so far as being [true or perfect] *jen* is concerned, it would only be a drop in the great ocean! However, within all the heavens, or without all the heavens, so far as *jen* is concerned, neither can we add to this [imperfect and limited development of it].

REFERENCES

[1] See above, Book Two, Part I, pp. 64-5.

[2] 精氣 the 'quintessential *ch'i*'.

[3] 汗氣 the 'sweat *ch'i*'.

[4] Taking 不 to be erroneously inserted before 至.

[5] In a passage elaborating on this a little farther on, the author remarks that 'this will thus be the ultimate attainment of the survival of the fittest according to natural evolution'. (Original text, p. 436.)

[6] The author points out that monkeys have speech, and men must learn this speech so that they may train monkeys to be servants. Parrots also have the ability to transmit words, to sing, and to dance.

[7] Correcting 蛜 to 蜈 ; a reference to a minute creature mentioned in several old writings such as *Yen Tzu Ch'un Ch'iu* and *Lieh Tzu*. According to *Tz'u Hai*, the same name is also found written as 焦蜈 , or 鷦蜈.

[8] Correcting 蜨 to 睫.

[9] The Chinese equivalent of the fabulous roc (see *Chuang Tzu*, I, 1).

[10] This was actually said by Mencius (see *Mencius*, I, A, 7.8: 'With regard to animals, the Gentleman, having seen them alive, cannot bear to see them die; having heard their [dying] sounds, he cannot bear to eat their flesh. This being the case, the Gentleman stays far away from the kitchen').

[11] 惟其無盡．收以盡盡之 A plausible rendering, but not one of which I am completely confident.

PART X

ABOLISHING BOUNDARIES OF SUFFERING
AND ATTAINING UTMOST HAPPINESS

I n the beginnings of man he suffered because of hunger, and so he sought the fruit of the grasses and trees, and the flesh of birds and beasts, to fill himself. If he could not get flesh and fruit, then he suffered. If he got and ate them, filled up on them, satiated [himself] with them, then he was happy. He suffered because the wind and rain and mist attacked his body, and so he wrapped [himself in the bark of] grasses and trees, and wove hemp and *ko*¹ [into garments] to cover his body. If he could not get them, then he suffered. If he got and wore them, then he was happy. He suffered because he did not obtain [satisfaction of] his human (i.e. sexual) desire, and so he sought a mate to embrace. If he could not get [a mate], then he suffered. If he got one, then he was happy. Later, there were wise ones who 'in pursuing affairs added refinements'² to the old ways. [Taking] food, they cooked it, roasted it, mixed it, and so increased [men's] happiness. [Taking] clothing, they [used] silk [material], made it gay with the 'five colours and the six hues',³ [devised] gowns, caps, and sandals, and so increased [men's] happiness. (Similarly with dwellings, and with gratification of sexual desire.) The increase of happiness is [caused by] that which more suits and better accords with man's spiritual soul and bodily soul, which heightens and expands [man's] enjoyment and pleasure. The inability to attain this happiness is suffering. [Suffering] is the spirit knotted-up, the body wounded, [the soul] melancholy and downcast. [The capacity for] increased happiness is limitless; [the capacity for] increased suffering is also limitless. The two are related faculties. Daily to bend our thoughts more earnestly to means of seeking happiness and avoiding suffering: this is to progress.

(This is what all the sages have had as their purpose, with all their material inventions and social techniques. We may judge them by the one criterion of the extent to which they have increased human happiness and decreased human suffering. Their methods must also be judged as valuable or not, according to the times and the environment.

(In One World everyone will live in public housing. Outside of their regular rooms at their place of work, everywhere they will find great hotels, whose beautiful and pleasant accommodations defy description. They will be of several grades, according to the money the guest wishes to spend. There will be four better kinds: 'movable rooms' [i.e. electrically powered cars that run on tracks], 'flying rooms', or, 'flying ships',[4] and [marine] ships. The people of this age will love to travel.) The grasses and trees are the most stupid, and therefore flourish but do not move about. The sheep and swine are not so stupid as the grass and trees, and are able to move about, but cannot go far. As for the great *p'eng*-bird and the yellow *ku*-bird,[5] [they fly] a thousand *li* with a single movement [of their wings]. In antiquity, [men] aged and died without leaving their native village;[6] [thus] they were like the grass and trees. In the Middle Age, [men] travel about like sheep and swine (i.e. only short distances). In the Age of Complete Peace-and-Equality, then they will be like the great *p'eng*-bird and the yellow *ku*-bird.

(All public and private residences will have to pass the inspection of the health authorities. Public hotels will be equipped with air-conditioning, electrical heating, massaging machines. There will be fast, electrically propelled ships on the water, equipped with every comfort and pleasure—even to gardens—and many people will live on these ships. On land there will be automobiles. These will be developed to the point that they will seat perhaps several hundred persons, and will go at great speeds. Perhaps they will be electrically powered; or it may be that they will be powered by some new fuel. Horse-drawn carriages will be used only for hauling short distances, or they may be entirely replaced by the electrical vehicles.) Therefore, at the beginning of One World, [people] will live on mountain tops; at the middle [period of that age], they will live on the sea; later, they will live in the air.

(There being no private homes, everyone will dine together, like a great convention. There will be no slaves or servants, but their functions will be performed by machines, shaped like birds and beasts.[7] One will order by telephone, and food will be conveyed by mechanical devices—possibly a table will rise up from the kitchen below, through a hole in the floor. On the four walls will be lifelike, 'protruding paintings'; music will be playing, and there will be dancing. All this will stimulate the appetite. In all these things there will be refinement and moral uplift.

(At this time, people will eat their food in a liquid form—the essences extracted from solid matter. These essential juices will be more easily absorbed by the body than are the solids. There will be vapours which will be inhaled to give a joyful intoxication, but without harm to the body.[8] By imbibing only the essences of foods, man's life will be prolonged.

(There follows a short section repeating the discussion [see above, Part IX] regarding non-killing of animals. There will be three stages within the Age of Complete Peace-and-Equality itself: The Age of Disorder, in which meat will still be eaten; the Age of Increasing Peace-and-Equality, in which the flesh of birds and animals will no longer be eaten; the Age of Complete Peace-and-Equality, in which even insects and fish will no longer be eaten, and in which all forms of life possessed of cognition will be equal. Equality will not extend to the vegetable kingdom, for man must eat to preserve himself, and because these forms of life are not possessed of the cognitive faculty, and hence are not to be included in the domain of *jen*.

(Clothing in this time will be made of materials and patterns suitable to weather conditions and to working comfort. They will have great variety and beauty, but will indicate no distinctions between people, except for the badges of honour for *jen* or knowledge. There will be constant progress in the use of all kinds of implements to advance civilization. Music will play a great part in all phases of human life. People will shave off all hair except for that in the nose [which fulfils the function of straining dust and impurities from the air]. This is on the ground that the nearer we are to the beasts, the hairier; the more civilized we become, the less hirsute. Furthermore, lack of hair contributes to cleanliness.[9] Men and women will bathe several times daily, in water which will leave them fragrantly scented. This is not a matter of perfuming in the present manner, so that a woman will be more attractive as a sexual plaything. Rather it is like the matter of hair: thereby humans are farther elevated above the filthy, foul-smelling beasts. 'The beauties of the present age will still not equal the ugly of the Age of Complete

Peace-and-Equality.' Even the toilet facilities of that time will be made pleasant with music and fragrant odours and mechanical contrivances for flushing away the filth.) For the time when people go to the toilet is the time when they are most tranquil and with-drawn from the hubbub [of the world]. If there is that whereby to lift their thoughts above this world (literally, move their thoughts of abandoning the world), to [inspire] their imaginations beyond the mundane (literally, ideas of discarding forms), then their souls will of themselves [rise] far [above] the worldly level.

(Everyone will receive a daily medical check-up. All phases of life will be under the supervision of the medical authorities. Contagious diseases will be eradicated. The whole earth will be made clean and healthful. About the only ailments remaining will be external ones, easily treated with medicines. Thus, although there will be public hospitals, they will be almost empty; the sick will comprise only those who are about to die [of old age]. In the case of the latter, should their sufferings be acute, and the doctors agree that there is no hope of improvement, then they may be mercifully put out of their agony by electrocution . . . People of this time will attain to longevity of from a hundred or two hundred, to over a thousand years, due to progress in medical science, clothing, and diet.

(The search for longevity, for the art of becoming a spirit or immortal [shen-hsien], may be carried on only by those who have returned with twenty years of service the twenty years of support and education received from the public.[10] Those who wish to retire from the world to carry on these [Taoistic] or Buddhistic practices may, therefore, do so after the age of forty. These capabilities will be the highest attainment of One World. But they may not interfere with the public service owed by everyone, or else the work of the world might be neglected, and civilization retrogress.)

Christianity takes reverence for God (t'ien) and love for men as its teaching of the Good; it takes repentance of sin and judgment after death as its [means of making people] frightened of [doing] evil. In the Age of Complete Peace-and-Equality, [people] will naturally love others, will naturally be without sin. Comprehending the natural workings of evolution, they will therefore not reverence

God. Comprehending the impossibility (literally, difficulty) of limitless numbers of souls occupying the space [of 'Heaven'], they therefore will not believe in a Day of Judgment. The religion of Jesus will therefore, when we have attained One World, be extinct.

Islam speaks of the bonds of states, rulers, subjects, husbands, and wives. By the time we have entered [the Age of] One World, it will thus [already] be extinct. Although possessed of a soul, [yet for man] always to adduce God [in support of his] actions: such [a Way] is crude and superficial, and lacks sufficient substantiation. One World of Complete Peace-and-Equality is then the ideal of Confucius. Having arrived at this time, Confucius's theory of the Three Ages will have been completely fulfilled. However, the *I* [*Ching*] speaks of the alternations (literally, dispersing and gathering, or dissipating and growing) of *yin* and *yang*; [this theory] may be propagated, but [its workings] will not be apparent.[11] For, the sickness being over, there is no need to use medicines;[12] the shore having been reached, the raft [of Buddha's teachings] may likewise be discarded.

Therefore in the Age of One World only the studies of [the art of becoming] a spirit or immortal,[13] and of [becoming] a buddha,[14] will be widely practised. For One World is the ultimate Law of this world; but the study of immortality, of longevity without death, is even an extension of the ultimate Law of this world. The study of buddhahood, [a state] without birth or death, [implies] not [merely] a setting apart from the world, but [an actual] going out of this world; still more, it is a going out of One World. If we go this far, then we abandon the human sphere and enter the sphere of immortals and buddhas. Hereupon, the study of immortality and buddhahood then begins. [Comparing the two], the study of immortality is too crude, its subtle words and profound principles are not many, and its [ability] to intoxicate men's minds is limited. As for the universality and subtlety of the study of buddhahood, it extends to the point where the speaking of words is discontinued, and the activities of the mind are terminated. Although having sage-wisdom, not to move a hand (i.e. to remain quiescent): such [self-]containment is yet more profound. And further, there are also the mysterious arts of the Five Vanquishings[15] and the Three

Brilliants;[16] the application of [their] supernatural powers is still more singular.

Therefore after One World there will first be the study of immortality. After [that] there will be the study of buddhahood. The inferior knowledge is the study of immortality; the superior knowledge is the study of buddhahood. After [the studies of] immortality and buddhahood will come the study of roaming through the heavens. I have another book [on that subject].[17]

REFERENCES

[1] 葛 A plant of the bean family with fibres from which cloth is woven (*Pueraria thunbergiana*).

[2] 踵事增華 A stock phrase.

[3] 五色六章 From *Li Chi*, 'Li Yüan'. Commentary explains that the 'five colours' are blue (or green), red, yellow, white, and black; while the 'six hues' are the same plus 'heaven-black'. (See *Tz'u Hai*, under 六章 .)

[4] These are apparently envisaged as gas balloons rather than airplanes. On p. 442 of the original text we are given a description of what the earth looks like from these 'flying rooms'. (See also above, Part VIII, p. 260, n. 8. It is possible that in this description we have an indication of a post-1905 date for composition of at least this part of the *Ta T'ung Shu*.)

[5] For the *p'eng*-bird, see above, Part IX, n. 9. The yellow *ku*-bird 黃鵠 is a similar creature, first mentioned in *Ch'u Tz'u*, 'Pu Chü' 卜居 .

[6] A reference to *Tao Te Ching*, 80, which is quoted just before in our text (but which is not in section I have selected for translation).

[7] See also above, Part IX, p. 269, n. 6.

[8] Our author specifically says 'like the Indian *ma-chi chiu* (蔴及洒)'. What this may be, I do not know. Marijuana might be intended, according to the sound, and from the fact that this narcotic is made from hemp. However, the *chiu* indicates a liquor.

[9] Our author suggests that, shaving being the nuisance it is, a new 'medicine' will then be in use, one application of which will prevent the further growth of hair.

[10] Compare above, Part VIII, Chapter XV.

[11] i.e.—I take it—when One World has been attained, the principle of

fulfilment inevitably being followed by decline will no longer be operative.

[12] This sounds like a proverbial saying; but I have not succeeded in verifying it.

[13] 神仙, or as below, 仙學. The principal objective of 'religious' Taoism.

[14] 佛學 I have thus rendered, since our author here is definitely referring to this specific objective within the general area of Buddhism.

[15] 五勝 The cycle of the five elemental forces—metal, wood, water, fire, earth—which successively overcome each other in the processes of nature.

[16] 三明 Sun, moon, and stars, according to Tung Chung-shu (? 179-? 104 B.C.). (See *Tz'u Yüan.*)

[17] See above, Part I, p. 67, interlinear note.

BIBLIOGRAPHY

This bibliography is divided into three sections: (I) Chinese and Japanese Language Materials; (II) Western Language Materials; (III) Miscellaneous Materials. The first two headings are self-explanatory. Under the third, there will be found a few items which pertain only indirectly to our subject, but which will give the interested reader an introduction to other aspects of K'ang Yu-wei's career. In this section have also been listed the reference works which have been relied upon most frequently during the writing of this book.

The bibliography is short, and possibly even at that a little over-generous. K'ang Yu-wei, as one of the prominent figures in recent Chinese history, has been mentioned of course in most of the works dealing with that period. Usually he is treated merely as the leader of the One Hundred Days of Reform. Thus far, there has appeared in Western languages no book-length study of him as scholar and philo-sopher, and only one book-length study of him at all, namely, Franke's *Die Staatspolitischen Reformversuche K'ang Yu-weis und seiner Schule*. In most of the Western language materials listed below, treatment of him is brief, sketchy, inadequate, and often erroneous. There has been no translation of his really original work, *Ta T'ung Shu*, into any language. In Chinese and Japanese the situation on the whole is better, with several biographies, and one book-length treatment of *Ta T'ung Shu*, namely, Tadokoro's *Cosmopolitan Thought in China*. The histories of Chinese philosophy or thought include a chapter on him, usually considering him as the last of the Ch'ing philosophers. However, these chapters are nearly always based on Liang Ch'i-ch'ao's summary in his *General Discussion of Ch'ing Dynasty Scholarship*. They hardly offer much to a student interested in serious research on K'ang's thought. The books of this type which are listed are certainly not a complete coverage, but it would serve no purpose to add to them.

I have thought it may be helpful to give the reader something more than a bare title to go by, and so have added brief comments in many cases. In Section III the listing of basic reference tools may appear superfluous—rather like listing Webster's dictionary. Yet it seems to me only just that we should acknowledge the labours of those upon whose compilations we all depend for our own productions. Unnecessary though it may be to tell the student of Chinese that one has had Mathews's dictionary at hand every hour of the translation process; yet it will do no harm to state that indebtedness. Since it is by virtue of such works as *Tz'u Hai* that we are able to assume some slight appearance of erudition in our footnotes, courtesy as well as honesty should impel us to express our gratitude. As K'ang Yu-wei says somewhere in this book, 'requital is a basic principle'.

A few writings have been cited in the body of the book which are not included in the bibliography, as they were used only incidentally, and do not in themselves bear on our subject.

SECTION I

CHINESE AND
JAPANESE LANGUAGE MATERIALS

Chang Po-chen (張伯楨): *Biography of the Gentleman from Nan Hai* (南海先生傳), 1932.

Chao Chi-pin (趙紀彬): *Chinese Philosophical Thought* (中國哲學思想). Shanghai: Chung Hwa Book Store, 1948. [See Chapter X, Section 3 (pp. 207–9), on K'ang Yu-wei.]

Chao Feng-t'ien (趙豐田): 'Draft Chronology of Mr. K'ang Ch'ang-su' (康長素先生年譜稿). *History Annual* (史學年報), vol. II, no. 1, 1934; published by the History Society of Yenching University, Peiping; pp. 173–240. [The most important biography of K'ang Yu-wei yet to appear, based on K'ang's own *Chronology* for the first forty-year period, and on a large number of other sources.]

Chiang Wei-ch'iao (蔣維喬): *History of Chinese Philosophy during the Last Three Hundred Years* (中 國 近 三 百 年 哲 學 史). Shanghai: Chung Hwa Book Store, 1932 and 1936. [On K'ang Yu-wei, see pp. 105–17. Not much on *Ta T'ung Shu*, and that mostly taken from Liang Ch'i-ch'ao.]

Ch'ien Mu (錢穆): *History of Chinese Scholarship during the Last Three Hundred Years* (中國近三百年學術史). Shanghai: Commercial Press, 1937 (2 vols.). [A much more extended and detailed survey than the preceding item. On K'ang Yu-wei, see Chapter XIV (pp. 633–709); this chapter also includes a study of T'an Ssu-t'ung and his *Jen Hsüeh*, and its relation to *Ta T'ung Shu*. One of the few important works on our subject.]

Ch'ien Mu: 'Critique of K'ang Yu-wei's Scholarship' (康有為學術 述評). *Tsinghua Journal* (清華學報), vol. XI, no 3, July 1936; pp.583–656. [This article is reprinted, with minor changes, in the author's work cited above.]

Ch'ing Draft History (清史稿). [See 'Biography of K'ang Yu-wei (康有為傳), in vol. CXI, *Lieh Chuan*, pp. 251–260 (the final biography of this *ts'e*, occupying four pages).]

Fujihara Tei (藤原定): 'K'ang Yu-wei and Sun Wen' (康有為と 孫文). An article in a book edited by Saneto Keisho (實藤 惠秀), entitled *Modern Chinese Thought* (近代支那思想). Tokyo: Kōfū Kan (光風館), 1942; pp. 79–92.

Fujihara Tei: *Modern Chinese Thought* (近代支那思想).Toyko: Chūō Kōrin Sha (中央公論杜), 1941. [See Chapter VII, 'K'ang Yu-wei's Utopian Thought', pp. 78–91. A good summary.]

Fung Yu-lan (馮友蘭): *History of Chinese Philosophy* (中國哲學史). Shanghai: Commercial Press, 1934 and 1941 (2 vols.). [Generally considered the best work on its subject yet to appear. On K'ang Yu-wei, see vol. II, Chapter XVI, Section 2, pp. 1012–21. (For English translation, see under Section II below.)]

Ho Lin (賀麟): *Contemporary Chinese Philosophy* (當代中國哲學). Shanghai: Sheng Li Publishing Co. (勝利出版公司), 1945. [Dismisses K'ang in a few sentences (see pp. 3 and 4); a superficial and biased work.]

Kamiya Masao (神谷正男): *History of Contemporary Chinese Thought* (現代支那思想史). Tokyo: Seikatsu Sha (生活杜), 1940. [Translation of Parts I–IV of Kuo Chan-po's *History* (see below).]

Kamiya Masao: *Problems of Contemporary Chinese Thought* (現代支那 思想の問題). Tokyo: Seikatsu Sha, 1940. [A compilation trans-lated from several sources, including Kuo Chan-po's *History* (see below), and Ts'ai Shang-chih's (蔡尚志) *Chinese Thought of the Last Thirty Years* (近三十年來の中國思想界   ).]

K'ang Yu-wei (康有為): *One World* (大同書). With hand-written preface by the author; preface by the editor. Edited by K'ang's pupil, Ch'ien Ting-an (錢定安). Shanghai: Chung Hwa Book Store, 1935. [The first edition containing complete text. This is text used in the present translation.]

One World (Parts I and II only). San Francisco: Sai Gai Yat Bo Publishing Co., A.C. (After Confucius), 2480 (1929). With a frontispiece photo-portrait of the author.

One World (Parts I and II only). See *Compassion Magazine*, below.

NOTE: A bibliography of K'ang's writings will be found in the work by Lu & Lu, listed below; Chao's 'Draft Chronology', listed above, also, has a partial bibliography of works on and by him.

Kimura Eiichi (木林英一): *Studies in Chinese Realism. Reflections on its Scholarly Standpoints* (中國的實在觀の研究、何學問的立場の反省) Tokyo: Kōbundō Shobo (弘文堂書房), 1948. [See Part II, essay entitled 'The Thought of *Ta T'ung Shu* and its Character' (pp. 191–289). (This essay was written in 1943, according to the preface, p. 11.) Important.]

Kuo Chan-po (郭湛波): *History of Chinese Thought During the Past Fifty Years* (近五十年中國思想史). Peking: Jen Wen Book Store, 1936. [On K'ang Yu-wei, see Chapter I, pp. 5–17. I took my notes from the revised MS. loaned by the author, which he hopes to have published under the title *History of Contemporary Chinese Thought*. There were only minor revisions in this chapter.]

Liang Ch'i-ch'ao (梁啓超): *General Discussion of Ch'ing Dynasty Scholarship* (清代學術概論). Shanghai: Commercial Press, 1934 (first edition was published in 1921). [On K'ang Yu-wei, see Chapters XXIII and XXIV (pp. 126–37). This is the source for most of the summaries of K'ang and his works, particularly *Ta T'ung Shu*.]

Liang Ch'i-ch'ao: *Biography of K'ang Yu-wei* (康有為傳). Shanghai: Kuang Chih Book Store (廣智書局). Written in 1901; republished in 1907 and 1908; 48 pages. [A brilliantly concise yet revealing picture of the man and his ideas and methods, written by his most eminent pupil. The biography was written before Liang and K'ang drifted apart; it is our best source for the pre-exile K'ang, not in narrative detail, but in its appraisal of the teacher as educator, philosopher, religious thinker, political theorist, etc.]

Lu Nai-hsiang (陸乃翔) and Lu Tun-k'uei (陸敦騤): *Biography of Mr. K'ang Nan-hai* (康南海先生傳). Privately printed by the

K'ang family, 1929. (Only vol. 1 published); 56 double pages. [This work is probably not available in many places outside of China—or even in China; K'ang Yu-wei's son, Shou-man, kindly loaned me his copy while I was in Taipei, Formosa, from which I had photographic prints made. This biography, by two pupils of K'ang, offers an advantage over Liang's of covering the later period also in its subject's career. It is more factual and detailed, but less intimate and illuminating, than Liang's *Biography*. It contains a bibliography of K'ang's writings.]

Onogawa Hideyoshi (小野川秀美): 'The Formation of the Reformatory Thought at the End of the Ts'ing Dynasty' [translation of title in Journal] (清末變法論の成立). *Journal of Oriental Studies* (Tōhō Gakuhō 東方學報), no. 20, March 1951. Published by the Research Institute of Humanistic Studies, Kyoto University (the former Oriental Research Institute), pp. 153–84.

Onogawa Hideyoshi: 'Political Thoughts and the Evolution Theory at the End of the Ts'ing Dynasty' [translation of title in Journal] (清末の思想と進化論); *ibid.*, no 21, March 1952, pp. 1–36.

Compassion Magazine (不忍雜誌). Founded and written by K'ang Yu-wei. Published in Shanghai, February to November 1913. [See the present work, Book One, Chapter I, p. 20.]

Sung Yün-pin (宋雲彬): *K'ang Yu-wei* (康有為). Shanghai: Commercial Press, 1951, and San Lien Publishers, 1955. [The author is so prejudiced against his subject that one wonders why he bothered to make this study.]

Tadokoro Yoshiyuki (田所義行): *Cosmopolitan Thought in China. [A Study] Centring on K'ang Yu-wei's Ta T'ung Thought* (中國に於ける世界國家思想康有為の大同思想を中心として). Tokyo: Hirano Hinoyasu (平里廣安), 1951; iv, 228 pages. [The only book-length study in any language, so far as I am aware, of *Ta T'ung Shu*.]

Watanabe Hidekata (渡邊秀方): *General Discussion of the History of Chinese Philosophy* (中國哲學史概論). Translated from the Japanese by Liu K'an-yüan (劉侃元). Shanghai: Commercial Press, 1926. [See Part IV, Chapter VIII, on K'ang Yu-wei (pp. 193–201).]

Wu Tse (吳澤): *K'ang Yu-wei and Liang Ch'i-ch'ao* (康有為與梁啓超). Shanghai: Hua Hsia Book Store (華夏書店), 1948;

202 pages. [Concerned with politics, and of only marginal interest to our subject.]

Yang Yu-chiung (楊幼烱): *History of Chinese Political Thought* (支那政治思想史). Translated from the Chinese by Murata Shiro (村田孜郎). Tokyo: 1940. [See Part III, 'Present-day Political Thought', Chapter XI, Section 2, on the K'ang-Liang School. Unimportant; mostly taking Liang Ch'i-ch'ao's ideas.]

SECTION II

WESTERN LANGUAGE MATERIALS

Brière, O.: 'Les courants philosophiques en Chine depuis 50 ans (1898–1950).' *Bulletin de l'Université l'Aurore*, Shanghai; no. 40, sér. III, tome 10, October 1949. [See pp. 562–3.] (English translation of this work, by Laurence G. Thompson, entitled *Fifty Years of Chinese Philosophy*, was published by Allen & Unwin, London, 1956.)

Chen Huan-chang: *The Economic Principles of Confucius and his School.* New York, 1911 (2 vols.). [A Columbia University doctoral dissertation. Important; written by a pupil of K'ang Yu-wei, and presenting a detailed explanation of the views of Kang and his group as to interpretation of the Classics.]

Forke, Alfred: *Geschichte der Neuren Chinesischen Philosophie.* Hamburg, 1938. [See Book III, A, 19. Jahrhundert, II. Schule des K'ang Yu-wei (pp. 575–97).]

Franke, Otto: *Studien zur Geschichte des Konfuzianischen Dogmas und der Chinesischen Staatsreligion: das Problem des Tsch'un-Ts'iu und Tung Tschung-schu's Tsch'un-Ts'iu Fan Lu.* Hamburg, 1920.

Franke, Wolfgang: *Die Staatspolitischen Reformversuche K'ang Yu-weis und seiner Schule. Ein Beitrag zur Geistigen Auseinander-Setzung Chinas mit dem Abendlande.* Hamburg, 1935. [A dissertation published in *Mitteilungen des Seminars für Orientalische Sprachen an der Friedrich-Wilhelms-Universität zu Berlin*, Jahrgang XXXVIII, erste Abteilung: Ostasiatische Studien; pp. 1–83. The only book-length treatment of the subject in a Western language. See also review by J. J. L. Duyvendak in *T'oung Pao*, sér. II, tome XXXIII, 1937; pp. 95–100].

Fung Yu-lan: *A History of Chinese Philosophy.* Translated from the

Chinese by Derk Bodde. Princeton, 1951 (vol. I, 2nd edition) and 1953 (vol. II). [On K'ang Yu-wei, see vol. II, Chapter XVI, pp. 679–691. On 'new text' and 'old text' philosophical developments, see vol. II, Chapters II and IV. The many additions and explanations by the translator make this English version helpful to the Western reader.]

Fung Yu-lan: *A Short History of Chinese Philosophy.* Edited by Derk Bodde. New York, 1948. [On K'ang Yu-wei and related subjects, see Chapter XXVII (pp. 319–31); on Tung Chung-shu and Kung Yang theory, see Chapter XVII (pp. 191–203).]

Hsü, Leonard Shihlien: *The Political Philosophy of Confucianism. An Interpretation of the Social and Political Ideas of Confucius, his Forerunners, and his Early Disciples.* London, 1932; 258 pages.

Hughes, E. R.: *The Invasion of China by the Western World.* London, 1937. [Important for picturing the general socio-intellectual milieu of K'ang and his contemporaries. Remains the only adequate survey of its subject.]

Hummel, Arthur W.: *The Autobiography of a Chinese Historian. Being the Preface to a Symposium on Ancient Chinese History (Ku Shih Pien) translated and annotated by Arthur W. Hummel* . . . Leyden, 1931. [A doctoral dissertation. Although this work contains no reference to *Ta T'ung Shu*, it does show the influence of K'ang Yu-wei on the younger contemporary scholars, and is good background on the general intellectual situation in contemporary China.]

Hummel, Arthur W.: (Editor.) *Eminent Chinese of the Ch'ing Period (1644–1912).* Washington, D.C., 1943 and 1944 (2 vols.). [A monumental work, indispensable for students of this period of Chinese history. K'ang Yu-wei is found in the article on T'an Ssu-t'ung (since he lived on into the Republican period, and is thus excluded from a separate entry according to the plan of this work).]

Hummel, William F.: 'K'ang Yu-wei, Historical Critic and Social Philosopher, 1858–1927.' *Pacific Historical Review*, vol. IV, 1935, pp. 343–55.

Hummel, William F.: *The Role of Historical Criticism in the Chinese Renaissance of Today.* Typescript, unpublished doctoral dissertation, University of Southern California, 1931. [On K'ang Yu-wei, see pp. 40–67.]

Legge, James: *The Li Ki.* Sacred Books of the East, vol. XXVII; Oxford,

1885. [See Book VII: 'The Li Yun, or Ceremonial Usages . . .' (pp. 364–93).]

Levenson, Joseph: *Liang Ch'i-ch'ao and the Mind of Modern China.* Cambridge (Mass.), 1953. [On K'ang Yu-wei, see Index.]

Lin Mousheng: *Men and Ideas. An Informal History of Chinese Political Thought.* New York, 1942. [See Chapter XV, 'K'ang Yu-wei, the Last of the Confucians' (pp. 215–29).]

Lung Chieng-fu: *The Evolution of Chinese Social Thought.* Typescript, unpublished doctoral dissertation, University of Southern California, 1935. [See Chapter IX on K'ang and *Ta T'ung Shu*. Abstract of this dissertation was published by U.S.C. Press in 1941, Social Science Series, no. 23, 40 pages.]

Richard, Timothy: *Forty-Five Years in China.* New York, 1916. [On K'ang Yu-wei, see Index. Richard, a missionary of catholic interests and broad vision, was influential in the reform movement of the late 1890s (see the present work, Book One, Chapter I, p. 24, n'.).]

Tjan Tjoe Som [Tseng Chu-sen] (曾 珠森): *Po Hu T'ung. The Comprehensive Discussions in the White Tiger Hall.* Leiden, 1949 (2 vols.). [A doctoral dissertation, treating of the great council of scholars held in A.D. 79, at which the attempt was made to clarify and arrive at final decisions on disputed points in the Classics. This work will be found very helpful in understanding the controversy of the 'new' and 'old text' schools.]

Soothill, William E.: *Timothy Richard of China.* London, 1924.

Teng Ssu-yü, Fairbank, John K., and Sun, E-tu Zen: *China's Response to the West. A Documentary Survey (1839–1923),* vol. 1, Cambridge (Mass.), 1954. [Of general interest, so far as recent Chinese intellectual history is concerned; not much on K'ang.]

Thomas, Elbert Duncan: *Chinese Political Thought. A Study Based Upon the Theories of the Principal Thinkers of the Chou Period.* New York, 1927. [See Chapter IV, 'The State', especially pp. 44–7, which deals with *ta t'ung.*]

Tseng Yu-hao: *Modern Chinese Legal and Political Philosophy.* Shanghai, 1930. [See Chapter II, 'K'ang Yu-wei (1858–1927) as a Reformer and Political Scientist' (pp. 39–64).]

Tsuchida Kyoson: *Contemporary Thought of Japan and China.* London, 1927. [Chapters X and XI deal with Chinese thought, briefly but well. On K'ang Yu-wei, see Chapter X, pp. 194–201.]

Wilhelm, Richard: *The Soul of China*. Translated from the German by John H. Reece. New York, 1928. [Reflections and remembrances of a sensitive German missionary-scholar, much of whose interest lay in Chinese thought. On K'ang Yu-wei, see pp. 76–81.]

Woo Kang [Wu K'ang]: *Les Trois Théories Politiques du Tch'ouen Ts'ieou, Interpretées par Tong Tchong-chou d'après les principes de l'école de Kong-yang*. Paris, 1932 (250 pages). [Good for background on the Kung Yang School, of which K'ang was the latest, and one of the principal, adherents.]

Wu Kuo-cheng: *Ancient Chinese Political Theories*. Shanghai, 1933. [Originally a doctoral dissertation, Princeton University. For a brief discussion of the *ta t'ung* theory and translation of the 'Li Yün' passage, see pp. 298–300.]

SECTION III

MISCELLANEOUS MATERIALS

Berneri, Marie Louise: *Journey Through Utopia*. Boston, 1951.

Bland, J. O. P., and Backhouse, Edmund: *China under the Empress Dowager. Being the Life and Times of Tzu Hsi*. London, 1910. [See especially Chapters XII through XV, pp. 178–245, for an account of the Hundred Days of Reform.]

Cameron, Meribeth: *The Reform Movement in China, 1898–1912*. Palo Alto (California), 1931. [A Stanford University doctoral dissertation; the only book-length treatment of its subject in English—written, however, entirely from Western-language sources.]

Chinese Historiography Society, editors (中國史學會主編: *The Reform (Movement) of 1898* (戊戌變法. Published in Shanghai by Shen Chou Kuo Kuang Company (神州國光社), 1953: 4 volumes. Publication no. 8 of the 'Collectanea of Materials on Modern Chinese History.' This work collects in one place the most comprehensive group of materials on the subject. It includes the *Chronology* by K'ang Yu-wei as well as much else on and by him.

Franke, Wolfgang: 'Eine Reisebericht Kang Yu-weis über Deutschland', *Sinica*, vol. VIII, 1933, pp. 188–92.

Hertzler, J. O.: *The History of Utopian Thought*. New York, 1923.

Laidler, Harry W.: *Social-Economic Movements. An Historical and Comparative Survey of Socialism, Communism, Co-operation, Utopianism, and Other Systems of Reform and Reconstruction.* New York, 1944.

Mumford, Lewis: *The Story of Utopias.* New York, 1922.

Negley, Glenn, and Patrick, J. Max: *The Quest for Utopia. An Anthology of Imaginary Societies.* New York, 1952.

(*North China Daily News*): *The Emperor Kuang Hsü's Reform Decrees, 1898.* Reprinted and published at the *North China Herald* office, 1900 (61 pages).

Reference works used most importantly during composition of this book:

Chu I-hsin (朱翊新), compiler: 標準學生字典 Taipei: World Book Co., 1952 (revised edition).

Fenn and Chin: *The Five Thousand Dictionary.* Peking, 1940, 5th edition, photolithographed in Cambridge (Mass.), 1944.

Kenkyusha's New Japanese-English Dictionary. American edition, offset reprint, Cambridge (Mass.), 1942.

K'o Huai-ch'ing (柯槐青), compiler, and Ho Kung-ch'ao (何公超), reviser: 成語手冊 Taipei: Hsin Lu (新魯) Bookstore. 2nd combined edition.

Langer, William D. (compiler and editor): *An Encyclopedia of World History.* Boston, 1948 (revised edition).

Li Chi (李籍): 日本現代人名地名表 Chungking: Cheng Chung Book Store, 1945.

Mathews, R. H.: *A Chinese-English Dictionary. Compiled for the China Inland Mission.* Shanghai, 1931; revised American edition, photolithographed in Cambridge (Mass.), 1945.

Morimoto Kakuzō (森本角藏): 四書索引 Tokyo: published by the author; 2nd edition, 1933.

P'ei Wen Yün Fu. Shanghai: Commercial Press edition of 1937, in 7 vols.

Rose-Innes, Arthur: *Beginners' Dictionary of Chinese-Japanese Compounds.* American edition, photolithographed in Cambridge (Mass.), 1945.

Tz'u Hai. Shanghai: Chung Hwa Book Co., 1938.

Tz'u Yüan. Shanghai: Commercial Press, 1939 (combined original text and supplement edition).

Yeh Shao-chün (葉紹鈞): 十三經索引 Shanghai: K'aiming Book Store, 1934.

ADDENDUM

Hahm Hong-keun (咸洪根): 'Kang Yu-wei and his Principle of Ta-tung' [translation of title in journal] (康有為의 思想에對하여 ― 大同思想을 中心으로 ――). *The Korean Historical Review* (The Ryoksa Hakbo), vol. 1, no. 4, September, 1955. Published by the Korean Historical Association, Seoul, pp. 435–87. (A good survey, but written in hangul.)

INDEX

THE END

Printed in the USA/Agawam, MA
August 5, 2013

578620.030